A Dynamic Approach to Economic Theory

This book contains a set of notes prepared by Ragnar Frisch for a lecture series that he delivered at Yale University in 1930. The lecture notes provide not only a valuable source document for the history of econometrics, but also a more systematic introduction to some of Frisch's key methodological ideas than his other works so far published in various media for the econometrics community. In particular, these notes contain a number of prescient ideas precursory to some of the most important notions developed in econometrics during the 1970s and 1980s.

More remarkably, Frisch demonstrated a deep understanding of what econometric or statistical analysis could achieve under the situation where there lacked known correct theoretical models. This volume has been rigorously edited and comes with an introductory essay from Olav Bjerkholt and Duo Qin placing the notes in their historical context.

A valuable addition to the scholarship in this area of economic history, this will prove invaluable to all those interested in Frisch, economic theory or the history of economic thought.

Olav Bjerkholt is Professor of Economics at the University of Oslo. **Duo Qin** is Professor in Economics at School of Oriental and African Studies, University of London.

Routledge studies in the history of economics

A Dynamic Approach to Economic Theory

The Yale Lectures of Ragnar Frisch, 1930

Edited by
Olav Bjerkholt and Duo Qin

LONDON AND NEW YORK

First published 2010
by Routledge
2 Park Square, Milton Park, Abingdon, Oxon OX14 4RN

and by Routledge
711 Third Avenue, New York, NY, 10017, USA

Routledge is an imprint of the Taylor & Francis Group, an informa business

First issued in paperback in 2013

© 2010 Ragna Frisch Hasnaoui. Introduction, selection and editorial
matter, Olav Bjerkholt and Duo Qin

British Library Cataloguing in Publication Data
A catalogue record for this book is available from the British Library

Library of Congress Cataloging in Publication Data
A catalog record for this book has been requested

ISBN: 978-0-415-56409-0 (hbk)
ISBN: 978-0-415-74619-9 (pbk)
ISBN: 978-0-203-84552-3 (ebk)

Typeset in Times New Roman
by Wearset Ltd, Boldon, Tyne and Wear

Contents

Illustrations

Figures

Boxes

Foreword
Teaching economics as a science: the Yale lectures of Ragnar Frisch

Ragnar Frisch was one of the founding fathers of econometrics as a scientific discipline. With a wide-ranging knowledge of mathematics, statistics and economics, he was one of a quadrumvirate of Norwegians who developed much of the basis for modern econometrics (the others were Trygve Haavelmo, Olav Reiersøl and Herman Wold). Frisch was one of its most creative thinkers, and indeed invented many of the concepts commonly used today, and the corresponding nomenclature. He was also one of its most active participants, and played a crucial role in the foundation of the Econometric Society, and the creation and funding of its main journal, *Econometrica*. Frisch was the first recipient of The Sveriges Riksbank Prize in Economic Science in Memory of Alfred Nobel, jointly with Jan Tinbergen in 1969. In turn, Haavelmo was awarded the prize 20 years later.

This fascinating edition of Frisch's previously unknown Yale lectures by Olav Bjerkholt and Duo Qin reveals many insights into both his thinking and his actions at the start of the 1930s, an ominous period for the world economy with the onset of the Great Depression. The timing with the largest downturn since then, induced by the financial crisis, is coincidental, but not incidental. In his 1951 will, Frisch left his papers to the University of Oslo Library and assigned Haavelmo and Reiersøl the task of arranging the contents for publication. So far, the only Frisch manuscripts to have been published are the Poincaré lectures, and now at last the Yale lectures have been edited.

Bjerkholt and Qin have not only edited Frisch's Yale lectures, but have also written an excellent and insightful editors' introduction, which both seeks to describe the context of events around Frisch's visit to Yale in 1930 (leading to the Econometric Society) and to elucidate the material in his lectures. Frisch was never the easiest writer to understand – his *Autonomy* paper is a classic thereof. Thus, explaining what Frisch was lecturing on is crucial to facilitating the re-absorption of his ideas. Both editors have a proven track record in the scholarship of the history of econometrics (see, for example, Bjerkholt 2005; Qin 1993), and must be congratulated for combining their skills and extensive knowledge to bring this work to fruition.

It is important to establish what was known historically, and how it related to other ideas, both internal to the discipline and external. I have always been struck by the subtlety of earlier analyses, and as shown in Morgan (1990) and Hendry and Morgan (1995), many earlier insights in econometrics have been forgotten. For example, Bjerkholt and Qin interpret Frisch's ideas on equilibrium in light of the more recent developments of equilibrium-correction mechanisms and exogeneity.

A remarkable recent example is the re-discovery of the work of Bradford Bixby Smith, a prescient, yet ignored, researcher (see Mills 2009). Smith's two main publications (1926 and 1927) anticipated a great deal of what came later: permanent versus transitory innovations; difference versus trend stationarity; common-factor restrictions; general-to-specific modelling; and forecasting in the face of unanticipated structural breaks, which reads like a list of 1970–90 research! Yet he was only cited four times, then forgotten (once by Mordecai Ezekiel, the author of the most famous textbook of the time, *Methods of Correlation Analysis* (Ezekiel 1930)), despite having published in the leading journal, and being part of a group at the US Department of Agriculture which included Charles F. Sarle, the first winner of the Babson Prize (Gordon and Kerr 1997). If such important contributions published in major journals can be completely forgotten and need to be painstakingly rediscovered, a valuable role remains for archival study.

Haavelmo and Reiersøl took up Frisch's interests in data analysis and econometric theory and greatly advanced the set of methods, particularly in Haavelmo (1944) and Reiersøl (1945). Both types of technique are still dominant today. Bernt Stigum is perhaps the inheritor of Frisch's idea on axiomatizing economic theory seen as a purely cognitive model (which Stigum calls 'toy actors in a toy economy' (Stigum 1990)), necessitating building bridges from the axioms to empirical reality. Thus, this research line initiated by Frisch in the early 1930s remains vibrant, like so many other ideas and developments discussed in his Yale lectures. That is why 80-year-old lecture notes deserve notice.

David F. Hendry
February 2010

References

Bjerkholt, O. (2005) 'Frisch's econometric laboratory and the rise of Trygve Haavelmo's probability approach', *Econometric Theory*, 21: 491–533.

Ezekiel, M. (1930) *Methods of Correlation Analysis*, New York: Wiley & Sons.

Gordon, D.V. and Kerr, W.A. (1997) 'Was the Babson Prize deserved? An enquiry into an early forecasting model', *Economic Modelling*, 14: 417–33.

Haavelmo, T. (1944) 'The probability approach in econometrics', *Econometrica*, 12: 1–118.

Hendry, D.F. and Morgan, M.S. (1995) *The Foundations of Econometric Analysis*, Cambridge: Cambridge University Press.

Mills, T.C. (2009) 'Bradford Smith: a forgotten time series econometrician', Loughborough University.

Morgan, M.S. (1990) *The History of Econometric Ideas*, Cambridge: Cambridge University Press.

Qin, D. (1993) *The Formation of Econometrics*, Oxford: Clarendon Press.

Reiersøl, O. (1945) 'Confluence analysis by means of instrumental sets of variables', *Arkiv for Matematik Astronomi och Fysik*, 32: 1–19.

Smith, B.B. (1926) 'Combining the advantages of first-difference and deviation-from-trend methods of correlating time series', *Journal of the American Statistical Association*, 21: 55–9.

Smith, B.B. (1927) 'Forecasting the volume and value of the cotton crop', *JASA*, 22: 442–59.

Stigum, B.P. (1990) *Towards a Formal Science of Economics*, Cambridge, MA: MIT Press.

Acknowledgements

The manuscript is part of the Ragnar Frisch Archive at the National Library of Norway, in accordance with a will written by Ragnar Frisch already in 1951. The will put upon the literary executors, who are now long dead, to arrange for publication 'if they find anything of sufficient interest'. After having retrieved and studied the Frisch manuscript in 2007 we received most valuable advice and encouragement to go ahead with publication from Peter C.B. Phillips, Yale University.

We have been happy for the interest shown by Routledge and grateful for the evaluation given by three anonymous referees.

We owe sincere thanks for technical support and assistance in preparing the Frisch manuscript with its intricate graphs for publication to Sarah White and Emily Qin and to Tina Victoria Engelsrud, Henning Øien and Sigurd Galaasen, assistants at the Department of Economics, University of Oslo. We are grateful for excellent service from the Manuscript Collection at the National Library of Norway in accessing the documents about the run-up to the establishment of the Econometric Society, carefully preserved by Ragnar Frisch, and drawn upon in our introduction.

Editors' introduction

Teaching economics as a science: the Yale lectures of Ragnar Frisch

Olav Bjerkholt and Duo Qin

Why should 80-year-old lecture notes in economics by Ragnar Frisch have any interest today? We shall try to answer the question in this introduction and also prepare the reader for what he/she will find in them.

The lecture series for which these notes were prepared was given by Ragnar Frisch as Visiting Professor at Yale University in the autumn of 1930. The timing deserves particular attention – the eve of the foundation of the Econometric Society. Frisch's lecture series lasted well into December 1930. The Econometric Society was founded on 29 December 1930 in the Statler Hotel, Cleveland, Ohio, in between other events at the annual joint meetings of the American Economic Association, the American Statistical Association, and other professional associations.

The Econometric Society was founded as a programmatic association, with the primary goal to scientify economics. Physics was set as the scientific ideal, as referred to in the Constitution. The Econometric Society was the first international organization in economics. At the time, it was of less importance in the United States than in Europe, where scholars from different countries were brought together at the annual Econometric Society meetings and speeded up the exchange of methodological and theoretical ideas considerably. The membership remained small until long after the Second World War. But many young budding talents were attracted to the Society almost from the beginning, as reflected in Nobel economics laureates over the first 20 years of the Prize, many of whom had acquired the membership in the 1930s or 1940s. The success of the Society is perhaps far beyond what its founders had expected.

A key to this success was the financial support of Alfred Cowles III, which allowed the Society to publish its own journal, *Econometrica*, from 1933.[1] In the very first issue Joseph Schumpeter wrote programmatically on behalf of the Econometric Society:

> We do not impose any credo – scientific or otherwise – and we *have* no common credo beyond holding: first, that economics is a science, and, secondly that this science has one very important quantitative aspect. We are no sect. Nor are we a 'school'.

> (Schumpeter 1933)

But what did Schumpeter, and those he spoke on behalf of, mean by economics being a 'science' and this science having 'one very important quantitative aspect'? What, indeed, were the ideas about economics and science of those 16 people who took part in the 'organization meeting' which declared the Econometric Society as established? Ragnar Frisch, the second youngest of the 16 founders, was, in fact, the kingpin of everything revolved around at the founding of the Society and has cast lasting impact on its future development that few of the other founders have.

It is therefore important to recapitulate the evolvement of Frisch's idea about econometrics in association with the founding of the Econometric Society and its journal, which went back as early as 1926. Of the large amount of Ragnar Frisch's archival remains, his Yale lectures stand out as the single most important work representing the spirit of the founders of the Econometric Society. At first sight, these lecture notes may read loose and tedious. In fact, 'econometrics' is nowhere used or mentioned in the notes. But these notes were not prepared for a showpiece marking the start of econometrics. They were simply for the lectures Frisch chose to give as a visiting professor at Yale. However, as they were prepared at a time when his mind was very much concerned with bringing to fruition the idea of an econometrics society, these notes provide us with invaluable information of his frame of mind on the matter.

In order to fully extend the historical importance of Frisch's Yale lecture notes, we shall present a blow-by-blow story of how the Economic Society was finally founded in 1930, with emphasis on Frisch's role (see pp. 2–10). Many of documents drawn upon here have never been published and have never been drawn upon in the accounts of these events. We then describe briefly how the Yale lecture notes came into being in connection with Frisch's contribution to econometrics of the time. In the final section we comment in some detail on the text of the lectures, relating them to Frisch's later works and subsequent developments in economics and econometrics.

The quest for the scientization of economics

Studies on the history of econometrics have given plenty of coverage on the role of the Cowles Commission in the formation of econometrics. Surprisingly, far less has been written on the history of the Econometric Society and the background of its establishment. The summary facts about the foundation of the Econometric Society, as stated by various authors, are often drawn from incidental remarks in Christ's (1952) history of the first 20 years of the Cowles Commission. Christ's account is, however, incomplete and somewhat incorrect.[2] Furthermore, it conveyed the impression that the Econometric Society was rooted in the United States. But, as we shall show here, it was an idea conceived and nurtured in Europe, and replanted to the more fertile ground in the United States when the occasion arose. The man at the centre of all this was Ragnar Frisch. The history would probably have been very different without Frisch's active involvement and participation.

Let us trace back to Frisch's essay, 'Sur un problème d'économie pure' (1926a). The essay has been cited more for its opening lines where the term '*économétrie*' (econometrics) was coined, than for its substantive content. It was undoubtedly a lucky strike as a coinage of terms, but it was also more than that.[3] While Frisch coined 'econometrics' in the first sentence of this essay, the second sentence defined the aim of 'econometrics' as that of turning economics 'into a science in the strict sense of the word'. There is a surprisingly, if not straight, intimate link from this coinage to the establishment of the Econometric Society in 1930 and the journal *Econometrica* in 1933. Exactly how and when Frisch was inspired to coin this term with its programmatic connotation is not known. It was stated in the essay that the work was done in Paris in 1923 but the opening paragraphs may have been added later. Frisch sent François Divisia a reprint of the essay soon after the work was done. An exchange of letters followed between the two men in 1926. In one letter, Divisia proposed that the inherent aim of 'econometrics' be supported by a suitable organization of some sort for scholars sharing an interest in a more scientific economics, including a journal of some sort. Frisch responded by proposing to name the journal 'Econometrica'.

Both Divisia and Frisch took meticulous care of this early correspondence and gave related documentary accounts on later occasions (see Divisia 1953; and Frisch 1970: 222–6, which is his Nobel Prize speech). After the exchange with Divisia, Frisch passed the ideas to Ladislaus von Bortkiewicz, Eugen Slutsky and couple of other European scholars.[4] These letter exchanges lasted into January 1927, when Frisch was preparing to go the United States in early February on a Rockefeller Fellowship.[5]

Once in the United States, Frisch set to turning the ideas into concrete plans. In the spring of 1927 he wrote a three-page memorandum which was mainly about 'the establishment of an international periodical devoted to the advancement of the quantitative study of economic phenomena, and especially to the development of a closer relation between pure economics and economic statistics'.[6] To support the journal, an organization was proposed, which was temporarily designed as a 'self-perpetuating executive committee' with representatives from five major countries, who had the power to appoint two editors, one American and the other one European, and an editorial secretary. The financial support was to come from an 'American endowment'.

The design was revised later. In July 1927 Frisch wrote again to Divisia from his summer recess at Glacier National Park, telling him that he had come to the conclusion that it would be preferable to have only one responsible editor. Furthermore, Frisch proposed Camille Colson or Divisia to be the editor!

In the autumn of 1927 Frisch rewrote and extended the memorandum to a five-page version dated October 1927.[7] Frisch had surely promoted these ideas as often as he could during travels to different universities in the United States. Schumpeter visited Harvard in 1927/8, arriving in September 1927; Frisch wrote to him from Berkeley and said that he would come to Harvard in November or December to discuss the plan with Schumpeter there. He was most likely the

European economist Frisch considered as his best ally. Their meeting certainly must have comprised a discussion of the extension of the memorandum. The revised memorandum is interesting because it mainly concerned the scientific aspect and is worth quoting at length:

> An important object of the Journal should be the publication of papers dealing with attempts at statistical verification of the laws of economic theory, and further the publication of papers dealing with the purely abstract problems of quantitative economics, such as problems in the quantitative definition of the fundamental concepts of economics and problems in the theory of economic equilibrium.
>
> The term equilibrium theory is here interpreted as including both the classical equilibrium theory proceeding on the lines of Walras, Pareto, and Marshall, and the more general equilibrium theory which is now beginning to grow out of the classical equilibrium theory, partly through the influence of the modern study of economic statistics. Taken in this broad sense the equilibrium problems include virtually all those fundamental problems of production, circulation, distribution and consumption, which can be made the object of a quantitative study. More precisely: The equilibrium theory in the sense here used is a body of doctrines that treats all these problems from a certain point of view, which is contrasted on one side with the verbal treatment of economic problems and on the other side with the purely empirical-statistical approach to economic problems.

In other words, it was a bold attempt to draw a line demarcating what was 'in' and what was 'out' with regard to publication in the journal. More importantly, the emphasis on 'equilibrium theory' placed the concept as the cornerstone to build on for the scientization of economics. Frisch was at the time highly concerned with the understanding and identification of business cycles, the emphasis may be related to his conviction that cycles were part of an equilibrium phenomenon rather than an independent state as opposed to an equilibrium state.

The rather strictly defined editorial policy was modified by an additional statement that the journal should accept papers 'of a more purely statistical character provided they deal with such statistical technique or such statistical data that they have a definite bearing on problems in the equilibrium theory'; and an even finer delimitation restricted the journal from publishing 'papers dealing with statistical technique in general', as such papers had other more appropriate publication channels.

Towards the end of his fellowship year in the United States, Frisch reported to Divisia in January 1928 that the prospect of getting financial support for a journal was bleak there (Divisia 1953: 26). It seems overwhelmingly likely that Frisch had raised the issue with a number of potential donors, including the Rockefeller Foundation, which financed not only a large number of fellowships in economics, but also empirically oriented economic research institutions in many countries. The effort seemed to have come to nothing.

There is one more event of interest before Frisch left the United States in early March 1928. On 29 February 1928, Frisch met Joseph Schumpeter and Gottfried Haberler in the Colonial Club at Harvard. Frisch recorded the minutes of their conversation.[8] According to the minutes, the conversation was more or less as a constitutional convention on econometrics (and very much a European one at that!). Paragraph 1 of the minutes put down the fundamentals: 'The terms *econommetric* and *econommetrics* are interpreted as including both pure economics and the statistical verification of the laws of pure economics, in essential distinction to the purely empirical manipulation of statistical data on economic phenomena' (our italics).[9] Then the minutes dealt with the journal, which was downgraded to a 'systematic, annotated bibliography of econommetric litteratur[!]', possibly issued as a supplement 'to some existing economic journal'. There were some details about the selection principles. The bibliography covered by the journal should comprise engineering, natural science and mathematical journals as these frequently would have articles which 'for methodological or other reasons are highly significant from the econommetric point of view'. The bibliography should naturally also allow proper review papers of 'more important contributions'.

The issue of an organization was also brought up. Some interesting points were made, although in a modest way. The minutes described it as 'an informal circle of scientists the world over interested in problems of econommetrics'.[10] The circle should be open to not only economists but also 'scientists in other fields, who by the nature of the problems have an affinity to econommetrics'. Cooperation with mathematicians was especially mentioned. And, not least important, the circle was given a name, undoubtedly put forward by Schumpeter: *Eranos Oekonommetrikos – an International Circle for the Promotion of Econommetric Studies.*

So what would the circle do apart from reading the journal of *Oekonommetrika*? A low-key realism seemed to have prevailed at the Colonial Club that day. Until more experience was gained the activity would have to be restricted to circulating a list of names and addresses to facilitate correspondence. The topic of 'possibilities of establishing regular courses of econometrics in colleges and universities' was the only one explicitly specified for the correspondence.

The meeting with Schumpeter and Haberler on the eve of his return to Europe was an important boost to Frisch in pursuing his bold dream, after failing to get financial support during his visit to the United States. Frisch travelled widely during his fellowship year and tried energetically to find and contact people who shared his interests and could become potential allies in his econometric cause. He didn't find many. Now, he prepared himself for taking the cause back to Europe. Frisch had already established contact with many Europeans who might be interested in econometrics and had got additional names from Schumpeter and Haberler.[11]

During his American visit, Frisch naturally visited Irving Fisher at Yale. Frisch was in a sense a pupil of Fisher, as he had been greatly inspired by Fisher's 1892 dissertation, which Frisch had studied in Paris (see Bjerkholt and

Dupont-Kieffer, 2010). The two men shared an interest in measuring marginal utility, as well as in promoting mathematical economics. Frisch also sought out Charles Roos at Princeton; Roos had been a student of Griffith C. Evans and was involved in promoting economics with the American Association for the Advancement of Science. The latter got him in contact with the Harvard polymath E.B. Wilson. Nothing much seems to have come out of Frisch's contact with Fisher or Roos in this period, however.

The theoretician that Frisch really had looked forward to meeting and enlisting in the support for econometrics in the United States was Allyn A. Young, who for some years had been at Harvard. Allyn Young gave Frisch, at his request for leading figures in the United States in mathematical economics, a list of eight names – Irving Fisher, H.L. Moore, Warren M. Persons, Holbrook Working, Frank H. Knight, Frederick C. Mills, Mordecai Ezekiel and E.H. Chamberlin. This list, wrote Young, 'includes practically everyone in this country who has a serious interest in the field of mathematical economics'. Frisch also asked Allyn Young about leading figures in statistical economics. Young passed Frisch's request to Mordecai Ezekiel of the USA Department of Agriculture. Ezekiel came up with a list of another eight names, but apart from Henry Schultz, the names were not as well known in the history of economics or econometrics.[12]

After returning to Oslo in early March 1928, Frisch drafted a memorandum in French.[13] Its structure and content was very similar to his memorandum of October 1927, with some additional ideas from the Frisch–Haberler–Schumpeter conversation. *Eranos Oekonommetrikos* was not mentioned explicitly. The importance of building a network along with the bibliography was set out. The memorandum ended with a suggestion that the chief editor and editorial staff had to be on the alert for the econometric cause and that, if the occasion arose, they should constitute themselves as a committee and take all possible measures to promote the econometric program, by initiatives such as convening an international congress or founding an international association.

There is a gap in Frisch's meticulously kept records after this document. The gap occurred at a time when Frisch's career came to a critical point, due to his father's death and the responsibility he felt for the family firm (see Bjerkholt and Dupont-Kieffer 2009, Editors' introduction). Frisch may have considered giving up his scientific career; at least he told Irving Fisher so in the spring of 1929. Fisher responded by arranging an invitation for him from Yale University for one year as a visiting professor on fairly generous financial terms. Frisch accepted the invitation and came to Yale in February 1930.

This American trip reignited Frisch's dream to promote econometrics. In the spring of 1930, Frisch lectured at Yale on a number of topics that interested him and worked intensively on several research ideas. He had ample contact with Fisher; they planned to write a book together and Frisch assisted Fisher in a number of odd jobs. Charles Roos dropped by, perhaps on more than one occasion. The interaction between the three men led them to the conclusion that the time was ripe for a renewed attempt to launch an econometrics association. In a letter to Schumpeter written on 11 June,[14] Frisch informed him that he would very soon receive important news about 'the plans of establishing an international association of mathematical economics'.

The plan was drawn up on 17 June 1930, when Fisher, Roos and Frisch met again in Fisher's spacious property on Prospect Avenue in New Haven. The three men drafted a five-page letter about 'the organization of an international association for the advancement of economic theory' and distributed it to a carefully selected list of leading scholars in a number of countries. In addition to the three signees, the list consisted of 28 names from 11 countries.[15]

The story thereon, up to the organization meeting in December, is well known in the literature. The 17 June letter is quoted at length by Divisia (1953).[16] It stated that the chief purpose of the association was 'to help in gradually converting economics into a genuine and recognized science' and that the term 'theory' used in connection with the organization should 'not be interpreted as synonymous with abstract reasoning only, but as including also the analysis of empirical evidence suggesting or verifying theoretical laws'. Interestingly, the term 'econometrics' was not introduced, neither for the name of the association, nor for the stated purpose of it. The letter went on to suggest four requirements for membership eligibility and asked the recipients whether they agreed to these requirements and whether each one considered himself eligible and interested in helping to form the association as one of its charter members. The requirements were stated as limiting membership to those who:

a   are thoroughly familiar with general economic theory,
b   have a working knowledge of mathematics as applied to economic theory and statistics,
c   have some knowledge of accounting,
d   have published an original contribution to economic theory or to the analysis of such economic statistics or accounting as have a definite bearing on problems in economic theory.
   (Letter to multiple recipients by Irving Fisher, Charles F. Roos and
   Ragnar Frisch, 17 June 1930, p. 1, Ragnar Frisch Archive,
   the National Library of Norway)

One may wonder where the 'accounting' requirement comes from. It seems rather unlikely to have come from Frisch. Some of the recipients found it irrelevant. Why was it not 'some knowledge of statistics' instead? Did the term 'statistics' carry too much ambivalence as to its connotation as a requirement? An additional question raised in the letter provides some indication of this unresolved difference among the triumvirate. It asked the recipients whether they think 'have some experience in handling statistical data' should be added to the four requirements.

The letter did not specify the exact meaning of the 'science' that economics should be converted into, apart from it being 'genuine and recognized'. Physics or other sciences were not mentioned. Nor was there any trace of the idea of jumpstarting economics from scratch.[17] On the contrary the letter emphasized conversion rather than reconstruction of economics, as implied in the following quote:

> You will notice that in the requirements for eligibility we have put a good deal of emphasis on the quantitative character of economic theory. As you know, the quantitative movement in economics started on an a priori basis through the introduction of mathematics into economic theory. Afterwards and independently, empirical studies in mathematical statistics were made. Still more recently, a beginning has been made to bridge the gap between these two approaches. These attempts at putting economics on a scientific and quantitative basis by introducing numerical and statistical observations into the theoretical structure we consider as one of the most promising developments in modern economics, and one to which the association should give considerable attention. In our opinion, it will be largely through a constant and close connection between the abstract-rational and concrete-empirical points of views that the modern quantitative movement in economics will produce significant and lasting results.
>
> (Letter to multiple recipients by Irving Fisher, Charles F. Roos and Ragnar Frisch, 17 June 1930, p. 3, Ragnar Frisch Archive, the National Library of Norway)

The quote conveyed the understanding, shared perhaps both by the triumvirate and most of the recipients, that the task at hand was to build upon existing theory, enhanced through greater emphasis on mathematics in the formulation of theory, and particularly through 'bridging the gap' through theoretical and empirical work. In particular, the last sentence in the quote can be recognized as an early and rough version of the key sentence in the Constitution of the Econometric Society (see below, p. 9). The pre-eminence of theory in this bridge-building was even related to the practical criteria for future membership, as the letter explicitly proposed to prevent those who thought they could do empirical analysis of economic problems 'without reference to fundamental theoretical principles' from joining the association:

> We believe that the association should not include those who have merely treated economic problems empirically, without reference to fundamental theoretical principles. If you and the others consulted are in sympathy with us in laying down this policy, mathematical statisticians as such will not be included. They will only be included if they satisfy all the requirements (a) to (d). In practice, the line may be difficult to draw. On this we would like to have your judgment.
>
> (Letter to multiple recipients by Irving Fisher, Charles F. Roos and Ragnar Frisch, 17 June 1930, p. 3, Ragnar Frisch Archive, the National Library of Norway)

In addition to consulting the recipients on this potentially sensitive barrier for membership, the letter also asked for responses on a number of other points, such as people to be invited for membership, the proposed association's activities, its envisaged journal and its content as well as editorial policy, etc. The letter tentatively named the journal as *Oekonommetrika* for the recipients' opinion.

Of the 28 recipients of the 17 June letter, 26 responded, some at great length. Frisch summarized their responses into a 13-page document with a digest of answers.[18] The triumvirate subsequently decided to go ahead to the next stage of organizing a meeting during the joint meetings of the American Economic Association, the American Statistical Association, the American Mathematical Society and the American Association for the Advancement of Science. A draft 'Constitution of the Econometric Society' was agreed by the triumvirate in November and enclosed in an invitation letter for the 'organization meeting', which was sent to a list of 84 names on 29 November 1930, exactly a month prior to the due date of the meeting. The list covered the majority of European countries as well as Japan, China, Brazil and Algeria. One month in advance was of course relatively short notice for overseas recipients. Few, if any, might at all have considered the possibility of attending.

It was in the draft Constitution that the name 'Econometric Society' appeared for the first time. The draft Constitution also set out key phrases that would serve as signposts for the association and its journal in years to come. As an explanatory subtitle, the Society was called 'An International Society for the Advancement of Economic Theory in its Relation to Statistics and Mathematics'. In paragraph 1 on the 'Scope of the Society' its main object was set out as:

> to promote studies that aim at a unification between the theoretical-quantitative and the empirical-quantitative approach to economic problems and which are penetrated by a constructive and rigorous way of thinking similar to that which has come to dominate in the natural sciences.[19]

Interestingly, the triumvirate appeared to be quite uncertain of the name, as could be seen from the following almost apologetic statement in the invitation letter:

> As to the name of the society, we consider it essential that the name should indicate quite clearly the specific object which the society has in view. If the society is formed with the scope we have suggested, it seems advisable to coin a word, since no current single word will connote exactly the correct idea. So far, we have been unable to find a better word than 'econometrics'.
> ...
> We are aware of the fact that in the beginning somebody might misinterpret this word to mean economic statistics only. But if the complete subtitle of the society is always given in the official publication and in the letterheads of the society, and if the members and fellows of the society persist in using

the word 'econometric' and 'econometrics' in their proper sense, we believe that it will soon become clear to everybody that the society is interested in economic theory just as much as in anything else.

(Letter to multiple recipients by Irving Fisher, Charles F. Roos and Ragnar Frisch, 29 November 1930, p. 3, Ragnar Frisch Archive, the National Library of Norway)

Their hesitancy turned out to be unwarranted as the name was very quickly accepted. The letter further stated that at the organization meeting 'a President of the society and a Council will probably be elected'. At least probability was there from the very beginning!

The organization meeting finally took place on the night of the first day of the annual meetings of the professional associations in Cleveland. The attendance was, however, not impressive. Only eight from the list of 83 turned up in addition to Roos and Frisch. Irving Fisher was absent due to conflicting commitments. But the attendance comprised heavyweights – Harold Hotelling, Henry Schultz, Joseph Schumpeter and E.B. Wilson. The other four from the list were William Ogburn, J. Harvey Rogers, W.A. Shewhart and J. Wedervang, a professor of economics at the University of Oslo, whom Frisch had helped to arrange a visit to study the US education system. Schultz may have fitted Frisch's ideal description of an econometrician better that anyone else. Hotelling was considered the best statistician in the United States by Frisch. Sadly, Allyn A. Young had died from influenza in 1929, after returning to England in 1928.

But among attendees there were six people who were not on the list. Three were eminent mathematicians: Karl Menger, visiting from Vienna, Norbert Wiener and Oystein Ore, a Norwegian Professor at Yale. Frisch was a member of the American Mathematical Society (and not of the AEA or ASA). The mathematicians were probably brought over by him from the AMS sessions. The other three were Frederick C. Mills, M.C. Rorty and Carl Snyder, the latter two were stalwarts of the ASA (and together with Wilson and Ogburn successive presidents of ASA from 1928 to 1931).

It is interesting to observe that theoretical economists were almost absent from the Cleveland meeting. This reflected perhaps the state of American economics of the time, which was strongly influenced by the German historical school, noticeably different from the situation in Europe, where economics was dominated by theoretical economists. It seems odd, however, that none of the econometrically oriented American agricultural economists invited showed up.

Emergence of econometrics and the Yale lecture notes

The historic Cleveland meeting and Frisch's intimate involvement set a unique background for the Yale lecture notes. It is remarkable and almost surprising that Frisch made himself a pivotal figure during the foundation of the Econometric Society and was widely recognized and respected as such soon afterwards. We must note that Frisch was not at all well established in 1930, especially in comparison with Fisher. He was just a visiting professor at Yale, not yet having a professorship in his home country. He had not published in any international economic journals. Moreover, his educational background was unimpressive – only a two-year economics program at the University of Oslo.

Frisch was almost a self-taught man. He became proficient in many branches of mathematics through studying in Paris in the early 1920s and he might have felt much more at home among mathematicians than among economists.[20] But Frisch's interest in economics had never left him since his university days. The drive for the scientization of economics was certainly inspired by advances in natural sciences, but the underlying motivation was the need for social improvement as much as purely intellectual interests. His Paris treatise (1926a), published in a Norwegian mathematical journal, was an attempt at introducing an axiomatic approach in economics and, at the same time, a bold heuristic attempt at confronting theory and data.

Subsequently, Frisch's attention moved from mathematics to statistics. He defended a doctoral dissertation in statistics in Oslo in 1926. He was in his statistical period while visiting the United States in 1927–8. There, he completed two major works. One was about the analysis of time series, with particular regard to the identification of business cycles. The work was widely distributed as a mimeograph in 1927. It occupies a prominent place in the history of econometrics (see Morgan 1990; Bjerkholt 2007). The other work was the essay 'Correlation and scatter', completed in 1928 and published in 1929 (Frisch 1929a). It puts forward a very comprehensive approach to the analysis of statistical data. However, the work did not attract wide interest due partly to its use of matrix methods and partly to its publication in a journal which had rather limited distribution outside Scandinavia. In the same year, he also published a paper on the meaning of 'static' and 'dynamic' in Norwegian in a Danish journal (see Frisch 1929b). The discussion laid the foundation for the Yale lecture notes.

In fact, the Yale notes are not just a summary of his previous studies,[21] they also present us with a comprehensive picture of Frisch's thinking of what economics should be as a scientific discipline. They offer us a vital piece of evidence showing the coming into being of a systematic framework, upon which modern econometrics was to be established into a formal sub-discipline of economics over a decade later by his student, Haavelmo, and a group of young researchers at the Cowles Commission (see Qin 1993). The notes could be seen as a timely herald of the founding of the Econometric Society and also a forceful justification for the rapid rise of Frisch into the leadership position of the Society.

The Yale lecture notes were also taken at a time when Frisch was approaching the prime of his innovative research. He accumulated an inventory of theoretical ideas and developed them substantially during his fellowship year in the United States. The result was a flow of papers appearing in major journals in the United States, UK, France and Germany during the early 1930s. The best known of the papers are 'Pitfalls in the statistical construction of demand and supply curves' (Frisch 1933a), 'Propagation problems and impulse problems in dynamic economics' (Frisch 1933b) and the Poincaré lectures (see Bjerkholt and Dupont-Kieffer 2009). His output in the early 1930s also comprised two monographs: *New Methods for Measuring Marginal Utility* (1932) and *Statistical Confluence Analysis* (1934). The Yale lecture notes offer valuable insight to these forthcoming works, and also to other ideas that he was working on but never got published properly. The present publication of the lectures has finally made those ideas openly available.[22]

Readers who have read Frisch's research papers and monographs before may be surprised at how plain and verbose the Yale lecture notes read, which contrast sharply to the abstruse and sometimes taciturn style of writing in his published works. We should feel lucky to learn Frisch's general thinking in such a comprehensive and easily comprehensible way. Evidence from the Ragnar Frisch Archive tells us that Frisch had the idea of producing a textbook out of his Yale lecture series when these notes were prepared. In a report form to Yale University submitted in the first term of 1930–1 (i.e. the autumn term), Frisch wrote, as item 3 in the section 'Research and Publication', the following: '"A Dynamic Approach to Economic Theory." This is an attempt at developing some parts of economic theory from an angle admitting of statistical verification. The manuscript is now being dictated. Will be a book of about 200 pages.' The lecture notes have a subtitle: 'Lectures at Yale University beginning September, 1930'. According to the report quoted above, the lectures were for a small course of 13 students (six registered students and seven visiting students) at the Graduate School. But Frisch must have thought of the plan for a book during his first teaching term at Yale, which started in February. The very first lecture was delivered on the 13 February 1930, entitled 'What is meant by economic theory?' Frisch prepared a five-page note for that lecture (Ragnar Frisch Archive). The note was extended into a 24-page manuscript, dated April 1930, with the title 'What is economic theory?', which later became the first section of Part I of the Yale lecture notes.

During the spring term, Frisch also lectured on the topics of time-series analysis and of productivity theory. The latter topic was planned to come out as a separate book,[23] while materials from the former topic were to become part of the Yale lecture notes, as shown from the planned content list in Box I.1 (see section 3, 'the separation of short-time and long-time components in an empirical time series' of Part III). The actual existing manuscript of Part III consists of only two sections, one as an introduction and the other section 1 according to the planned list. Some basic features of economic time series were discussed in the introduction section (see the relevant discussion in the next part), paving the way to the planned section 3. In the Archive, there is a pile of lecture notes taken by students who attended Frisch's autumn course. Box I.2 presents a list of the lectures covered by these notes. It is clear from the table that the topic of time-series analysis was taught in a number of the lectures in November and December 1930.

Box I.1 Planned contents list of the Yale lecture notes

I General Consideration on Statistics and Dynamics in Economics

1   What is economic theory?
2   A discussion of the fundamental distinction between a static and a dynamic economic theory
3   The static and the dynamic conception of an equilibrium
4   Structural, confluent and fictitious relations in economic theory

II Dynamic Formulation of Some Parts of Economic Theory

1   A dynamic analysis of marginal utility
2   A dynamic formulation of the law of demand
3   A simple case of steered oscillations. The reaction problem
4   A simple case of initiated oscillations
5   Dynamic analysis of a closed economic system

III Statistical Verification of the Laws of Dynamic Economic Theory

1   Types of clustering in scatter diagrams and the non-significance of partial correlations
2   General principles regarding the possibility of determining structural relations from empirical observations
3   The separation of short-time and long-time components in an empirical time series
4   The phase diagram. Phase elasticities and structural elasticities. The comparison problem in time series components
5   Critical remarks on some of the recent attempts at statistical determination of demand and supply curves
6   A new theory of linear regression. The diagonal and the arithmetic mean regression. The invariance problem
7   A statistical analysis of selected groups of data by the methods developed in the present course

This table of contents is only tentative. New Sections may be added during the course. At the end of the course a corrected table of contents will be inserted instead of the present one.

Box I.2 also tells us that the first few lectures in October were on the topic 'steered vs. free fluctuations', which matches with section 3 of Part II in the planned content list shown in Box I.1, another unwritten section of the manuscript.[24] Actually, section 2 of Part II is well represented in the students' notes if we scan through them. The notes recorded a microdynamic system of a market with demand and supply/production side and with a stock of (unsold) goods. It was represented by dynamic equations with numerical parameters displaying

Box I.2 Yale students' notes

Oct. 17, 1939   Lecture V
II.3 Steered oscillations and free oscillations.
Oct. 21, 1930   Lecture VI
II.3 Steered vs. Free fluctuations (Impulse vs. Propagation) (cont.)
Oct. 24, 1930   Lecture VII
II.2 A Dynamic Formulation of the Law of Demand. Illustrations of Steered, Semi-Steered and Free Oscillations.
Oct. 28, 1930   Lecture VIII
III.1 Types of Clustering in Scatter Diagrams and the Non-Significance of Partial Correlations.
Oct. 31, 1930   Lecture IX
Correlation Study in n Variables.
Nov. 4, 1930   Lecture XI
Collective Scatter and the Correlation Coefficient.
Nov. 7, 1930   Lecture XII
Regression. Time correlation in Two Variables.
Nov. 11, 1930   Lecture XII
III.4 The Phase Diagram.
Nov. 18, 1930   Lecture XIV
Linear dependency in cyclical curves. III.3 The separation of short-time and long-time components in empirical time series.
Nov. 25, 1930   Lecture XV
Second Difference Operation: K. Simple Addition Operation: H. Weighted Moving Average Operations: M, G.
Dec. 2, 1930   Lecture XVI & XVII
Effect of K and H on sin function (concluded). More General Operation: Ω.
Dec. 5, 1930   Lecture XVIII
Preparatory Smoothing of Time Series. Graphical short hand method of determining any number of components providing all differences in wave order are large.
Dec. 9, 1930   Lecture XIX
Treatment of Empirical Time Series. Case I: One cyclical component and no trend. Case II: One cyclical component and a trend.
Dec. 12, 1930   Lecture XX
An initial digression demand-supply (related to the Pitfalls paper). Case II (cont.); Case III: Two cycles and No Trend.
Dec. 16, 1930   Lecture XXI
Some examples of key equations.

price and stock dynamics. In fact, the same model was used in his Poincaré lectures in 1933 (see Bjerkholt and Dupont-Kieffer 2009: lecture 4).

Frisch must have intended, when he collected and kept these students' notes, to use them as reference when he had time to carry on writing those unfinished sections of the planned contents. Scanned images sampled from the students' notes are given in Figures I.1 and I.2. It is historically interesting to note from

Figure I.1 that the concepts of 'propagation' and 'impulse' were discussed in the fifth lecture on 17 October. That serves as strong evidence that Frisch's had by then more or less worked out the overall ideas for his macrodynamic model paper (1933b), as mentioned previously.

Interestingly, Frisch's plan for the book could be grander than the planned content list, as indicated from the endnote of the list in Box I.1, 'New Sections may be added during the course. At the end of the course a corrected table and contents will be inserted instead of the present one'. Unfortunately, Frisch never

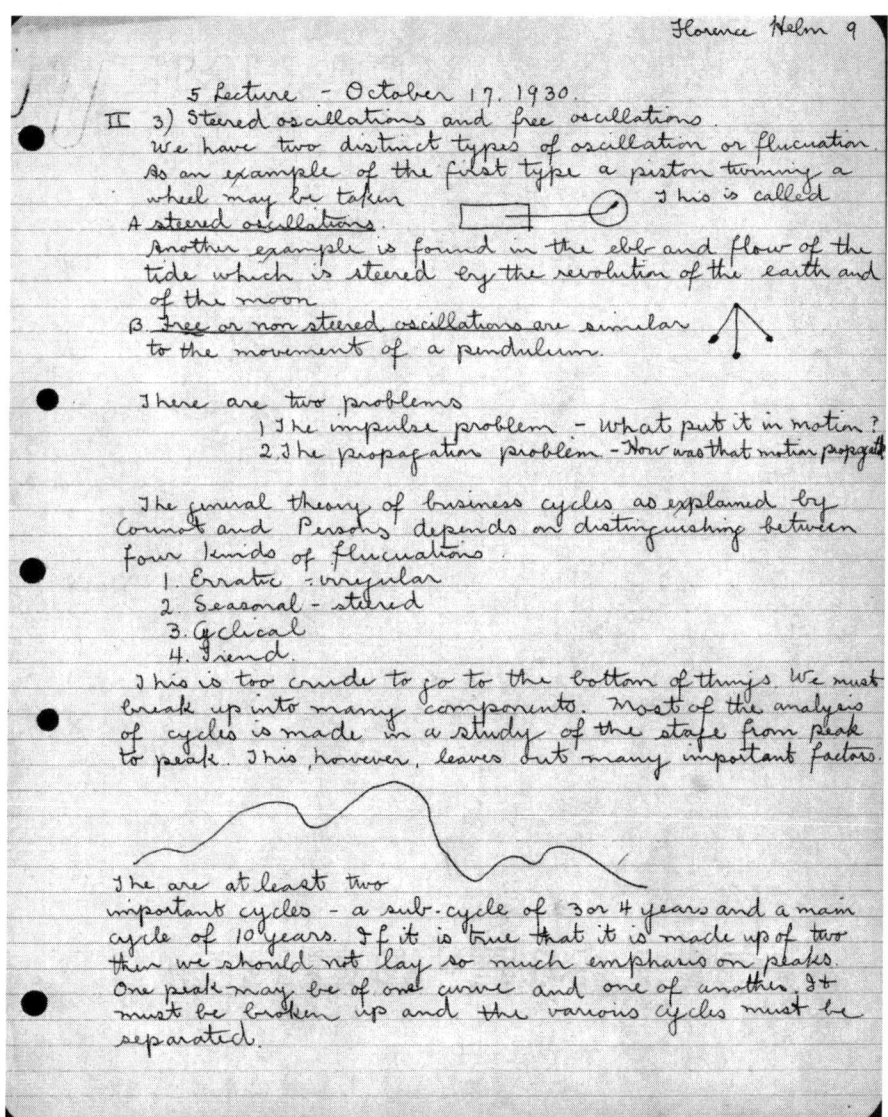

Figure I.1 Scanned lecture notes by students: Lecture 5. (source: Frisch Archive).

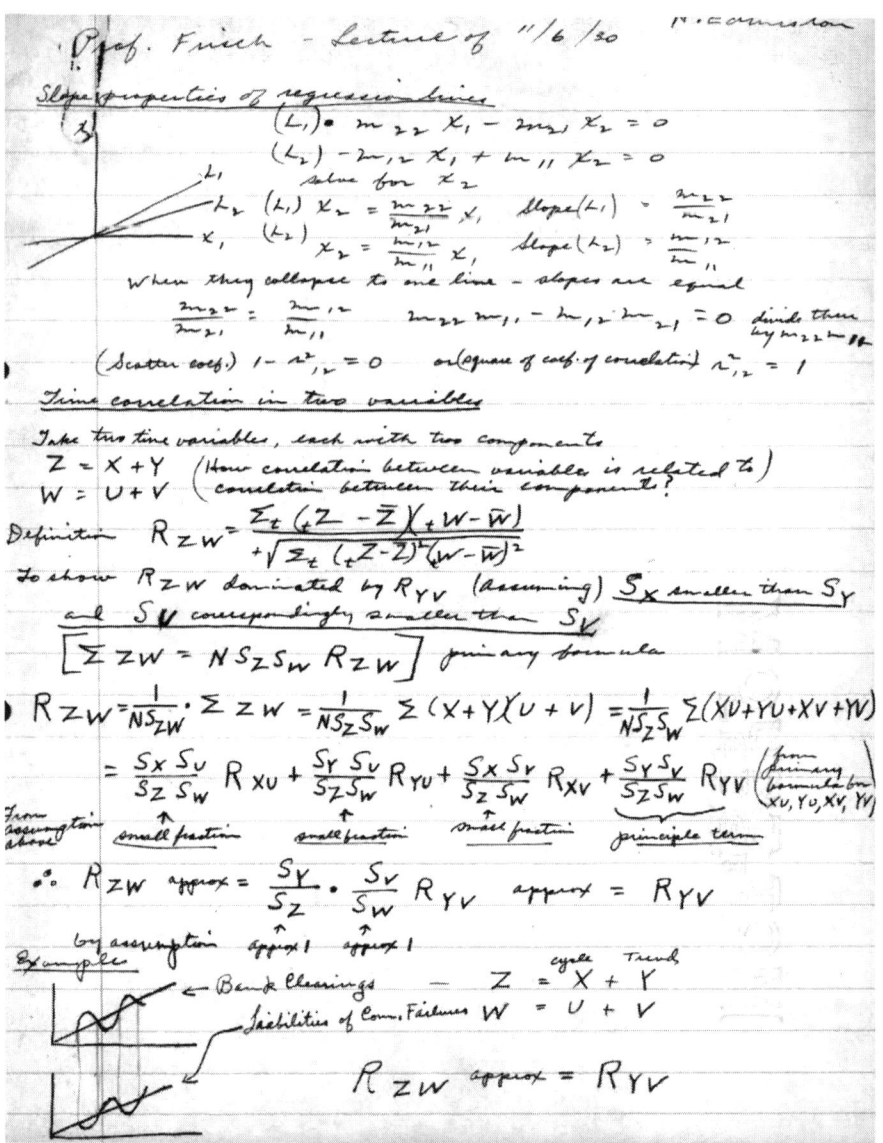

Figure I.2 Scanned lecture notes by students: Lecture 12 (source: Frisch Archive).

found the time to finish even the planned contents after delivering the Yale lectures. He was appointed Professor in Oslo from 1 July 1931 and secured funding from Rockefeller Foundation to set up a research institute in Oslo, which was establish at the beginning of 1932. Meanwhile, he became more and more involved in the affairs of the Econometric Society as Council member, long-time editor, president, organizer, contributor and also a key figure in every way in the pre-Second World War European meetings of the Econometric Society. He got himself involved with the Cowles Commission as well. With mounting commitments from various activities, the idea of a textbook became a shelved and forgotten dream.

The Yale lecture notes from a historical perspective

The lecture notes were incomplete and not ready for publication, as described above. The notes were distributed in very limited numbers as carbon copies bound in folders.[25] The lecture notes are rendered here exactly as they were written down and distributed in 1930, apart from correction of misprints and minor infelicities, and replacement of the handwritten graphs by computer based reconstructions.

In addition to the editing duty, we shall also make an attempt to provide some commentary discussion on the three parts of the existing lecture notes from the perspective of the history of economics and econometrics.

Part I, general considerations on statics and dynamics in economics

What is economic theory?

This section is arguably the most philosophical writing by Frisch. His primary attention is to bridge statistical modelling with macrodynamics in economics. His general motivation is to model economics after science disciplines such as 'astronomy, physics and biology' (p. 29). From a scientific perspective, he argues that economics is in need of 'a new fusion between theory and observations' (p. 30) and maintains that '*the true theorist in economics has to become at the same time a statistician*' (p. 30). It recapitulates his definition of econometrics as the unification of 'statistics, economic theory, and mathematics', later reflected in his formulation of the aim of Econometric Society – 'unification of the theoretical-quantitative and the empirical-quantitative approach to economic problems and that are penetrated by constructive and rigorous thinking similar to that which has come to dominate in the natural sciences' (Constitution of the Econometric Society adopted 1930, published *Econometrica*, 1, 106–8). In his subsequent lectures and writings, Frisch only gave summary statements on the matter.

The essential medium of the unification is model building. Frisch describes models as creation of the intellectual mind of investigators, who are 'sovereigns in the model world' so long as 'the rules of formal logic' are maintained (p. 32). Crucially, the creation should serve the primary purpose of 'transobservational invention' (p. 33). The invention is embodied mainly in two key components: new concepts/objects and new relations. Once models are created, the investigators would engage in exploring them. Here, Frisch carefully distinguishes two types of regularities: empirical laws, i.e. 'something which exists in the real world', and rational laws, i.e. 'something which exists in the model world'.

Frisch maintains that 'between them there is a gap, which can never be bridged' (p. 34). The continuous attempt to narrow the gap by the investigators reflects the second purpose of model building: to 'understand' and 'explain' empirical regularities. Further elaboration of that purpose leads to discussion of two concepts: causality and probability.

Frisch takes an instrumental viewpoint about 'causality'. He is opposed to the 'animistic' connotation of causes, i.e. the belief of causes as 'something imperative which exists in the exterior world' (p. 36). Instead, he advocates a scientist's expedient attitude of utilizing causal description as a means to digest and simplify the giant mass of observations. Frisch refers to that as 'scientific causality' and points out that its main attribute is 'the *direction* of causality' (p. 37). Such directional relations form the essence of models representing the modelers' description and explanation of the exterior observations. It is interesting to note that Frisch's instrumental viewpoint has maintained its dominance not only in the Cowles Commission work on identification issues with respect to simultaneous-equation models, e.g. Koopmans (1949), up to the subsequent invention of Granger causality (1969) in econometrics, but also in mainstream economic methodology, e.g. Friedman (1953).

As for the concept of 'probability', Frisch carefully distinguishes three notions: 'frequency, probability and belief', or 'empirical, abstract and personal probability'. In the context of model building, Frisch relates frequency or empirical probability with the empirical world, abstract probability with the artificial model world and belief or personal probability with irrational behavior, and cautions against the confusion of personal belief with abstract probability. The discussion again shows that Frisch is not anti-probability as commonly believed, as forcefully argued by Bjerkholt (2005).

A discussion of the fundamental distinction between a static and a dynamic economic theory

Here, Frisch criticizes explicitly the Austrian static equilibrium approach as being inadequate in characterizing dynamic movements in economics. His dynamic analysis bears the discernible influence of the Scandinavian school of thought, e.g. Wicksell. But he moved significantly further than Wicksell on the subject and his innovative conceptualization was to overarch the Cowles Commission paradigm of structural econometrics.

Frisch starts his introductory exposition by emphasizing that 'the distinction between statics and dynamics is a *distinction between two different ways of thinking, not a distinction between two different kinds of phenomena*' (p. 44). The exposition relies closely on his previous (1929b) work. Here, Frisch describes static laws as 'variations with regard to certain alternatives' whereas dynamic laws explaining 'how one situation grows out of the preceding' (p. 45); or in other words, 'dynamic theory is sequential while the static theory explains things without taking account of the time order of the events' (p. 49). In view of the time dimension underlying all phenomena, Frisch further classifies static analysis into two types: *instantaneous* type and *asymptotic* type (p. 49). The latter, referred to as 'asymptotic-static' type, is essentially a 'long run' feature (p. 49). The concept is further extended in the subsequent section when he comments on the notion of equilibrium.

In the present section, Frisch also discusses several pairs of concepts, e.g. stationary versus shifting phenomena, one-dimensional versus several dimensional analysis, short-time versus long-time components. Here, what is particularly interesting in terms of econometric methodology is his discussion on the '*ceteris paribus*' clause. Frisch remarks that 'the meaning of ceteris paribus is one of the points in economics which has been the subject of the greatest amount of loose and cheap reasoning'. He maintains that 'ceteris paribus has no meaning *unless we have already constructed a model world with a several dimensional relationship*' as that would enable us 'to *specify* which these "other things" are that shall be assumed constant'. Therefore, 'ceteris paribus regards the nature of a *model* world' rather than the '*exterior world*' as it is impossible to specify which these other things are (p. 55). Moreover, he uses *ceteris paribus* as a condition for the validity of individual explanatory variables in a several dimensional analysis, i.e. a multiple relation setting. He points out that these explanatory variables must possess the property of 'free variability' with respect to each other in order to allow for the *ceteris paribus* clause. This attribute effectively rules out the problem of multicollinearity, a concept which was yet to be developed.

Analytical and historical dynamics

Frisch defines 'historical dynamics' as the method of applying dynamic principles to specific phenomena which have happened, and 'analytical dynamics' as the method of generalizing the phenomena into abstract formulation. It is discernible from the discussion that Frisch's position was to promote econometric research in analytical dynamics, and that he thus regarded it vitally important to define dynamic, as opposed to static, in a manner as precise as possible. Subsequently, he extended his definition of dynamics in association with the concepts of equilibrium versus disequilibrium (Frisch 1936); and he also augmented his position into 'an ideal programme for macrodynamic studies' (see Phelps Brown 1937: 365–6), as well as his eloquence to convert Tinbergen from the 'historical' method to the 'structural' method (Tinbergen 1935, 1938).

The notion of an equilibrium. Assumption-equilibrium and situation-equilibrium

Here, Frisch draws an interesting distinction between 'assumption' equilibrium as against 'situation' equilibrium. The distinction was first discussed in his 1926 paper (1926b). Here, the distinction is discussed in the context of a parametric model of a set of interdependent variables. An 'assumption' equilibrium amounts to a normative statement, a certain possible solution of the model, which bears no relevance to the issue of whether the solution could be fulfilled in reality.

The issue of relevance is pertinent to 'situation' equilibrium, which describes a positive state, a real situation where the characterization of certain assumption-equilibrium happens to be fulfilled. Frisch further categorizes situation-equilibrium into two types: stationary equilibrium where values of the variables concerned are asymptotically static/constant, and moving equilibrium where the 'long time components' (long-run values) of the variables are moving/trending together with time. Remarkably, the latter type conceptualizes the essence of cointegration analysis which was developed over 50 years later (see Engle and Granger 1987). But more remarkably, Frisch's conceptualization goes further to the dynamic situation of what is known nowadays as the error-correction mechanism (ECM), for example see Hendry (1995: Section 7.10). In Frisch's description, ECM is termed as a 'stable' equilibrium in which the equilibrium state would attract small deviations (errors) back to itself (i.e. a negative feedback system), whereas the equilibrium would be 'unstable' if it stimulates small deviations further away from the equilibrium (i.e. a positive feedback system). As mentioned above, Frisch's present discussion foreshadows his 1936 paper.

Structural, confluent and artificial relations in economic theory

The discussion here is intimately related to the correspondence of empirical analysis with theoretical analysis, although the mathematical relations that Frisch uses to define the three concepts are extremely simple, too simple perhaps for any useful econometric models. Nevertheless, his definition exposes the very essence of structural econometric modelling. Frisch spells out two conditions for a structural relation under the implicit assumption that the relation is set within a constant parameter model. His first condition – the relation 'holds good identically in the variables involved', amounts to the ideal situation when there exists a perfect fit of the explained variable given the values of the explanatory variables. His second condition – the relation 'holds good even though we do not assume any particular side relation to be fulfilled', effectively rules out the possibility of a so-called 'structural break'. In other words, it requests that the model should remain valid even under the situation when the way by which a certain explanatory variable is generated has been altered. The condition precedes the formal definition of 'super exogeneity' for over half a century (see Engle *et al.* 1983). It effectively removes the ground of Lucas' critique (1976). In Frisch's terminology, what the Lucas critique attacks has nothing to do with structural relations but only 'confluent' relations, i.e. those relations that meet the first condition but not the second.

Frisch defines artificial relations as those which fulfil neither of the two conditions. Interestingly, this definition is close to Yule's (1926) description of nonsense regression.

Part II, dynamic formulation of some parts of economic theory

In the planned contents list, Part II comprises the following sections:

1 A dynamic analysis of marginal utility
2 A dynamic formulation of the law of demand
3 A simple case of steered oscillations. The reaction problem.
4 A simple case of initiated oscillations
5 Dynamic analysis of a closed economic system

As it turned out only the first of these five sections was included in the lecture notes and, furthermore, the manuscript itself strongly suggests that even this first section is incomplete. Part II is devoted to a presentation of Frisch's prime areas of methodological innovation in theorizing. The key concepts here are *dynamics*, *axiomatization* and *marginal utility*. The plan was to display how *dynamization of theory* should be conducted, but the actual lecture notes are little more than preliminaries towards such a dynamization. The second key concept is *axiomatization*, which again is closely connected to the third, *marginal utility*. Frisch viewed axiomatization as a crucial element in the theoretical quantification programme. He had pioneered axiomatization in economics by demonstrating how the postulation of a utility function could be replaced with an axiomatic structure from which the existence of a utility function could be proved (see Frisch 1926a). His 1926 work (1926a) had made a strong impression on many of those who had had an opportunity to study it. The work was reviewed and commented on in various journals but mainly with emphasis on the empirical part of it. Here, Frisch's discussion on axiomatization is set in a much more developed conceptual framework. But just as he comes to promising a statement and discussion of the axiomatic system the notes are cut off abruptly. We don't know for sure what was actually covered in the lectures.

The quantification or measurability of marginal utility was a common interest between Frisch and Irving Fisher. By Frisch's own testimony it was Fisher's 1892 dissertation that had inspired and convinced him that it was possible to fulfil Jevons' dream of achieving empirical measurement of marginal utility. In 1925 Fisher made, without being aware of the forthcoming Frisch (1926a), an effort at empirical estimation of marginal utility, only to recognize that Frisch had chosen a better approach. After Frisch's arrival at Yale in 1930, they set out to write jointly a monograph on utility measurement. Their plan somehow aborted; instead, Frisch completed the manuscript of a monograph entitled *New Methods for Measuring Marginal Utility* while at Yale in 1931 and had it published in 1932. The monograph shows how utility reasoning and measurement methods could be very helpful in various policy areas. It does not pursue axiomatization or dynamization of the utility concept. Frisch wanted to deal with those topics in the lecture series.

Frisch (1929b) had, as discussed under Part I above, introduced his ideas about *static* and *dynamic*, which soon became adopted among mathematically oriented economists. But Frisch (1929b) had also made a first attempt at dynamizing the marginal utility concept.[26] It seems likely that Frisch had intended to use that material in this part as well.

A dynamic analysis of marginal utility

There are three subsections in this single section of Part II. In the first two, Frisch discusses current theoretical controversies on the use and understanding of the utility concept. In both cases Frisch holds the mainstream position and presents the arguments in a lucid and persuasive manner.

Subsection (2.1.1) is on the controversy between psychological vs. the behaviourist approach to utility measurement. The two key proponents Frisch holds up for are F.Y. Edgeworth and Irving Fisher, respectively. The psychological approach is very closely associated with Edgeworth. It had more adherents in the UK than elsewhere but was on a losing edge. Fisher represents the opposite view, which discards the relevance of unobservable psychological processes and argues for an approach where acts of individuals' choices constitute the basis for a quantitative definition of utility. It should be noted that Vilfredo Pareto was a better known protagonist for the anti-psychological approach than Irving Fisher, although Fisher's 1892 work was earlier than Pareto's. Frisch seemed to prefer Fisher's dissertation for its quantitative approach, as shown from his discussion here.

An interesting detail in Frisch's non-sectarian presentation of the controversy is his embrace of an argument by Slutsky in his 1927 critique of Böhm-Bawerk, an article Frisch received as a reprint from Slutsky. Slutsky also sent Frisch his 1915 article on demand theory. Somehow Frisch has not mentioned it. Actually few were aware of the existence of Slutsky's 1915 work at the time.

In subsection (2.1.2) Frisch presents the controversy between adherents of a utility concept as something that is needed for economic analysis and those who argue for an economic theory based only on observable market phenomena free of any utility reasoning. The latter view was represented foremost by Gustav Cassel in his famous book *Theoretical Social Economics*. Frisch argues for the utility reasoning with respect to 'internal price analysis' as opposed to 'external price analysis'. Frisch describes the latter 'as a dogma that the pricing process should be studied exclusively by external notions, strictly avoiding the notion of utility' (p. 86).

Frisch is a strong proponent of letting theory guide the empirical and statistical analysis. Only on the basis of behaviouristic theory could price and consumption analysis 'be raised from a blind and busy collection of data into the dignity and significance of a scientific investigation' (p. 86). This argument is elaborated by two illuminating examples set in simple mathematical terms. The first example illustrates how the demand curve is derived from a utility structure rather than just being postulated; the second is about the derivation of properties of a labor supply curve. Years later the 'external analysis' has resurged in a more sophisticated form of the revealed preference approach in demand theory.

The axiomatic foundation of utility definition in subsection (2.1.3) is the only part where Frisch breaks new ground. He sets his axiomatic approach on the basis of 'fictitious interrogation experiments' and distinguishes the key concepts of 'choice object' versus 'choice situation'. Frisch elaborates on the conceptual framework, including some dynamic elements, but his presentation is hampered by the fact that the axiomatic system and the relevant discussion is not included in the lecture notes as a necessary prerequisite. It is unlikely that Frisch presented his lectures without touching upon the axiomatic system itself.

A strong proof of Frisch's awareness of the necessary prerequisite is his Poincaré lectures, given at the Henri Poincaré Institute in Paris two to three years later. The first topic of the lectures is the axiomatic approach, which is presented as a much more enhanced system than the original one set out in Frisch (1926a). Unfortunately, his Poincaré lectures remained unknown to the public until about 75 years later (see Bjerkholt and Dupont-Kieffer 2009).

Part III, statistical verification of the laws of dynamic economic theory

A short statement of some of the classical formulae in correlation and linear regression analysis

Most of this long section is devoted to simple description of correlation and regression theories. Nevertheless, Frisch has not forgotten to relate the theories to economics. In particular, he is concerned with the special features of time-series data. That is best seen from his application of Pearson's principal component theory,[27] as an alternative to Yule's (1926) nonsense regression analysis, to the case of two time-series variables, each is assumed of being made of a strong time trend component and a cyclical component. The application demonstrates how misleading it would be to look at the correlation coefficient of the variables if the aim of the investigator is to study the relationship between the cyclical parts (short-time components) of the variables, since that coefficient is dominated by the correlation of the trend (long-time) component. Frisch uses the case to show 'the necessity of decomposing our time series before analyzing their interrelationships' (pp. 136–7). Note that the above conclusion is at odds with the view from many present-day business cycle studies that Frisch is the founder of the Frisch–Slutsky impulse-propagation structural modelling approach (see Frisch 1933b) as opposed to the time-series decomposition and measurement approach led by the NBER (National Bureau of Economic Research).

Another interesting part of Frisch's discussion of economic time series is in his 'preliminary remarks on the phase diagram' (pp. 141–7). The discussion is focused on how to relate variables whose cyclical components are similar in length but different in timing. He shows how lagged correlation coefficients could be used for the purpose, the essential intuition underlying the modern-day Granger causality test (1969).

Types of clustering in scatter diagrams and the non-significance of partial correlation

This section demonstrates Frisch's main concern over the exploratory use of correlation and regression analyses for economic inference. He is preoccupied with two problems – the problem of variable choice (i.e. the missing-variable problem) and the lack of variable variations in data samples (similar to the multicollinearity problem due to inadequate sample data information). From the standpoint of a theoretical/economic model being linear and deterministic, Frisch sees the two problems as being closely entangled. Nevertheless, his focus is on the situation where the correct and complete model is unknown. He attempts to tackle it first by decomposing the variations of a modelled variable into three parts: 'systematic variations', 'disturbances' and 'accidental variations'. The classification is defined by what he views as the nature of explanatory variables. The variations are 'systematic' when all the relevant explanatory variables are correctly included; 'disturbances' occur when one or a few highly significant variables are missing whereas 'accidental variations' are the result of omitting variables which are unimportant and negligible. When the complete set of the relevant variables is undecided, or in his words the set is 'not closed', 'partial correlation coefficients will be undefined'. Therefore, the modeller should realize that 'partial and multiple correlation coefficients are not primarily descriptive of the character of the systematic variations, but are essentially indicators of the presence of accidental variations and disturbances' (p. 165). In other words, modellers should view them as indicators of incomplete and possibly mis-specified models. Unfortunately, this interpretation of his left almost no trace in the mainstream econometrics to be established during the 1940s.

Frisch then discusses ways to determine if certain variables should be excluded from the variable set and when the variable set comes 'near to being closed' (complete) by means of studying the scatter diagrams. The discussion lays the foundation of his bunch map method in *Statistical Confluence Analysis* (1934), as well as the notion of 'irreducibility' versus that of 'redundancy' (Frisch 1938). Although his technical pursuit has not turned out to be as fruitful as he expected, much of his conceptual insight remains thought-provoking, especially his cautious interpretation of the classical correlation parameters.

Noticeably, Frisch's cautious attitude towards the role of statistical analysis in the verification of economic theories preceded his taking the firm position of the structural model approach (1938), an approach which was to dominate econometrics, via the collective work of the Cowles Commission, for years to come. In that respect, the present lecture notes provide us with a wider and clearer historical background upon which the setting to that powerful modelling approach was laid.

Notes

1 Alfred Cowles also funded the Cowles Commission at Colorado Springs in 1932, a research facility devoted to promote the scientific aims of the Econometric Society (see Christ 1952). He originally wanted to call his new enterprise The Econometric Foundation, which, indeed, would have been a suitable name, but had to find another solution as European Council members reacted negatively. The Commission moved to Chicago in 1939 and was affiliated to the University of Chicago. In 1955, it moved to Yale University and changed its name to the Cowles Foundation.

2 Christ may have relied upon Roos (1948), whose accounts of these early events are less reliable than the documentary sources quoted here, as is his unsubstantiated assertion that Irving Fisher had tried to establish an econometric society in 1912.

3 See Bjerkholt and Dupont (2010) for more on Frisch (1926a). Frisch was extremely fond of coining terms – in several languages – but only 'macroeconomic/microeconomic' can match 'econometric' with regard to international success of acceptance.

4 The Ragnar Frisch Archive has a handwritten list by Frisch of 14 letters, written shortly before his departure for the United States, entitled *Letters relating to 'Oeconometrika'*, with columns for 'date', 'from', 'to' and 'brief summary of the content', as if Frisch already felt convinced of the historical importance of his initiative and these early letters. The first letter was dated 4 September 1926 and the fourteenth letter 17 January 1927. Note that Frisch in the first letter to Divisia had spelt the name of the journal, which still was a pie in the sky, as 'Econometrica'. In the ensuing years Frisch used about five more names, accommodating persuasive advice from different quarters.

5 Frisch had a three-year fellowship from the Laura Spelman Rockefeller Memorial but intended to spend the last two years in Europe (possibly because the terms did not allow Frisch's wife, Marie, to accompany him to the United States). Soon after Frisch returned to Europe his father fell ill and died. Frisch felt obliged to surrender the fellowship for family reasons and the bottom fell out of his scientific career (see Bjerkholt and Dupont-Kieffer 2009: xviii–xix).

6 Deposited at the Ragnar Frisch Archive, the National Library of Norway. The document was just entitled *Memorandum*, with no date or author given. Divisia received the memorandum in a letter of 22 May 1927, and quoted it at length in Divisia (1953: 24–5). The archive also has a draft version of Divisia's memorandum.

7 Deposited at the Ragnar Frisch Archive, the National Library of Norway. The new version bypassed the question of one or two editors and mentioned only 'editorial staff'. The name of the journal had become *Oekonommetrika*!

8 The typewritten minutes were entitled 'Abstract of Conversation between Professor Schumpeter, Dr. Haberler and Dr. Frisch on Possible Measures to Promote the Study and Teaching of Econommetrics', Ragnar Frisch Archive, the National Library of Norway. The key points occupied two and half pages with additional two pages of a list of people from 18 European countries, who were 'suggested as susceptible to support the work, or as being able to give information about such persons'. With the minutes in the archive were also 17 page of handwritten notes on the stationery of the Colonial Club, Cambridge, MA, which on closer scrutiny can be identified as ten pages by Frisch, four by Schumpeter, and three by Haberler, mostly of names and comments related to proposed names. Schumpeter's pages also had a nicely drawn map of northern Italy.

9 Schumpeter, who had strong credentials in classical languages, particularly Greek, argued consistently on the double 'mm' in the coined new term on logical and etymological grounds.

10 This mirrored Divisia's reaction to Frisch's proposal in 1926 of an international association, namely that the first aim ought to be a 'cercle restreint' (see Divisia 1953: 22–3).

11 Among the many names of potential interest floated on the table in the Colonial Club,

several were distinguished pure mathematicians, such as Felix Hausdorff and Constantin Caratheodory.

12 The other seven named by Ezekiel were Bradford B. Smith, Hugh B. Killough, Elmer Rauchenstein, Clyde Chambers, Edward M. Daggitt, C.F. Sarle and G.C. Haas.

13 Deposited at the Ragnar Frisch Archive, the National Library of Norway, in the form of a five-page carbon copy of a typewritten document dated April 1928; there was also a handwritten draft dated April 1928 as well.

14 Schumpeter was expected to be visiting Harvard again in late September that year.

15 By country of affiliation the numbers and names were: United States 10 (T.N. Carver, J.B. Clark, J.M. Clark, G.C. Evans, M. Ezekiel, I. Fisher, H.L. Moore, W.M. Persons, C.F. Roos and H. Schultz), Italy 5 (L. Amoroso, C. Gini, U. Ricci, T. de Pietri Tonelli and G. del Vecchio), France 4 (C. Colson, François Divisia, J. Moret and J. Rueff), United Kingdom 3 (A.L. Bowley, J.M. Keynes and A.C. Pigou), Germany 2 (L. von Bortkiewicz and J.A. Schumpeter), Sweden 2 (G. Cassel and B. Ohlin), Austria 1 (H. Mayer), USSR 1 (E. Slutsky), Poland 1 (Wl. Zawadski), Denmark 1 (H. Westergaard) and Norway 1 (R. Frisch).

16 Quotes from the letter are from the copy in the Ragnar Frisch Archive at the National Library of Norway.

17 After the Econometric Society was established there were apparently occasional calls in the United States for a break with the past and a complete reconstruction of economics.

18 Only G. Cassel and A.C. Pigou did not respond. The typewritten document put together by Frisch was entitled 'International Association of Economists. Digest of Answers to Letter of Invitation to First List', dated 12 October 1930, deposited at the Ragnar Frisch Archive, the National Library of Norway. It is a highly interesting 13-page document to assess the international interest and, indeed, enthusiasm over the idea of an econometric association but we leave it aside here.

19 Although it is not known how these key formulations of the Constitution came about the formulations, it is worth noting that they were strikingly similar to formulations used in Frisch (1926a, 1926b).

20 For more on Frisch's background and early career, see Bjerkholt and Dupont-Kieffer (2009) and Bjerkholt and Dupont (2010).

21 In the Archive, Frisch kept his translation of parts of his 1926a work from French into English, and also his 1926b work from Norwegian into English. The translation was dated May 1930. Much of the translated materials were used in Part I of the Yale lecture notes.

22 Notice that section 5 of Part II in the planned content list is clearly suggestive of his macrodynamic modelling work (1933b) and section 5 of Part III from the list foreshadows Frisch's (1933a) essay. Unfortunately, both sections were left unwritten in the manuscript.

23 In the same report quoted above, Frisch wrote as item 4: ' "Marginal and Limitational Productivity." This is an attempt at clarification in the theory of productivity. Will be a book of about 150 pages. Most likely to be published by the Yale University Press'.

24 Frisch later moved from the concept of 'steered' to 'bound' in respect of business cycle analysis; his view was that the cycles were generated as 'free', i.e. inherent in the economic system, rather than 'bound', i.e. induced through exogenous shocks.

25 It was recorded on a sheet, dated 2 December 1930 and glued to the inside back cover of the Yale lecture notes kept in the Archive, that 11 copies of the lecture notes had been distributed. The recipients included Schumpeter, Furniss (i.e. Edgar Stephensen Furniss, at the time Dean of Graduate School, Yale University), and most of the students who attended the course.

26 The discussion of marginal utility and dynamization in Frisch (1929b) is in sections 4–7, which were not included in the 1992 translation.

27 Note that Frisch discussed principal components earlier in his (1929a) paper.

References

Bjerkholt, O. (ed.) (1995) *Foundations of Modern Econometrics: The Selected Essays of Ragnar Frisch*, Vol. I, Aldershot: Edward Elgar.

Bjerkholt, O. (2005) 'Frisch's econometric laboratory and the rise of Trygve Haavelmo's probability approach', *Econometric Theory*, 21: 491–533.

Bjerkholt, O. (2007) 'Ragnar Frisch's business cycle approach: the genesis of the propagation and impulse model', *European Journal of the History of Economic Thought*, 14: 449–86.

Bjerkholt, O. and A. Dupont-Kieffer (eds) (2009) *Problems and Methods of Econometrics: The Poincaré Lectures of Ragnar Frisch, 1933*, London: Routledge.

Bjerkholt, O. and A. Dupont (2010) 'Ragnar Frischs's conception of econometrics', *History of Political Economy*, 42: 21–73.

Christ, C.F. (1952) 'History of Cowles Commission, 1932–1952', in *Economic Theory and Measurement: A Twenty Year Research Report 1932–1952*, Chicago: Cowles Commission for Research in Economics, pp. 3–65.

Divisia, F. (1953) 'La Société d'Econométrie a atteint sa majorité', *Econometrica*, 21: 1–30.

Engle, R.F. and C.W.J. Granger (1987) 'Co-integration and error correction: representation, estimation and testing', *Econometrica*, 55: 251–76.

Engle, R.F., D.F. Hendry and J.-F. Richard (1983) 'Exogeneity', *Econometrica*, 51: 277–304.

Friedman, M. (1953) *Essays in Positive Economics*, Chicago: University of Chicago Press.

Frisch, R. (1926a) 'Sur un problème d'économie pure', *Norsk Matematisk Forenings Skrifter*, Oslo, Series 1, No. 16, 1–40; translated by John Chipman and issued as: 'On a problem in pure economics' in J.S. Chipman, L. Hurwicz, M.K. Richter and H. Sonnenschein (eds) (1971), *Preferences, Utility, and Demand: A Minnesota Symposium*, New York: Harcourt Brace Jovanovic, pp. 386–423.

Frisch, R. (1926b) 'Kvantitativ formulering av den teoretiske økonomikks lover' ['Quantitative formulation of the laws of economic theory'], *Statsøkonomisk Tidsskrift*, 40: 299–334.

Frisch, R. (1929a) 'Correlation and scatter in statistical variables', *Nordic Statistical Journal*, 1: 36–102.

Frisch, R. (1929b) 'Statikk og dynamikk i den økonomiske teori', *Nationaløkonomisk Tidsskrift*, 67: 321–79; translated (sections 1–3) as 'Statics and dynamics in economic theory', *Structural Change and Economic Dynamics*, 3 (1992): 391–401.

Frisch, R. (1932) *New Methods of Measuring Marginal Utility*, Tübingen: Verlag von J. C. B. Mohr (Paul Siebeck).

Frisch, R. (1933a) 'Pitfalls in the statistical construction of demand and supply curves', *Veröffentlichungen der Frankfurter Gesellschaft für Konjunkturforschung*, Neue Folge Heft 5, Leipzig: Hans Buske Verlag, pp. 1–39; also in Bjerkholt (1995: 208–40).

Frisch, R. (1933b) 'Propagation problems and impulse problems in dynamic economics', in *Economic Essays in Honour of Gustav Cassel*, London: Allen and Unwin, pp. 171–205; also in Bjerkholt (1995: 311–45).

Frisch, R. (1934) *Statistical Confluence Analysis by Means of Complete Regression Systems*, Oslo: Universitetets Økonomiske Institutt.

Frisch, R. (1936) 'On the notion of equilibrium and disequilibrium', *The Review of Economic Studies*, 3: 100–5.

Frisch, R. (1938) 'Statistical versus theoretical relations in economic macrodynamics', paper submitted to the Business Cycle Conference at Cambridge, UK, 18–20 July 1938; reissued in Bjerkholt (1995: 272–87) and in D.F. Hendry and M.S. Morgan (eds) (1995) *The Foundations of Economic Analysis*, Cambridge: Cambridge University Press, pp. 407–19.

Frisch, R. (1970) 'From utopian theory to practical applications: the case of econometrics', *Réimpression de Les Prix Nobel en 1969*, pp. 213–43.

Granger, C.W.J. (1969) 'Investigating causal relations by econometric models and cross-spectral methods', *Econometrica*, 37: 424–38.

Hendry, D.F. (1995) *Dynamic Econometrics*, Oxford: Oxford University Press.

Koopmans, T.C. (1949) 'Identification problems in economic model construction', *Econometrica*, 17: 125–44.

Lucas, R.E. (1976) 'Econometric policy evaluation: a critique', in K. Brunner and A.H. Meltzer (eds) *The Phillips Curve and Labor Markets*, Carnegie-Rochester Conference Series on Public Policy, Vol. 1, Amsterdam: North-Holland.

Morgan, M.S. (1990) *The History of Econometric Ideas*, Cambridge: Cambridge University Press.

Phelps Brown, E.H. (1937) 'Report of the Oxford Meeting, September 25–29, 1936', *Econometrica*, 5: 361–83.

Qin, D. (1993) *The Formation of Econometrics: A Historical Perspective*, Oxford: Clarendon Press.

Roos, C.F. (1948) 'A future role for the Econometric Society in international statistics', *Econometrica*, 16: 127–34.

Schumpeter, J.A. (1933) 'The common sense of econometrics', *Econometrica*, 1: 5–12.

Tinbergen, J. (1935) 'Annual survey: suggestions on quantitative business cycle theory', *Econometrica*, 3: 241–308.

Tinbergen, J. (1938) 'On the theory of business-cycle control', *Econometrica*, 6: 22–39.

Yule, G. (1926) 'Why do we sometimes get nonsense correlations between time series?', *Journal of the Royal Statistical Society*, 89: 1–64.

1 General considerations on statics and dynamics in economics

1.1 What is economic theory?[1]

If we take the words 'science' and 'scientific' in their old-fashioned restricted sense, we may perhaps say that astronomy is a field of study which is 'scientific' more than any other of the fields of study having as their object the exploration of the exterior world. The reason for this, it seems, is that in astronomy the fusion between theory and observation has been realized more perfectly than in the other fields of study. When astronomy is a science, it is not because it has an abstract theoretical structure, nor is it because it is built on minute prolonged observations, but it is because the astronomical observations are *filled into* the theoretical structure. It is this unification that raises astronomy to the dignity and significance of a true science.

Also in economics we have had theoretical speculations, but most of the time it has not been that kind of theory which is built with a view to being verified by observations. Economic theory has not as yet reached the stage where its fundamental notions are derived from the technique of observations. On the other hand, we also have had observations in economics, plenty of them. In the last century there has been accumulated an overwhelming statistical and historical material on economic facts. But these observations have not been guided and animated by constructive theoretical thinking in the same way as the astronomical observations. Theory and observations in economics have gone along in a more or less disconnected way. There have been cycles of empiricism and rationalism. At times when it became too obvious that economics did not progress so rapidly as, for instance, astronomy, physics and biology, even though theoretical thinking had been applied to it, some economists would lose confidence altogether in theoretical thinking in this field and plunge themselves into a pure empirical fact collection in the hope that such a blind grappling with facts should reveal something of the nature of the complicated phenomena with which the economist is faced. Then again when it became obvious that such a pure empiricism did not lead anywhere, theoretical speculations in economics had a revival and the abstract-minded type of people ruled the ground for a while. The latest phase of such a cycle is the reaction which is now little by little coming forth against the superficiality of the extreme institutionalists.

This situation, it seems to me, is very unfortunate. What is needed more than anything else in economics now is a new fusion between theory and observations. We need a theoretical structure more than anything else. But it must be a theoretical structure which is such that it is capable of being connected directly or indirectly with actual numerical observations. *The true theorist in economics has to become at the same time a statistician.* He has to formulate his notions in such a way that he gets a possibility of ultimately connecting his theory with actual observations. This will be stimulating, not only for the observational work, but for the abstract speculations themselves. I know of no better check on foggish thought in economic theory than to have the theorist specify his notions in such a way as if he were to apply the notions immediately to some actual or hypothetical statistical material.

Whether or not the economist shall be able to realize such a fusion between theory and observations is an important issue which has far-reaching consequences for mankind's future. Man has proved sufficiently intelligent to create a huge economic machine capable of producing a great variety of useful things. But he has not been sufficiently intelligent to understand how to *handle* this big machine. He stands beside his big machine, not knowing how to steer it, only hoping that the running of the machine will be not too disastrous to him. The picture, I think, is not exaggerated. We may only think, for instance, of the situations which occur again and again in the production cycle; huge productive forces, machinery and labour being idle at the same time as there are millions of people who want very badly a great variety of things which could be produced by the idle machinery and labour.

Not only has man been able to create a big economic machine which he cannot handle, but he is making it bigger and bigger and more complicated all the time. He is constantly getting more and more handicapped in his attempt to steer it. If he shall ever catch up with it will depend on whether or not the science of economics will prove itself capable to cope with the new situations that constantly arise. It is a race of life and death, and man is certain to lose if he does not succeed in developing economics into the state of a true science, that is, a study based not only on fact collection, but also on constructive theoretical thinking.

The present lecture will be devoted to an analysis of the nature of economic theory and its place within the whole system of economics. Later in the course we shall make a humble attempt at formulating some parts of economic theory in such a form as to make an empirical verification possible. We shall also try to carry through some such verification by an intensive analysis and utilization of actual statistical material.

There are five types of mental activities in which the scientific worker has to engage.

1   *The descriptive procedure.* One sort of question that the scientist has to answer is: what happened? What is the situation? What course did the events follow? In order to answer these three questions he has to engage in

descriptive, historical and experimental work. In some sciences, like economics, direct experiment is more or less impossible and the scientist must
rely largely on the descriptive and historical answers to the questions here
considered.

2   *The understanding procedure.* Another sort of question that the scientist has
to answer is: why did it happen? Why did this situation exist? Why did the
events follow the course they did? The answer to these questions constitutes
the rational part of the investigation. By the power of his mind the scientist
tries to bring some reasonable order into the happenings and the things he
observed.

3   *The prediction procedure.* The questions here are: what will happen? What
will the course of events be in the future? In order that this sort of questions
shall have a meaning, the phenomenon considered must be such that it
cannot easily be controlled by man. If it can be fairly completely controlled,
no forecasting problem exists.

4   *The human purpose decision.* Here the questions are: what do we wish shall
happen? What do we wish the situation to be? The three first sorts of questions are exclusively of an intellectual character. On the contrary the sort of
questions here considered are of an ethical or moral sort. It cannot be
answered unless we adopt some sort of a standard of social values. If the
answer to such a question shall be socially significant, it must, of course, in
some way or another weigh the opinions of different individuals. It is not a
question of what you or I personally think in this matter, but of what is a
socially fair position.

5   *Social engineering.* The question here is: what can we do to produce such
happenings or such situations? This last sort of question is the most complicated we can ask. In order to give a significant answer to this sort of question, we have to build on an analysis of all the first four sorts of questions.

Now as to theory. What part of the mental activities mentioned above constitutes
theory? The answer might be different accordingly as we interpret the word
theory in a narrower or a broader sense. Some people have a tendency of inter-
preting 'theory' as synonymous with research in general. If this is done theory
would, of course, include all the five mental activities tabulated. This, however,
would not be in accordance with the common usage of the word and would also
be scientifically rather a useless interpretation. We shall here take theory to mean
the type of scientific work which comes under the heading (2). It is the attempt
at *understanding*, at bringing a rational order into things which constitutes the
essential feature of theory as we shall here take the word. We now proceed to a
closer analysis of the nature of theory as thus defined, emphasizing in particular
the place of theory within economics.

The observational world itself, taken as a whole in its infinite complexity and
with its infinite mass of detail, is impossible to grasp. Taken in its entirety, in its
immediate form of sense impressions, it resembles, so to speak, a jelly-like mass
on which the mind cannot get a grip. In order to create points where the mind

can get a grip, we make an intellectual trick: in our mind we create a little *model world* of our own, a model world which is not too complicated to be overlooked, and which is equipped with points where the mind can get a grip, so that we can find our way through without getting confused. And then we analyse this little model world instead of the real world. This mental trick is the thing which constitutes the rational method, that is, theory. The system of straight lines, circles, etc., of geometry is an intellectual model of the straight lines, circles, etc., which occur in the real world. The economic market in the abstract sense is a model of really existing markets, etc. Instead of the expression 'model world', we could also use the expressions, 'schemes of thought' or 'system of fictions'.

When we create the model world it is up to ourselves to decide which features and characteristics the model world shall have and what kind of relations shall exist between the various phenomena and groups of phenomena in the model world. This we can do because we are sovereigns in the model world, so long as we do not break the rules of formal logic.[2]

This does not mean, of course, that our decisions regarding the constitution of the model world are ruled completely by free fantasy or caprice. *The model world shall serve a purpose.* It shall help to adopt a way of thinking that will ultimately be useful in our fight for control over nature and social institutions. It shall picture those indefinable things in the real world which we might call 'essentials', meaning by that, of course, essentials with regard to our own ends.

What kind of criterion have we, then, by which to judge if our model world conforms to this ideal? We have no such criterion – none that can be formulated as a definite logical rule. We have nothing except a mysterious, inborn 'sense of smell' which as a rule will guide us so that we finally get on the right track. This is precisely the reason why the scientist is to be considered a logical sovereign in his model world. He is just like a wise, absolute monarch. He uses his prerogatives with tact and care. *He knows that this is the only way of ultimately obtaining his ends.* He listens to the suggestions of facts but takes care to consider them non-obligatory.

The laws of the model world will often consist only in typification, an idealization of some observed empirical law. We observe, for instance, empirically that a given market will most frequently be able to absorb a greater quantity of an article, the lower the price. And having observed this, we create a model world with a demand curve, sloping downward.

But often the investigator will equip his model world with something more than this. By a heroic guess, he will add something which is entirely outside the body of observation at his disposal. It is exactly in this kind of heroic guess, transgressing the observational facts, that the great constructive minds distinguished themselves from the average scientific worker.

This something which the constructive imaginative mind adds to the observations can either be a new kind of objects, not resembling anything which is known from actual observations, or it can be a new relation between phenomena which are by themselves well known from actual experiences but which have never been observationally related, because nobody has thought of it, or because the phenomena are of such a kind that they cannot be observed together directly with the given technique of observation.

A classic example of the first kind of transobservational invention is the creation of a model world equipped with atoms. The atoms were, at the time of their introduction into science, something far beyond the range of direct actual observations. Later methods of observing the atoms were introduced. Still later the atom concept again changed, indeed so completely that one can perhaps say that at present all there is left of the atom is a differential equation. This recent change in the conception is only an example of the fact that we disregard a model world as soon as we get upon the idea of another model world which 'smells' better. This change in the notion of an atom is not essential in this connection. The essential thing in which we are here interested is the undisputable fact that the introduction of the transobservational notion of an atom into science has contributed immensely towards a better understanding of the fundamental problems of modern physics and chemistry.

As an example of the second kind of invention, one could take the discovery of the relation between the diminishing return of land and the fact that rent exists.[3] Both facts were well known long before Ricardo, but the relation between them was not seen until revealed by the abstract speculations of Ricardo.

In the model world of Ricardo, rent arises, not because land *has* a productive power (as had been maintained by the Physiocrats and by Adam Smith), but because this productive power of land is *limited*. Without having realized what this point contains, one will never be able to understand the phenomenon of rent in the real world.

Another example is Toricelli's discovery of the relation between the pressure of the atmosphere and the experience that fluids will mount in a vacuum. Any number of other examples could, of course, be cited.

The distinction which we have here made between two kinds of transobservational creations, one introducing a new 'object' and the other introducing a new 'relation', is of course only a conventional one, and not one of principle, amongst others because the very distinction between 'object' and 'relation' depends on the point of view. Something which is a 'relation' in a microcosmic model world might be an 'object' in a macrocosmic model world. The distinction which is here essential is the distinction between the empirical, descriptive part of the investigation and the transobservational creations.

Having created our little model world, we start out to explore it. This seems paradoxical. Should it be necessary to explore something which we have ourselves created? It certainly is in many cases. When we create a model world, i.e. define a scheme of thought, it is generally impossible at once to overlook all the consequences involved in the definition laid down. Most frequently this can only be done by systematic investigations. We only have to think of what is meant by a mathematical discovery. This kind of investigation constitutes an essential part of the rational process, namely the rational deduction. The creation of the model world itself constitutes the rational induction.

Strictly speaking, the distinction between induction and deduction can also be made within that part of the investigation which we called the empirical part. This would give an empirical induction and an empirical deduction. Whether this distinction is made or not, it should be noticed that the distinction between induction and deduction is not the same as the distinction between empiricism and rationalism. This point is not always kept clear.

The regularities which are revealed by the empirical method we shall call *empirical laws* and the regularities which exist in our model world we shall call *rational laws*. These two laws are fundamentally different. Between them there exists a gap, which can never be bridged. The empirical laws are something that exist in the real world, and which therefore have to be *discovered*. The rational laws, on the contrary, are something that exists in the model world, and which are therefore *created* by the mind of the investigator. An empirical law is something on the permanency of which we can never be sure. Even if the regularity in past experience is very great we might sooner or later discover an exception to the rule. Or even the nature of the law might change. Nothing of this sort can happen to a law in the model world. We can be absolutely certain of this, because it is ourselves who have created the law. And we have conceived of it so as to be something permanent and something which admits of no exceptions. The fact that a law expresses something necessary, something which does not admit of exception is an infallible criterion that the law in question belongs to a model world, not to the real world.[4]

We are now in a position to describe more fully what we mean by the words 'explain', 'understand', etc., which we used to indicate the second object of the scientific investigation.

Reduced to their ultimate terms these words mean nothing else than to construct a model world where the occurrence of some particular regularity (or phenomenon) is a sufficient condition for the occurrence of some other regularity (or phenomenon).

Suppose for instance that we have at hand a certain observational material, W, where we have traced a certain empirical regularity (relationship) F. We want to 'explain' why this regularity exists. Let us imagine that we have constructed a model world, w, which is equipped with a certain kind of idealized regularity (relationship), f, that gives a mental picture of F. The model world, w, will of course contain a number of other relationships. Some of these may be only typifications of some observed phenomena and regularities.

Suppose, for instance, that the regularity e in w is a typification, a mental picture of the empirical regularity E. Others of the relationships of the model world, say, a, b,... may be of an independent rational character, not resembling anything which is actually observed or observable. That is, there is nothing in W that corresponds to a, b,....

If our model world is such that the presence of e involves the presence of f (the conclusion being drawn either directly or indirectly through a, b,...), and if in the actual material at hand not only F but also E is present, then we may say that we have 'explained' F by E.

The argument is in point of principle not very different in case the empirical thing to be 'explained' is an individually determined event instead of an empirical law *F*.

As an example of this mental procedure let us consider an elementary argument in monetary circulation. We construct a model world where the various pieces of circulating medium have a given velocity of circulation, where we have some well defined methods of payment, etc. If there is an increase in the amount of circulating medium in this model world we can show by way of reasoning, involving velocities of turnover, individual prices, etc. (amongst others certain things that cannot be observed directly), that the price level will increase. And if we have actually observed a case where we had both an increase in circulation and a rising price level, we might try to 'explain' this situation by the model world just considered. In case we do so, we would have in terms of the above notation:

F=actually observed increase in the amount of circulation
E=actually observed increase in price levels.

It should be noted that in this procedure we must always make sure that the phenomenon considered in the model world, *e*, is really a sufficient reason for *f*. *e* must entail *f*, *no matter what the other features of the model world are*. It is only in this case that we have really obtained a significant explanation. If we notice, for instance, a higher suicide rate amongst married men than amongst unmarried, it would be premature to 'explain' the higher suicide rate by the marriage. Splitting the material according to age groups, we could see that it is not the marriage as such but the higher age of the married man that must be used as an explanation of the higher suicide rate.

So far we have considered the 'explanation' as being something that can be described by one single factor. This is not always the most powerful way to think. Also in our intellectual activities we act according to the old saying 'Divide and rule'. Instead of constructing a model world where there is a single event, *e*, that is a sufficient condition for the event, *f*, we may construct a model world where *f* is entailed by the *coincidence* between several events $e_1, e_2, \ldots, e_n$. The way to proceed would then be to study separately the effect of each of these features $e_1, e_2, \ldots, e_n$. A simple example is the following: a steamer going up a river with the speed of 15 knots, and the stream running with a speed of three knots, would give the steamer a net velocity (with respect to the bank of the river) of 12 knots. Here we have:

f=net velocity of steamer
e_1=gross velocity of steamer
e_2=velocity of the stream.

As an example in economics, we may consider such a thing as the principle of diminishing return from land. Much of the objections against the validity of this principle are due to an overlooking of the fact that this principle only regards one phenomenon, e_1, in a group of phenomena, e_1, e_2,... that determines the return from land. Actually there are here at least two principles acting against each other, just as in the case of the steamer on the river. One principle is that if the state of technique is given and if we have to press more yield from the soil by adding more labour, plowing deeper etc., this will, after a certain point, entail a decreasing relative return. (We may here consider the relative return as defined by the ratio between the money value of the total product and the money value of the variable factors, assuming prices to be constant. It is unnecessary here to go into further detail of definition.) On the contrary, if we add more inventions, that is to say, introduce a change of technique in our model world, we might have, not a decreasing but an increasing return when we increase the amount produced. This is only another expression for the fact that we now think of the phenomenon e_2: the state of technique in its relation to total product, instead of the phenomenon e_1.

So far I have avoided the word 'cause', and for most purposes it would be perfectly possible to do without it altogether. This would have the advantage of avoiding much confusion and superficiality which has been introduced into the discussion of the logic of science by this scholastic term. However, it would probably be impossible to rid the language of this notion, so we had better take it up and see what it contains.

The everyday conception of a cause is animistic. We think of a cause as something that governs or directs the general phenomenon in much the same way a general is directing his troops. Obviously we have gotten this idea from a psychological introspection of ourselves. We know that in many circumstances we have the ability of influencing the course of events by exerting our own will-power. And on this pattern we have built the fiction of governing causes. In other words, we think of a cause as something imperative which exists in the *exterior world*. In my opinion this is fundamentally wrong. If we strip the word cause of its animistic mystery, and leave only that part which science can accept, nothing is left except *a certain way of thinking*, an intellectual trick, a shorthand symbol, which has proved by itself to be a useful weapon, legitimate or illegitimate, in our fight with nature and social institutions. As I see it the scientific (as distinguished from the scholastic), problem of causality is essentially a problem regarding our way of thinking, not a problem regarding the nature of the exterior world. The scientific (as distinguished from the scholastic) answer to the question 'what is a cause?', does not read: it is such and such a phenomenon. If any scientific answer is possible it must read: it is such and such a way of thinking.

The important question to the scientist is not to know whether a cause is 'true' or not, meaning by the word 'true' something objective in the exterior world. The only criterion to which he attributes any importance is the 'convenience' and 'expediency' of the cause. By that he means its instrumental value in helping towards digesting the giant mass of observations in such a way that these observations can ultimately be utilized with success in man's fight for control over nature and the social institutions. He does not care if there exist in nature divine laws of the 'governing' type. All in which he is interested is that the course of the universe shall be such that he can successfully apply his mental trick with the model world.

The main aspect of the problem of the scientific causality is the *direction* of causality, i.e. the distinction between a thing from which the relationship originates (a cause) and the thing in which it terminates (an effect). This distinction, as I see it, is intimately related to the logical distinction between a necessary and a sufficient condition.

In the model world *w* we assumed *e* to be a sufficient condition for *f*. In other words, *e* always entails *f*, while the occurrence of *f* does not necessarily involve *e*. We can now, without running the danger of being animistically misinterpreted, say that this means: '*E* is a cause of *F*'. The fact that *f* might occur without entailing *e*, excludes the possibility of *F* being the cause of *E*, so that the direction of causality is here well defined.

Note that *e* and *f* are relations in the model world. It is on *e* and *f* that the logical mechanism operates. *E* and *F* are the empirical relations which *e* and *f* are picturing. The conclusions regarding *e* and *f* are strictly legitimate from the logical point of view. The extension of the argument to the corresponding empirical things *E* and *F* is illegitimate, but, as experience shows, often a very successful way of thinking. This is just the basic idea of the mental trick involved in the philosophy of the model world.

What would have happened if we had assumed *f* to be a sufficient condition for *e*, instead of *e* being a sufficient condition for *f*? In this case *f* would always have entailed *e*, while *e* might have occurred without entailing *f*, and we would consequently say: '*F* is a cause of *E*'.

In both these two cases the direction is well defined, but in none of the cases has there been a question of *the* cause. In the first case *E* was one of several possible causes of *F*, and in the second case *F* was one of several possible causes of *E*. How can we construct the notion of *the* cause, and still preserve the idea of a *directed* relationship?

If we assume that *e* is not only a sufficient but also a necessary condition for *f*, we get rid of the plurality of causes, there is now nothing except *e* that could entail *f*. But the limiting case here considered where we get rid of the plurality of causes is at the same time the case where the cause *direction* disappears. In fact, if *e* is a necessary condition for *f*, *f* must also be a sufficient condition for *e*. We could consequently just as well say that *F* is a cause of *E* as the reverse. In reality, none of these expressions would be plausible. The only plausible expression would now be that '*E* and *F* are two mutually dependent things'.

In order to establish a notion of *the* directed cause, we shall apparently have to make appeal to some new principle outside the principle of the sufficient condition. This new principle, as I see it, is the *principle of partition of model worlds*. The principle can best be explained by an example. Suppose we have constructed a model world, w_{ef}, where *e* and *f* occur, and *e* and *f* are mutually conditional. This means that *e* is the necessary and sufficient condition for *f*, and consequently *f* also the necessary and sufficient condition for *e*. Furthermore, suppose that we have constructed another model world w_{eg} which does not involve f, but involves e and a third thing g, this g being in w_{eg} a sufficient condition for e. Finally suppose that we have, so far, no plausible reason to construct any model world w_{fh} with the following properties: not involving e, but involving f and a fourth thing h which is a sufficient condition for f.

In this case, e and f are no longer symmetrical. We have here a criterion *outside f* from which to judge if e is present, namely g. And this possibility takes, so to say, the form in our mind that e has a chance of entering the arena through some other gate than f, although e must, of course, entail f as soon as e has made its appearance on the arena. In other words, the curious idea here involved is that e is both a necessary and sufficient condition for f and that e has *nevertheless* a chance of coming into existence independently of f, while f has no such independent chance. This idea, as I see it, is basic for the conception of E as *the* cause of F.

Such a conceptional scheme is logically impossible without the partition of the model worlds. If it shall be possible to think of e as having a chance to come into existence independently of f, it must be in a model world different from the one where e is invariably related to f. If we should merge the two model worlds, w_{eg} and w_{ef} together, the resulting model world would still consist of only two things, namely g and e', where e' represents the simultaneous occurrence of e and f. And in this model world $w_{ge'}$, we would only have the simple relation that g is a sufficient condition for e'.

If by any chance our knowledge and understanding of the phenomena should develop in such a way as to make it plausible to create a model world w_{fh} not involving e, and being such that h is a sufficient condition for f, we would be forced to drop the idea that E is *the* cause of F. E and F would now be perfectly symmetrical. We could neither say that E is the cause of F, nor could we say that F is the cause of E. There is only one thing which could now be reasonably said: namely, that the joint phenomenon $E' = (E, F)$ may be caused either by G or by H.

Any number of concrete examples of the situations here considered can, of course, be given. For example,

E = introduction of smallpox bacilli into the blood
F = exterior symptoms of smallpox
G = condition under which smallpox infection takes place.

In the preceding lines I have made an essential point out of the distinction between the 'description' and the 'explanation' of observed phenomena. And I have connected this distinction with the distinction between the empirical and the rational aspect of science. If one's main concern is to discuss the difference between scientific rational and the scholastic rational point of view, one could be tempted to say that the entire science is only a description, including under this general term also the whole model world apparatus. The model world apparatus might then, perhaps, be classified as *indirect* description as distinguished from the truly empirical description. I believe, however, that nothing would really be gained by such terminology. And one would lose a very convenient term; namely, 'description' in the classical sense. That is why I have found it advisable to stick to the customary use of this word.

The point of view here developed has an obvious connection with the definition of *probability*. Without entering upon this question at any length, I shall make a few cursory remarks. As I see it, there are three notions which must be kept absolutely distinct if we shall have any hope of splitting the fog in the field of probability. I would prefer to call these notions by three different nouns; namely, frequency, probability, and belief. But since many people will probably persist in calling all of these notions probability, it will be convenient also to have three adjectives. As I see it, empirical, abstract, and personal probability would be three significant words. These words as I take them are not intended to carry any reference to the discussion which has taken place about the 'objective' and 'subjective' probability.

Empirical, abstract and personal probability are three notions, and each of them has their characteristic properties, just as the horse, the bull and the bear have each their characteristic features. I have a feeling that in the attempt at defining probability, one has often been trying to define the horse by its horns, the bull by its claws and the bear by its hoofs. As characteristic examples, one could mention the attempt to take the degree of belief as a basis of abstract probability, or the attempt to consider abstract probability as the limiting case of frequency, or the application of the principle of sufficient reason and the like.

As I see it, a plausible definition can be given in a much simpler way. First of all, there is no trouble in defining an empirical frequency. Sometimes the technical difficulties in making an actual observation might be great, but the very notion of an empirical frequency involves no difficulty.

Second, the abstract probability is, as I see it, nothing else than a *frequency* in a *model* world. Abstract probability, therefore, exists by the simple act of our declaration. We attribute those properties to it which we might find convenient for our purpose. In the simplest cases the most natural thing is to assume a finite or an enumerable set of objects with a certain number of characteristics, the objects being distributed in a certain way according to these characteristics. This is all we need to deduce the elementary laws of addition and multiplication of probability. In particular we can avoid the foggy notion of 'equally possible cases' altogether. When we come to repeated trials, we have to construct a somewhat larger model world with multi-dimensional distribution and we have to make a few more assumptions on the character of the distribution, but still the nature of the intellectual process involved will be essentially the same.

In this way we can build up the whole theory of probability without evoking any scholastic or artificial principle. I am hoping at some future date to publish a development of the theory of probability on these lines.

The correspondence between the model world of probability and the real world of frequency is just the same as between any model world and the real things which the model world is picturing, and a similar remark applies to the theory of sampling which is, after all, only a branch of probability. Although the theory of sampling bears a rather definite relation to the empirical method as such, it is essentially a 'theory', an analysis of a model world, according to the point of view here adopted. What actual experience has done for the theory of sampling is nothing more or less than it does in any case of a model world construction; namely, to present to the absolute monarch its non-obligatory suggestions regarding the rules and laws of the kingdom.

Third, *belief* is something irrational which cannot be explained restlessly in terms either of frequency or of abstract probability, and which can still less serve as a basis for the definition of any of these notions. Belief is some sort of personal conviction about things (past, present and future) which it is impossible to define in exact terms. We can say so much though, that belief is built on several elements, amongst which we usually find both abstract probability and actual observation of frequencies.

Let us take an example. Suppose I am the director of a Shipping Insurance Company and the problem comes up shall I or shall I not at a certain premium let my company cover the risk on a certain vessel which is sailing next Saturday to Green Harbour, Spitsbergen. The decision depends on my belief concerning what will happen on this voyage and the whole content of my mind, empirical and rational, goes to form this belief.

The observation of empirical frequency in the maritime insurance field has long ago suggested to me the idea of analysing such things by constructing a model world of probabilities. So I have done. I have on my desk and in my files a whole series of results, theoretical and numerical, concerning the risks of vessels according to size, age, etc., and according to the different waters, etc. How close does my model world fit the situation? What other conditions outside those considered in my model world of probability should be accounted for? Nobody can give an exact figure on this. I have to judge mostly by my 'sense of smell'. So, calculable and incalculable things, abstract and rational things, frequency and probability, enter into my mind to be balanced against each other through a mechanism of which I have myself some feeling, but which I should certainly feel at a loss to explain exactly. The result of the working of this mechanism is an opinon, a belief: yes, I think it is advisable to let my company cover this risk.

I know of nothing which has been so powerful in creating fog in the theory of probability as the confusion of personal belief with abstract probability, this notion which can be so brilliant when presented in its real sharp-edged, logical beauty.

So much for the nature of the 'theoretical' work, that is for the nature of the mental activity based on a model world. Now let us see why it is that this kind of work is so indispensable in our fight for control over nature and social institutions. The answer is a very simple one: the fact is that nature and social phenomena have such a peculiar *advertising policy* of their own. Often they make much noise and showing off of many things which are, after all, unessential for a real understanding of the phenomenon in question, and which are only apt to capture the pure empiricist and keep him at some laborious and sterile tasks of fact getting. The key to the phenomena is very often furnished by some feature which seems utterly unimportant from the empirical point of view. This is why the purely empirical and so-called institutional approach to economics is so danger-ous. If we go to our economic or social investigations under the motto that we shall 'let the facts speak for themselves', what we will hear will very often be childish talk. When it comes to really understanding a phenomenon, to gain an insight into its nature, not only to be familiar with its appearances, then the *dis-crimination*, this mysterious sense of smell which the real theorist uses in the construction of his model world, becomes basic. The only road to wisdom has been and will ever be to hear all things and *believe little*. That is why in the deeper problems of science the crucial contribution towards a real understanding of the phenomenon is always furnished by one of these heroic guesses trans-gressing observational facts.

We have seen it over and over again in the natural sciences. The most grandi-ose example is perhaps Einstein's theory of relativity. While grandiose, this example is, however, not easy to understand, so let us rather take some other examples which are less grandiose, but easier to understand.

Let us imagine a scientist who is watching the shifting aspects of the surface of water. An empirical description of the individual ups and downs of the surface of the water would not lead anywhere, however minute the description was. In order to gain a real understanding of the phenomenon, our scientist would have to introduce at least three different sets of *ideas*: first, the idea of the direct action of the wind on the surface of the water. This would account for the small waves. Next, the idea of the propagation of the long swells coming from the ocean. And third, the idea of ebb and flow caused by the attraction of the moon. Without introducing a model world containing these three kinds of waves, he would be hopelessly lost in his attempt at understanding the phenomenon.

Or let us take another example. Let us imagine that somebody wanted to explain the movement of the moon around the earth, and in order to do so, obtained the co-operation of a number of observatories on the earth. Let us imagine that he ordered all the available telescopes to be pointed at the moon and great effort to be made in patiently studying all the details of the moon's surface. The observations obtained in this way would be interesting enough in themselves, but they would not contain any significant contribution to the problem at hand: the explanation of the orbit of the moon. The man who indi-cated the road to a real explanation of the problem did it without any telescopes. His tools were just a pencil and a sheet of paper, and his name was *Isaac Newton*. In his imaginative mind he constructed a model world where bodies attracted each other with a force proportional to the masses of the bodies and inversely proportional to the square over their distances. He started exploring this model world and found that certain bodies would move in certain orbits, and one of these orbits which could be computed from the law of this model world was the orbit of the moon. The real discovery was brought about by a brain, not by a staff of patient observers. All the observational material would have been a dead mass if not animated by a theorist of genius.

It seems to me that much of the work which has been done in economics in the recent years in its significance is comparable to minute observations of the surface of the moon in order to find out its orbit. Let me take some examples.

I happened to read an article in the *New York Times* some months ago, where a contributor suggested that now the unemployment problem *had got to be solved*. According to him, a great investigation should now be directed towards the unemployment problem, getting all possible facts about unemployment. The kind of investigation which the man had in view was evidently a thorough statistical investigation getting information about how unemployment was in the different industries, in the different localities, what the age distribution of the unemployed was, what the social conditions of the unemployed were, and so forth. All this is well and good and some time all this information might be utilized, but it does not in the least have a bearing on that basic unemployment problem which the man had in mind. This problem is, namely, a problem which cannot be solved separately but only as one feature of the fundamental problem of the more or less rhythmic oscillations in economic systems. To get minute information on the various forms and geographical distribution of unemployment is just as irrelevant to this basic problem as it would have been to direct all available telescopes towards the moon in order to find out why the moon moved in its peculiar orbit around the earth.

A similar way of thinking manifests itself even among professed economists, although perhaps here it is not quite as pronounced. The following might serve as an example. Many of the recent elaborate investigations in business cycles and the various phenomena characterizing such cycles, are immensely valuable by putting the study of certain economic problems on a more definite basis. But it cannot be denied that in quite a few of these laborious investigations a great amount of work is wasted because the investigations have not been animated and directed by constructive theoretical thinking. And much of the work which has not been directly wasted, has the character of detail work which in itself is interesting, but which does not have that relevance to the basic economic problems which the empiricists engaged in this fact collecting think they have. One particular point revealing the unfortunate effect of the lack of a theoretical background in this kind of work is, for instance, the fact that most of the business cycle work of the institutionalists is done in what might be called the *peak-to-peak spirit*. An economic time series is considered in its totality as it stands and a thorough description is made of what happens from one peak through a bottom and to the next peak. In other words, the analysis is directed towards a discovery and description of *the* business cycle without any understanding of the necessity of breaking the problem up in different orders of waves. Such a procedure, it seems to me, is just as naïve as it would be for a scientist to patiently watch the shifting aspects of the water without breaking the problem up in the wind wave, the swell, and the ebb and flow problem.

Some understanding of this point has, of course, always been present in economic discussion, but the point is very far from being recognized to the extent it must be before we can hope for real progress in business cycle theory. It is true that such a thing as the seasonal fluctuations have always been more or less clearly recognized as a particular kind of variation that has to be looked upon as something different from other kinds of fluctuations in economic series. But there are other components which it is just as necessary to distinguish. In particular we must distinguish between the *sub cycle* with a duration of something between three and five years, and the *main cycle* with a duration of something between seven and 11 years. It is very probable that these two cycles must be explained by two completely different sets of ideas just as the wind waves and the swell must be explained differently. The ultimate explanation of the ups and downs of business cycles lies in the *interference phenomenon* between these two (and eventually other) cycles. It is in this interference phenomenon that the clues to the business fluctuation are to be sought. An analysis of statistical time series in the peak-to-peak spirit without even an attempt at separating the sub cycle and the main cycle, will therefore lead away from that which furnishes the real clue to the phenomenon.

Further analysis of the interference phenomenon between the sub cycle and the main cycle will, I believe, furnish an explanation of many of the business cycle puzzles of today. Many of those things which look like inexplicable irregularities when an economic time series is considered in its totality and analysed in the peak-to-peak spirit, will turn out to be nice regularities when the time series is analysed with a view to really determining its various components. It will, for instance, often turn out that a certain peak in the given series is produced by a peak in the sub cycles, while the main cycle is at its bottom in that same point, and so on. It is quite significant that those who insist the most on the non-regularity of the economic cycle phenomenon are exactly those who show the least understanding of what is meant by components in a time series.

Later in this course we shall go into detail in the method of time series analysis and we shall give further examples showing how the purely empirical approach to cycle analysis leads to superficial and non-significant results.

I have tried in this lecture to develop my view on theory and of its necessity in the construction of a really useful science of economics. As I see it, there are only two issues possible for the historical, institutional, and similar schools in economics. Either they have to accept theory and its far-reaching rational implications; they have to make theory serve their purpose, and by doing so, rise to the dignity of a science, or they have to alienate rationality and rest forever a pure narrative art – the art of collecting and filing data. The idea that it should be possible to 'explain' the things of this world by any other mental process than the one built on rationality, that is, on 'theory', seems to me a fundamental naïvety of the extremists of the historical and institutional schools in Economics.

1.2 A discussion of the fundamental distinction between a static and a dynamic economic theory

The dynamic as distinguished from the static analysis of economic problems is much talked about nowadays. There is quite a general feeling amongst economists that the type of economic theory which we have inherited from the classical and from the Austrian economists is insufficient as a basis for the explanation of modern economic life, and that we must in some way or another amend this theoretical structure and eventually make some important additions to it. It is also generally agreed that one of the things we have to add to orthodox theory is something which it would be appropriate to call *dynamics*, but there the agreement ends. Or more precisely expressed, the term agreement or disagreement does not apply to the situation. It is more correct to say that we do not know whether we agree or not, because we do not really know what we mean by a static and a dynamic theory in economics. Although this question has been much talked about, I think it is correct to say that there is still a very bad need for clarification in this field. What I shall try to do in this lecture is to make a modest contribution towards such a clarification.

From a mathematical point of view, the ideas involved are not at all new. As a matter of fact, the mathematical approach involved is rather trivial. But from the point of view of giving an economic interpretation to the mathematical notions, I would be inclined to say that there is some originality in my point of view. My endeavour has been to work the various ideas involved together into a consistent whole and to build up a clear-cut logical scheme which I hope might be of some help in pointing out what we are really trying to do in our attempt to elaborate a type of economic theory which is more powerful and more realistic than the orthodox static theory.

I shall not attempt to give any critical study of the opinions of the various authors in the field. This is just a practical procedure for saving time. It does not mean that I want to force my own point of view upon you. Anybody who wants to dig more deeply into the matter is invited to look up the literature and eventually present his criticism of the views set forth in these lectures.

The first point I want to emphasize is that in my mind the distinction between statics and dynamics is a *distinction between two different ways of thinking, not a distinction between two different kinds of phenomena*. This point is basic and much confusion has arisen from the fact that these two things have been mixed together. The phenomena as such can be *stationary* or *shifting*, but this distinction has nothing to do with the distinction between a static and a dynamic theory. We may speak of a static and of a dynamic analysis. But it is without sense to speak about a static or a dynamic phenomenon. I don't know of any discussion where the expression 'static phenomenon', 'static situation', or the like have been used, where the idea of the author would not have been expressed more precisely by saying 'stationary phenomenon' or 'stationary situation'. This will only serve as a preliminary remark to distinguish between two points of view often confused. We shall later go into a more detailed discussion of the notion of a stationary versus a shifting phenomenon.

What particular feature of our way of thinking is it then that constitutes the difference between a static and a dynamic theory? It is clear that these features have something to do with *time*, but time can enter into our mind in different ways. The problem is to know in what particular way time must enter in order to make the analysis a dynamic analysis. It is by no means true that any analysis where time enters is dynamic. Dynamics is something much more than statics plus time. Or rather, it is something entirely different from statics plus time.

Practically any scientific law can be looked upon as a systematic analysis of certain *variations*. Any law – static or dynamic – tells us something of how one thing (or a set of things) varies if some other thing (or some other set of things) varies. The difference between the static and the dynamic law rests in the fact that the variations involved in the law are of different kinds. The variations involved in the static law are not real variations in time, but formal variations that occur when we compare certain well-defined situations which we imagine are realized *alternatively*. The idea is: *if* the quantitative phenomenon *A* has such and such a magnitude, then the quantitative phenomenon *B* will have such and such a magnitude. Or more generally: if the constellation within the complex *A* is such and such, then the phenomenon *B* will be such and such. In other words, the variations considered in the static law are not variations with regard to time, but variations *with regard to certain alternatives*. In this sense, the static law is timeless. (But this does not prevent time from entering into the definition of certain magnitudes occurring in the formulation of the law. Output per unit of time may, for instance, occur.)

On the contrary, the dynamic law is a law whose aim it is to explain how and why a situation changes from one point of time to the next. The situations that are compared by the dynamic law are not alternative situations (as in the static law), but *successive* situations. In the static law the compared situations are equivalent alternatives. In the dynamic law we add a new principle by which the situations are ordered in a certain succession, namely, the time succession. It is just this time succession principle and the comparison between one situation and the following which is the essential point in the dynamic analysis.

It is in this sense that the distinction between statics and dynamics is a distinction between two different ways of thinking, that is, a distinction between two different kinds of analysis: a *static* analysis is an analysis by which we try to explain a certain thing by taking into account a set of other things that exist at the same point of time, and a *dynamic* analysis is an analysis in which we try to explain a certain thing by taking into account not only other things existing at the same point of time, but also things existing at some other point of time. Generally, these other points of time will be points of time in the past, so that we can say that the essential characteristic of the dynamic analysis is that it tries to explain *how one situation grows out of the preceding*.

We shall make the point clear by an illustration. Suppose that we want to investigate a set of two phenomena: the price p and the quantity traded x of a certain commodity in a certain market. The first thing we have to do is to *observe* the phenomena. First we observe at the point of time t' the price and the quantity.[5] Let the result of the observation be (p', x'). We will imagine that this observation result is written on a card. Then we make a new observation: at the point of time t'' we find the observation result (p'', x'') which is written on a new card, and so forth.

When we have obtained a sufficiently large observation material, we collect the cards. The observation of the phenomenon is finished and the analysis of the

observations commences. If the analysis is such that it does not make any difference whether we shuffle the cards before starting the analysis, then the analysis
is static. We would, for instance, have a static analysis if we tried, on the basis of
this material, to formulate the law that a high price corresponds to a small quantity, and vice versa. (The distinction between inductive and deductive laws is
here unessential. This question therefore requires no consideration here.) On the
contrary if the analysis is such that the order of succession and the time sequence
between the cards is an essential factor, then the analysis is dynamic. In the first
case, time is, so to speak, only an observational-technical variable. In the second
case, the course of time itself is essential. We could say that when the theoretical
law is *sequential*, then it involves a dynamic analysis.

So far, I have not mentioned the distinction between kinematics and dynamics. If one should take account also of this distinction, one would get the following scheme of analysis: first, we have statics; the law is not a law regarding
variation with respect to time. Second, we have a part of the analysis where such
variations occur. This second part will again have to be subdivided into two
parts, namely, kinematics and dynamics (in the restricted sense). Dynamics (in
the restricted sense) are based on the notion of *force*. In kinematics this notion
does not occur. In the following I shall not go into further consideration of the
distinction between kinematics and dynamics (in the restricted sense). That,
which in the following will be called dynamics (within economics), is the entire
non-statical part of the analysis. In those parts of economic theory where it is
possible to define a notion of force, it will also be possible to subdivide this non-
statistical part of the theory into a kinematics part and a part which is, in a more
restricted sense, dynamic.

When we adopt the dynamic point of view – the comparison between one
point of time and the following – we need some new notions which do not occur
in the static analysis. The most important of these notions is the notion of rate of
change with respect to time, that is, *velocity* with respect to time. More generally, one could speak of the *reaction* velocity of the system (or of the process)
for certain inciting agents. The notion of velocity with respect to time can be
illustrated graphically in the following way. Let us consider a train in movement.
We draw a *time series* showing how the distance covered varies as a function of
time: After one minute the distance covered is one mile, after two minutes it is
2.3 miles, and so forth. The slope[6] of this curve at a given moment of time represents the ratio between a small increment in distance and the corresponding
small increment in time, and this ratio is just the velocity with respect to time. It
is the velocity with which the distance grows per minute (in the particular
moment of time considered).

The slope of such a time series may vary from one moment of time to another.
We can represent this variation by drawing a new time series whose ordinate
represents the rate of change for the first curve. For this new curve we can again
(in every moment of time) compute the rate of change. This quantity (i.e. the rate
of change of the rate of change) is called the *acceleration* of the original quantity. Thus we could continue and consider rates of change of higher orders.

The rate of change with respect to time we shall designate by a point over the letter in question. Thus if X and V designate the total quantity which is respectively bought and produced of a certain commodity (since a certain point of time that is chosen as origin for time), then $x=\dot{X}$ and $v=\dot{V}$ designate respectively the buying and the production *velocity*. While the capital letters, X and V, have the denomination quantity (and nothing more), the small letters, x and v, have the denomination quantity per unit of time. This notation is consistently used in the following: the magnitudes $\dot{x}=\ddot{X}$ and $\dot{v}=\ddot{V}$ designate respectively the buying and the production *acceleration*. These magnitudes have the denomination quantity per unit of time.

When we compare two situations statically, it is in principle unessential whether the change from one of the two situations to the other takes place slowly or rapidly. But in the dynamic analysis this is an essential feature. We could therefore also formulate the distinction between statics and dynamics by saying that: *any law which is such that it involves both a certain magnitude and the rate of change with respect to time of this same magnitude is a dynamic law. All other theoretical laws are static.* It should be noticed that this definition requires not only that the law shall involve a rate of change with respect to time but that it shall involve also the magnitude in question itself. The reason for adopting this formulation is obvious. Any magnitude existing at a certain moment of time may namely be considered as the rate of change with respect to time of some other magnitude. This other magnitude is simply the integral of the first magnitude extended over time from an arbitrary origin of time up to the point of time considered. Therefore, if we said that a theoretical law is dynamic provided only that it contained a rate of change with respect to time, any theoretical law would be dynamic. For instance, the velocity, v, of production (i.e. the production per unit time) is nothing else than the rate of change with respect to time of the total production V counted from some arbitrary origin of time. And the mere fact that an economic analysis involves v does not at all make it dynamic, but it would be dynamic provided it involved at the same time $v=\dot{V}$ and V. And the analysis would also be dynamic if it involved at the same time v and $\dot{v}$. Similarly, if we analyse the relation between the price of a certain commodity, p, and the quantity traded per unit of time x, by assuming that there exists a demand relation $x=g\,(p)$ then the analysis is static, and the function g is nothing else than the static demand function. On the contrary, if we analyse the price and the quantity by assuming that there exists in any moment of time a demand relation of the form $x=G(p,\dot{p})$, then we make a dynamic analysis.

In view of the difference between the static and the dynamic analysis, it is obvious that there will be a definite difference in the *type of theoretical results* obtained from the two sorts of analysis. In the static model world the situation will at any moment of time be completely determined if the theory adopts a necessary number of assumptions. If this is the case, there can be no motion at all in the model world. Or more precisely expressed: the model world is only changed every time we make a change in our assumptions. And if we make a change in our assumptions and thus call forth a change in the situation in the static model world, we never ask the question whether this change, following a

change in our assumptions, takes place rapidly or slowly. The concrete significance of this feature of the static analysis is that we look upon all the phenomena
as being either of an *instantaneous* type or of an *asymptotic* type.

Considering a phenomenon as being of the instantaneous type means that we
look upon it as reacting immediately, quick as lightning, to a change in our
assumptions. Consider, for instance, the ordinary static demand schedule, that is
to say, the relation $p = f(x)$ between the price of a commodity p and the quantity
traded per unit of time x. Looking upon this relation as being of an instantaneous
character means this: if we assume the quantity brought to the market to change
from some initial magnitude x' to the magnitude x'', then according to the static
demand schedule the price will change from $p' = f(x')$ to $p'' = f(x'')$, and if we conceive of the demand schedule as an instantaneous relation, this change in p following our change in assumptions regarding x will take place immediately, that
is to say, with an infinite velocity. It does not take any time for p to adopt itself
to the new assumptions. No friction or inertia hampers its movement. It is in this
sense that we have to look upon the thesis that there exists in the static world
under a given set of assumptions, 'a perfect mobility but no motion'.

If we look upon the phenomenon as being of the *asymptotic-static* type, we
admit that the reaction velocity is not infinite, but we do not take account of it.
Instead of asking what the course of the phenomenon will be in the immediate
time following a change in our assumptions, we only ask what the final situation
will be in some more or less distant future when all the things following our
change in assumptions have had time to work out their effects. That is to say, we
consider only the asymptotic situation. For instance, let us again consider the
static demand curve, but now looking upon it not as giving an instantaneous relation between p and x, but as giving asymptotic relation. Suppose that the quantity brought to the market has been kept constantly at the level x' for a
considerable time, and that as a result of this, the price has also been kept stationary, namely, at the level $p' = f(x')$. Now let us assume that the quantity
brought to the market suddenly jumps to a new level x'' much higher than the
original level, and that this new level x'' is maintained stationary for a very long
time into future. What will the effect on price be? In an actual case, the price
will probably first drop very abruptly. Most likely it will drop so far that after a
short time a reaction takes place. The price will start rising. Then again it may
drop somewhat down. Probably it will fluctuate up and down for a while until it
finally finds a new stationary level. This new stationary level p'' will depend on
the new stationary level x'' for the quantity. The relation between the new stationary level of the price p'' and the corresponding level of the quantity x'' is just
the static demand relation considered as an asymptotic relation, that is to say, we
have $p'' = f(x'')$. The essential feature of this asymptotic static point of view is
that we disregard variations immediately following the change in our assumptions and only take account of the final situation that would come about provided
the assumptions of the static theory were approximately fulfilled in long enough
time to give the phenomenon time to react in accordance with these assumptions.
In actual life these assumptions will very seldom be fulfilled. It is in the sense

here considered that we have to take the statement that the static analysis is only concerned with what takes place in the 'long run'.

From these examples we see that a common feature both of the instantaneous and the asymptotic types of static relation is that no change can take place in the static model world unless we make a change in our assumptions. In the dynamic model world the situation is quite different. If we adopt in this model world a set assumptions sufficient to make the model world determinate, *we do not stop motion in it*. On the contrary, such a set of sufficient assumptions will determine a certain course of events in our model world from the initial point of time where the consideration starts. Thus in the dynamic model world there might take place a change in the situation even though we do not change our assumptions. This is one of the things that make the dynamic analysis a much more realistic and more powerful tool of investigation.

To sum up, we may say that the distinction between statics and dynamics is a distinction between two ways of thinking, two different mental procedures which we might use in our attempt at 'explaining' things, that is to say, between two different types of theory. And the essential feature which distinguishes these two types of theory is that dynamic theory is sequential while the static theory attempts to explain things without taking account of the time order of the events.

I shall now take up a series of other points of view which have often been more or less vaguely connected with the idea of a distinction between statics and dynamics, but which have in reality nothing to do with this distinction. We have already touched upon one such point of view, namely, the distinction between a stationary and a changing phenomenon. We shall now elaborate somewhat on this distinction and also mention a few other distinctions which it is important not to confuse with the distinction between statics and dynamics. There are in all, seven such distinctions which we shall take up, namely:

1   a stationary versus a shifting phenomenon;
2   a cross-section description versus a flux description;
3   data versus quaesita;
4   one-dimensional versus a several dimensional analysis;
5   short time versus long time components;
6   first order versus higher order approximations;
7   a theory versus a human purpose analysis.

This list of points of view seems rather inhomogeneous, and, prima facia, rather irrelevant to the distinction between statics and dynamics. However, all these points of view are sometimes confused with the distinction between statics and dynamics. It will therefore be worth while to see what they contain.

1.2.1 A stationary versus a shifting phenomenon

When we say that a phenomenon is stationary we can mean either that the phenomenon as revealed by our observations of it, does not shift with time. Or we can mean something more, namely, that there is nothing that tends to produce a change in the phenomenon. In other words, there are no forces at work that pull in the direction of changing the phenomenon. In the first case, we adopt *the pure descriptive point of view*; in the second case, we adopt the *explanation point of view*. This explanation point of view as it refers to the distinction between the stationary and a shifting phenomenon will be further discussed in Section XXX. Here we shall discuss the distinction between a stationary and a shifting phenomenon from the descriptive point of view.

A phenomenon that is quantitative in the sense that it can be described by one or several *magnitudes*, is stationary when these magnitudes are constant over time, otherwise the phenomenon is shifting, that is, changing (with time). It should be noticed that the variations here considered are actual variations with respect to time. They are not alternative variations of the kind we considered when defining a static analysis. A similar definition of stationary and shifting applies to non-quantitative phenomena.

If the phenomenon considered is uniquely defined, this distinction between a stationary and a changing phenomenon is quite obvious. However, in the very definition of the phenomenon there may lie something which needs further explanation in order to give a precise meaning to the distinction between stationary and changing. We shall consider three such things:

1   *Partial versus complete shifting.* When we speak of a stationary population, we may mean only that the size of the population, that is to say, the number of individuals in the population, is non-changing with time. As a rule, however, when we use this expression we usually mean something more, namely, that the age distribution of the population is also non-changing. Sometimes the expression, a stationary population, may even mean more: for instance, that the distribution according to occupation, according to income, etc., shall be non-changing. This shows that the notion of a stationary population can be given a wider and a more restricted meaning, accordingly as we think of the phenomenon 'population' as defined broadly or in great detail. It is therefore necessary to make our statement more precise, for instance, by saying that 'the population is stationary with respect to the characteristics *A*, *B*, and *C*', or the like.

Exactly the same reasoning can, of course, be applied to a great number of other phenomena, for instance, production, consumption, etc. And if we combine the production data with the data on population, we still get a great number of possibilities which must be taken into account. For instance, the case where total production changes while the production per capita is stationary.

The most specific notion of a stationary phenomenon that we can conceive of in economics is "the completely stationary society." Here not only population is stationary in all respects, but also production, consumption, etc.

2   *Microcosmic versus macrocosmic shifting*. Several phenomena can be looked upon both from a microcosmic and a macrocosmic point of view. We may, for instance, think of the separate individuals in a population or we may think of the population as such. The first is a microcosmic and the latter a macrocosmic point of view. Similarly, we may think of the individual capital objects or we may think of capital stock as such, etc. Each individual is born, lives his life, and passes away. If we look upon this particular individual we therefore get a picture of something decidedly changing. And yet it may happen that the population to which this individual belongs is stationary, both with regard to its magnitude and with regard to age distribution, and other characteristics. Similarly, the individual capital objects are produced, worn out, and discarded. And yet it may be that the capital stock as such is unchanging. In both these examples, the phenomenon considered is shifting in microcosmos but stationary in macrocosmos.

Between the points of view (1) and (2) there is a certain connection but they are not identical. In (1) we split the phenomenon into several characteristics. On the contrary, in (2) we divide it into several elements, each one of which is the carrier of the characteristics that are considered under (1).

3   *Velocity versus acceleration*. We have already defined the notion of velocity and the notion of acceleration. For instance, the production velocity u is the rate of production per unit time.[7] That is to say, it is the rate of change with respect to time of the total production U counted from an arbitrary origin of time. And the production acceleration $\dot{u}$ is the rate of change with respect to time of u. If we think of the notion of 'production' as being represented by u, then a 'stationary production' means that u is not changing over time; that is to say, $\dot{u}$ in any point of time. Quite generally, a quantitative phenomenon is stationary (in the descriptive sense with which we are concerned at present) when, and only when, its rate of change with respect to time is equal to 0. Now in many cases we may think of the 'phenomenon' considered as being represented either by a certain magnitude or by the rate of change of that same magnitude. The notion of what is stationary will differ accordingly. In the former case we would have a stationary phenomenon provided the velocity of the original magnitude, with respect to time, was equal to 0. In the latter case we would have a stationary phenomenon if the acceleration of the original magnitude was equal to 0. For instance, if we think of the total population as increasing with a constant percentage per year, then this can in a certain way be considered as a stationary phenomenon. The *growth* is stationary. In this case we attach the distinction between the stationary and the shifting to the *growth velocity* instead of to the population number itself. When we here say that the growth velocity is stationary, we mean the growth that appears when the population number is represented in a logarithmic scale. In this case a constant growth percentage is expressed by the fact that the variation of the population number with

time is represented by a straight line, that is to say, a line with a constant slope. We may go still one step further and attach the distinction between the stationary and the shifting to acceleration instead of attaching it to the velocity. In this case a phenomenon may be looked upon as stationary, even if its rate of change with respect to time is changing. In order to have an exact definition of the expression 'stationary', it is therefore necessary to specify which one of the notions: the magnitude itself, its velocity, or its acceleration (or eventually even higher order rates of change) we think of. In some cases this specification may be superfluous because the nature of the problem makes it obvious which one of these points of view we have to adopt. But there are many cases when an explicit statement is needed.

1.2.2 A cross-section description versus a flux description

There are two kinds of descriptions: one sort of description only states what the actual situation is at a given moment in time; another sort describes what the situation is in a series of consecutive points of time. The first is a cross-section description, and the second a flux description. For instance, a statement from a bank, giving the situation at the close of business of 30 June 1929, is a cross-section description. If we have several such statements, say, statements for every half year over a period of years, then we would know not only what the situation was at a given moment of time, but we would also have information about the *evolution* of the institution considered. That is to say, we would now have a flux description.

The length of the intervals of time between two consecutive pictures in such a cinematographic flux description is essential for the nature of the flux description. For instance, in the case of the bank statements, there may be a number of characteristics, the evolution of which we would not be able to follow as close as we want to by only having semi-annual statements. There are a number of transactions of which we would like to have monthly or weekly or even daily data. How short we want to have the intervals of observation depends entirely on the *time changing* nature of those characteristics we want to follow. Some characteristics change so slowly that it is no use having anything more than semi-annual data, while other characteristics may show significant variations within a much shorter time.

It should be noticed that we are here only concerned with the descriptive point of view. We have here not asked the 'why' of the phenomenon. This 'why' we may ask either within a phenomenon defined by a cross-section description, or within a phenomenon defined by a flux description. Even the introduction of this 'why' into the matter would not raise the question about the distinction between a static and a dynamic analysis. That is to say, the distinction between asking the 'why' in a cross-section described phenomenon and asking the 'why' in a flux described phenomenon, is by no means identical with the distinction between a static and a dynamic analysis.

Nor should the distinction between a cross-section description and a flux description be confused with the distinction between a stationary and a shifting phenomenon. We may have a cross-section description of a shifting phenomenon, just as we may have a flux description of a stationary phenomenon. In the latter case we would have that particular case where all of the cinematographic single-pictures are identical.

The three points of view here considered: statics versus dynamics, stationary versus shifting, and cross-section versus flux description, are often confused in the discussion about statics and dynamics.

1.2.3 Data versus quaesita

Any theory must have a certain basis from which it departs. In a sense a theory is nothing else than a mechanism by which certain things are derived from certain other things. Those things that are given we call the *data* of the problem and those things which are sought we call the *quaesita*.

The decision of what shall be looked upon as data and what as quaesita can not be made according to any mechanical rule. Much depends upon the point of view which is adopted. For instance, let us consider an ordinary static curve of demand. If we imagine that the price is given, we may derive from the demand curve a certain quantity traded per unit of time. In this case the price is looked upon as a datum and the quantity as a quaesitum. The demand curve itself is the "theory" by which quaesitum is derived from datum. Now nothing prevents us, of course, from reversing the argument. That is to say, look upon the quantity as a datum and the price as a quaesitum. Or more generally, we could consider the mutual dependency between price and quantity that is expressed by the demand curve. If this is done, the demand curve is no longer a 'theory' that operates with a datum and a quaesitum, but only a 'law' or an equilibrium condition, that in turn will enter as a datum in a more inclusive theory.

The distinction between data and quaesita does not coincide with the distinction between a stationary and a changing phenomenon. The datum can just as well consist in a magnitude that is changing with time as in a constant magnitude, and the same is true of quaesitum. Furthermore, none of these points of view coincide with the point of view adopted when we make the distinction between a static and a dynamic analysis. The following may serve as an example. Let us assume that there is given a static demand function of the form $p = f(x)$. Further let us assume as a datum a time series x_t showing what the quantity was (or is going to be) in each point of time over a certain interval. From this datum we may derive a certain time series p_t which shows what the price will be in each point of time. From the static demand curve here adopted we derive that this price will simply be $p_t = f(x_t)$. This is an example of a static analysis with a changing datum and a changing quaesitum. At the same time it is an example of a static analysis of a changing phenomenon. We would have a dynamic analysis of a stationary phenomenon if we analysed how the asymptotic level of price follows as the ultimate situation after a series of oscillations when the quantity traded jumps from one stationary level to another in the way described in one of our previous examples.

1.2.4 A one-dimensional versus a several dimensional analysis

A one-dimensional analysis is an analysis when we 'explain' a certain phenomenon, say, the quantity traded x of a certain commodity, by taking into account *one* other phenomenon, say, the price p of this commodity. For instance, the ordinary static demand function $x=g(p)$ is the expression of such a one-dimensional analysis.

A several dimensional analysis is an analysis where we explain a certain thing by taking into account *several* other things. For instance, if we consider the static law of demand as a relation expression how the quantity demanded x_1 of a certain commodity depends on the price p_1 of this commodity and also on the prices $p_2,\ldots, p_n$ of certain other commodities, then we make a several dimensional analysis.

This distinction between a one-dimensional and a several dimensional analysis is also one of these distinctions which must not be confused with the distinction between statics and dynamics. As a matter of fact, we may conceive of a one-dimensional analysis both in a static and in a dynamic way. The one-dimensional demand analysis is, for instance, static, if we take it in the form $x=g\,(p)$, but it is dynamic if we take it in the form $x=g(p, \dot{p})$. Similarly, a several dimensional analysis may also be conceived of either in a static or a dynamic way. Thus the several dimensional demand analysis is static if we take it in the form $x_1=g\,(p_1,\ldots,p_n)$, but it is dynamic if we take it in the form $x_1=g\,(p_1,\ldots,p_n; \dot{p}_1,\ldots,\dot{p}_n)$.

It should be noticed that even if we take time itself t into our relation as one of the variables, that does not in itself make the analysis a dynamic one. For instance, if we write the demand relation in the form $x=g\,(p,t)$ instead of the form $x=g\,(p)$, this only means that we have passed from a one-dimensional analysis (namely, looking upon x as depending on p alone), to a two-dimensional analysis (namely, looking upon x as depending on the two variables p and t). The confusion between the distinction: one-dimensional versus several dimensional analysis, and the distinction between statics versus dynamics, is one of the most common confusions in the current discussion about this matter.

The current idea of the 'ceteris paribus' clause so frequently imposed on an economic deduction is really based on the conception of a several dimensional analysis as distinguished from a one-dimensional analysis. The idea is this: we first conceive of a several dimensional analysis, that is to say, we explain the phenomenon A by $B_1,\ldots, B_n$. Then in order to simplify we say: if the constellation within the $(n-1)$ dimensional complex $B_2,\ldots, B_n$ is *given*, say, as $B_2^0,\ldots, B_n^0$, then the question of 'explaining' A is simply a question of explaining its relation to B_1. We argue: if the constellation of B_1 is such and such, say, B_1^0, then the constellation of A will be such and such, namely, A', provided, of course, that the constellation within the set $B_2,\ldots, B_n$ is all the time the one we assumed, namely, $B_2^0,\ldots, B_n^0$. It is this underlying assumption regarding the given constant constellation in the set $B_2,\ldots, B_n$ that constitutes the meaning of ceteris paribus. Thus the expression ceteris paribus has no meaning *unless we have already constructed a model world with a several dimensional relationship*. We must have this several dimensional relationship in order to be able to *specify* what these 'other things' are that shall be assumed constant, and further in order to be able to specify what the constant constellation in these other things shall be. To say that 'other things are equal' does not carry any sense if we cannot specify what these other things are and in which constellation they are to be kept equal. We must specify both the set $B_2, \ldots, B_n$ and also the particular constellation $B_2^0, \ldots, B_n^0$ within this set.

This shows that the true meaning of the expression ceteris paribus regards the nature of a *model* world. It has not any meaning to say that such and such a law would hold good *in the exterior world* 'if all other things are equal'. In the real world we have namely no possibility of specifying what these other things are. And if we should try to escape from this difficulty by making the generous statement that actually *all* conceivable things should be 'equal', then the meaning of the phrase ceteris paribus would simply reduce to the triviality that: 'the event A will happen provided nothing prevents it from happening'.

It should be noticed that in order to make an analysis truly several dimensional, there must not exist by the very nature of the problem any restriction on the free variability of the variables involved. For instance, if we say that the quantity demanded of a certain commodity x_1 is a function $x_1 = g(p_1, \ldots, p_n)$ we assume, that there is no governmental regulation to the effect that the price p_3 should always be, say, half of p_2, or anything of that sort. If there did exist such a regulation then we could simply substitute for p_3 in the formula, the magnitude $p_2/2$. That is to say, *we would have reduced the number of variables*. It is only if the variables involved are truly independent that it is legitimate to select some of them and keep them constant by the clause ceteris paribus. For instance, if there existed a governmental regulation as the one mentioned above, we could not discuss the influence of p_1 and p_2 on x under the ceteris paribus clause that $p_3 = \$3, \ldots, p_n = \$5$. This particular point will be further discussed in Section 1.5. The meaning of ceteris paribus is one of the points in economics which has been the subject of the greatest amount of loose and cheap reasoning.

1.2.5 *Short time versus long time components*

We shall now consider a special way of segregating the different effects in a theoretical relation; that is to say, a special way of utilizing the ceteris paribus idea. The following example will illustrate the point.

Let us consider the consumption of electric power for lighting purposes. The time series showing how this consumption fluctuates with time contains in it some very definite separate movements: first, we have the daily fluctuations, due to the fact that we use more light at night than in the daytime. Second, we have a weekly fluctuation, due to the fact that we use more light on some weekdays than on others. Third, we have a very pronounced seasonal fluctuation, because we use more light in the winter than in the summer. Then there will also be some more or less cyclical fluctuations because the consumption of electric power for lighting purposes moves in tune with the rhythm of good and bad times. Finally, there will be a very pronounced secular movement because this century has been the century of electric light development. Each one of the movements in this example may be looked upon as a separate phenomenon that goes its course more or less independent of the other movements. We may express this by saying that they are *time components of different order*. The daily fluctuation is a short time component as compared with the seasonal fluctuation, and the seasonal fluctuation is a short time component as compared with the business cycle component, and this again is a short time component in comparison to the secular movement. Vice versa, the seasonal fluctuation is a long time component in relation to the daily fluctuation, and so on.

Instead of thinking of the relation between one of these time components and any of the others, we may consider the relation between one of the components and the composite effect of all the higher components. This leads to the idea of the *normal* of the component in question. For instance, let us consider the seasonal fluctuation in our series. The higher components would then be the fluctuations due to the rhythm of good and bad times in business and the secular trend. (Within the business cycle fluctuations we may even distinguish a sub-cycle of a duration of something around three years and a main cycle with a duration of something around ten years, but for the present purpose the distinction between the sub-cycle and the main cycle is unessential.) The composite effect of the business fluctuations and the trend would be the normal around which the seasonal fluctuations are oscillating. Similarly, if we add to this the seasonal fluctuations and the weekly fluctuations we obtain the normal of the daily fluctuations. Quite generally we may combine these components in various sets and thus obtain normals of higher and lower order.

The characteristic feature by which we distinguish between the short time and long time components in this example is the *slowness* or the *rapidity* with which the component moves over time: the seasonal fluctuation moved more rapidly than the business cycle fluctuations and was therefore a component of a lower order. This idea of distinguishing between the various sorts of phenomena according to the slowness or rapidity with which they move can be extended to practically any of those things which we consider in economics. For instance, if we take the quantity traded per unit of time of a certain commodity, this quantity x can most of the time be decomposed into a seasonal component x_I, a sub-cycle x_{II}, a main cycle x_{III} and a trend x_{IV}. The way in which these various components make up the composite effect x, may be additive, multiplicative, or of some more complicated form. The fact that the components are additive means that we have

$$x = x_I + x_{II} + x_{III} + x_{IV} \tag{1}$$

and the fact that they are multiplicative means that we have

$$x = x_I \cdot x_{II} \cdot x_{III} \cdot x_{IV} \tag{2}$$

The passage from the case of multiplicative to the case of additive components may be performed simply by a logarithmic transformation. In fact, if we have the multiplicative case expressed by formula (2) and we introduce logarithms, we get

$$\log x = \log x_I + \log x_{II} + \log x_{III} + \log x_{IV} \tag{3}$$

That is to say, if we consider the phenomenon $\log x$ instead of the phenomenon x, we get additive components instead of multiplicative components. The more complicated cases where we have a mixture of additive and multiplicative components cannot be treated in this simple way. However, in economic data we will most frequently have the situation where all the components are straightforward multiplicative. That is what we shall assume most of the time in the statistical analysis later in this course. Consequently, we shall introduce logarithms instead of the actual data and perform the analysis on the assumption of additive components.

Often the idea of a slow or a rapid movement which is at the basis of the distinction between short time and long time components in economic phenomena, can be given some *rational* explanation, by taking into account the intrinsic structure of the system whose movement we consider. In production theory we may, for instance, classify the various factors of production in different groups according as they may be replaced or increased in capacity more or less rapidly. For instance, if there is an increase in the demand for automobiles, some of the factors of production can be made to react very quickly; for instance, the great bulk of labour used in the automobile industry (most of this labour does not take very long to train). Smaller machines may also be made to react rather quickly: their number and capacity may be increased within a comparatively short time, although perhaps not so quickly as the labour. The great machines and the organization of new plants are examples of things that it takes a considerable time to carry through.

The following is a mechanical illustration which represents the notion of time components of different orders. Suppose that we have a big pendulum, very long and with very heavy mass concentrated in its end. To the lower end of this pendulum we attach a shorter and lighter pendulum. To the lower end of this pendulum we attach a still shorter pendulum with a still smaller mass, and so on. Now suppose that we put the whole system into movement. If the mass of each pendulum is small in comparison to the mass of the next higher pendulum, there will be very little influence from the motion of the lower pendulum on the motion of the higher. Therefore, each pendulum will oscillate approximately as if it were a free pendulum. Now let us focus the attention on the movement of the smallest pendulum at the bottom of the system. Let us measure the horizontal distance from this smallest pendulum to the vertical that goes through the point of suspension of the whole system. And let us trace this distance as a time series. This time series will contain in it a number of components; first a short component, due to the fluctuation of the smallest pendulum at the bottom of the system, then a component with a longer swing due to the presence of the next higher pendulum, and so on. Finally there will be a component with a very long swing due to the presence of the largest pendulum. In short there will be small waves superimposed on large waves. Graphically the most important difference between the nature of these time components will be that the high components will have a much smaller *curvature* than the low components (except in those particular points where the low components change curvatures). In this example we can attach a very concrete meaning to the notion of normal. The normal of the lowest pendulum is at any moment of time the position of the next higher pendulum, and so on.

The distinction between short time and long time components is another one of these points of view that has frequently been confused with the distinction between statics and dynamics. As a matter of fact, these two points of view are entirely different. A short time component may be analysed statically or dynamically and the same is true of a long time component. The following might serve as an example. Suppose that we have decomposed the time series representing the quantity traded x of a certain commodity into the four above-mentioned components $x_I, \ldots, x_{IV}$. Further suppose that we have in a similar way decomposed the price p of this commodity into the four corresponding components $p_I, \ldots, p_{IV}$. This being done, it may be of considerable interest to compare p_I with x_I, and also to compare p_{II} with x_{II} and so on. Generally, it will not be of any great interest to compare the total magnitude x with the total magnitude p. Namely, the situation may frequently be that the relation between the short components, say, the relation between p_I and x_I, is of a different sort from the relation between the higher components, say, the relation between p_{II} and x_{II}. In an actual case we would probably find that if the first components, namely, the components no. *I* represent seasonal fluctuations, then we would have a rather definite static demand relation of the form $p_I = f(x_I)$, while the relation between p_{II} and x_{II} might be of a different sort. If the components no. *II* are components of the sub-cycle type, then a high magnitude of p_{II} would most frequently be associated with a high magnitude of x_{II}, contrary to what holds good for p_I and x_I that are related by the above static demand relation.

Both the relation between x_I and p_I and the relation between x_{II} and p_{II} here considered are of the static type, because there has not been a question of taking account of the rate of change of these quantities. If we had analysed the relation between x_I and p_I by assuming a dynamic demand relation of the form $x_I = g(p_I, \dot{p}_I)$, then we would have introduced a dynamic analysis, and it is obvious that such a dynamic analysis we can also make with regard to the relation between x_{II} and p_{II} and also with regard to the relation between x_{III} and p_{III} and so on.

A static demand curve in (x_{III}, p_{III}) coordinates would be a *long time normal demand curve*, as compared with a static (x_{II}, p_{II}) curve.

The following might serve as an example of the necessity of separating the time components before proceeding to the analysis: it is of no interest to compare the secular trend of pig iron with the secular trend of interest rates, amongst others, because there does not seem to be any secular trend at all in interest rates. On the contrary, it has a considerable interest to compare the short cyclical fluctuations in pig iron production with the short cyclical fluctuations in interest rates.

The failure to take into account the fundamental idea of the distinction between time components of various orders has a very unfortunate effect on the analysis of all sorts of economic phenomena that proceed more or less rhythmically. The whole significance of the analysis is more or less invalidated if one does not analyse the problem with a true understanding of what is involved in the separation of time components of different orders. The failure to see the difference between what I have called the *sub-cycle* (with a duration of something around three or four years), and the *main cycle* (with a duration of something around ten years), is particularly unfortunate, since it leads away from that point where in all probability the clue to the cycle phenomenon is to be found, namely, in the *interference* between the sub-cycle and the main cycle, as I have already mentioned in Section 1.1. Any investigation which fails to take account of this fundamental distinction is handicapped from the beginning.

Even the work of Wesley C. Mitchell, which has been of such a fundamental importance in making available new and basic information regarding the fluctuations of business activities is handicapped in this respect. It is true that Mitchell makes a few cursory remarks on the notion of components of different orders, but this is only in connection with the *trend idea*. In this connection he mentions, for instance, Wolfe's, Kondratiev's and Kuznets's work on what might be called the generation cycle. It is only as an attempt to analyse the nature of the *trend* that Mitchell considers the generation cycle. He never gets out of the scheme of thought originated by Cournot, namely, of considering the time evolution of an economic phenomenon as made up of four components: a more or less erratic component, a seasonal fluctuation, a cyclical fluctuation, and the trend. Mitchell seems never to have taken the position that the third of the above-mentioned components, namely, 'the cycle', contains in itself at least two components: the sub-cycle and the main cycle. It is true that he mentions Kitchin's work on the 40-month cycle but that is a purely incidental remark which has had no consequence for the way in which Mitchell attacks the whole problem. This attack is decidedly made in the peak-to-peak spirit looking upon 'the cycle' as an indivisible unit in itself. A characteristic example of how misleading the analysis becomes when one fails to distinguish between the sub-cycle and the main cycle is Mitchell's study of the *frequency distribution* of the length of 'the cycle', measured between two apparent bottom points (or between two apparent peaks) in the given composite time series. If it is true that the rhythmic changes of economic activities contain two distinct components, namely, the sub-cycle and the main cycle, then this concept of the length of the cycle measured from peak to peak does not express any significant feature of the data. This length does not give an adequate expression for the length of any of the periods in the underlying components, not to speak of the fact that one of the apparent peaks in the composite time series may indicate a peak in the sub-cycle, while the next following peak in the composite series may indicate a peak in the main cycle, so that the span of time between the two peaks *has nothing at all to do with a cycle length*. To form the frequency distribution of the length of 'the cycle' in this case is therefore, it seems to me, comparable to observing in each individual in a population the *average* between, say the height and the income of this individual, and then forming the frequency distribution of this average. Such a procedure has very little significance, to say the least. What does have significance is to consider the frequency distribution of the height by itself and also to consider the frequency distribution of the income. Similarly in cycle analysis: what has a meaning is to really decompose the curve and then form the frequency distribution of the period length for each component.

Another misleading feature of the peak-to-peak attach on 'the cycle' problem is the fact that the apparent difference in length between the rising parts and the falling parts of the given composite time series seems to contain a rather puzzling problem. If we attack the problem with a true understanding of the fact that the fluctuations in question represent an *interference* phenomenon, then the whole puzzle of this problem vanishes and only a purely geometrical triviality remains. If we construct, for instance, the composite curve containing a three-year sine curve and a ten-year sine curve, and we look at the apparent components, that is to say, the components measured from peak to peak in the composite curve, we will, of course, notice that the distance from a peak to the following bottom is shorter than the distance from the bottom to the following peak, so long as we are on the upward branch of the long cycle, while the reverse is true when we are on the downward branch of the long cycle. This is only what might be called a *retouch* phenomenon: peaks and bottoms in the composite curve are *displaced* with respect to the peaks and bottoms in the *underlying components*. It is only in the apparent components that we have the difference between the length of the rising and falling parts of the curve. *No such difference exists in the underlying components that we obtain when we perform a real decomposition of the given component curve.*

There is still another puzzle which is reduced to a pure triviality when we understand that the economic fluctuations represent an interference phenomenon, namely, the fact that our long cycle seems to contain an exact number of small cycles. This relation between long and short cycles is only something which shows up if we consider the given composite curve in the peak-to-peak spirit, that is to say, if we look at the *apparent* component instead of looking at the *underlying components*. It is due simply to the retouch phenomenon. The localization of the bottoms in the apparent long cycle is influenced very strongly by the localization of the bottoms in the underlying short cycle, because the convexity of the underlying short cycle is greater than the convexity of the long cycle. This will very often make it *appear* as if the bottom point in the long cycle coincided with a bottom point in the short cycle, and similarly for the peaks. This being so, it is obvious that it will appear as if the long cycle contained an exact number of short cycles.

1.2.6 First order versus higher order approximations

A theory is, as we have explained, an analysis of a model world. If this analysis shall have any meaning at all, it must more or less closely *fit the reality*. An absolute fit will never be obtained because of our limited capacity of thinking and of observation. But the fit may be more or less close. We may even in some cases conceive of a whole series of theories regarding one and the same phenomenon, the first theory giving the poorest fit, the second a better fit, the third a still better fit, and so on. These theories we would then say represent a first order, a second order, a third order, etc., approximation.

Such a series of approximations are dealt with not only because we were originally mistaken and then later gained better insight enabling us to develop a higher approximation. Sometimes we may *deliberately* consider a theory which we know gives a poorer fit to reality, than some other theory which we know of and which we could eventually utilize. When we do not utilize this better theory, it may be simply because this would be so much more painstaking. We use lower order approximation because this means an economy of time and effort and because we do not need, for the purpose at hand, a result that is any more accurate than the one obtained by the simpler theory.

The distinction between first order and higher order approximations should not be confused with the distinction between a one-dimensional and a several dimensional theory. Sometimes the closer fit to reality is obtained by introducing new variables. But sometimes it is obtained in quite a different way, namely by retaining the same number of variables as we had in the simpler theory but only conceiving of a more complicated relation between these variables.

Nor should the distinction between first order and higher order approximations be confused with the distinction between statics and dynamics. It is true that in many cases, perhaps in the majority of those cases which are at present arousing most of the actual interest of economists, the passage from the first order to a higher order approximation will actually mean a passage from a static to a dynamic theory. But that is only an expression for the present stage of economic theory. In point of principle the two distinctions are different.

1.2.7 A theory versus a human purpose analysis

As we have explained in Section 1.1, when we develop a theory we never introduce ethical considerations. We never ask the question, how can this or that phenomenon be related to a human purpose. This latter question is something which comes in by a much later stage in the approach, namely, under the fourth of those headings we put up in Section 1.1. This distinction between a theory and a human purpose analysis should not be confused with the distinction between statics and dynamics. The fact that these two distinctions are not identical is so obvious that it is sufficient merely to call attention to it. It is unnecessary to go into further detail. Surprisingly enough, however, the two distinctions have not infrequently been confused in the discussion about statics and dynamics.

I don't see any other explanation of this confusion than the following: historically the kind of theory which has been developed in economics has so far been only a first-order approximation theory. That is to say, it has given a rather poor fit to the observations. It has been rather unrealistic. On the other hand, those people who have been primarily interested in the human purpose analysis have as a rule had a very realistic attitude. They have indulged in empirical facts which have, of course, accounted for a better fit between their ideas and the real world (although their lack of constructive theoretical thinking has necessarily made their understanding of the phenomena somewhat superficial). In other words, theory has more or less been associated with a poor fit to reality while a human purpose analysis has been associated with a good fit. On the other hand, there has been a very definite feeling that the main object of the introduction of a dynamic analysis into economic theory should be to realize a better fit between theory and the realistic economic world. That is to say, we have also had the situation that the static theory has been associated with a pure fit to reality and dynamics with a good fit to reality. Perhaps this coincidence can account for the fact that sometimes theory has been associated with statics and a human purpose analysis has been associated with dynamics.

1.3 Analytical and historical dynamics

I now proceed to discuss the distinction between what we might call analytical and historical dynamics within economics. This distinction is not of the same fundamental nature as the distinction between dynamics and statics. Both the analytical and the historical dynamics attempt, namely, to explain how one situation grows out of the preceding. The distinction is of a formal and conventional sort. Historical dynamics is an attempt to analyse by dynamic principles those phenomena which have not yet been brought into rigorously formulated theoretical laws, and which must therefore be treated by a more or less vague or subjectively coloured reasoning. From a theoretical point of view it is the analytical dynamics which is the dynamics in the restricted sense.

The following is an example of a historical dynamic law: if we look upon the economic evolution of a society we will as a rule notice that as the density of the population increases, the economic machinery is made more complicated and more refined: we get specialisation of labour, machinism is developed, monetary and credit regime supersedes barter, on the labour market there are developed new institutes of law, for instance, collective bargaining, special labour courts, institutions of arbitration, etc. All these phenomena are more or less intimately connected. *In their historical development they determine each other mutually.* We may therefore speak of a law that governs the evolution, but it is not a law that can be formulated with the same abstract rigour as, for instance, a dynamic law of demand expressed by the equation $x = g(p, \dot{p})$. It therefore belongs to another type of theory.

Often the distinction between historical and analytical dynamics will be related to another distinction, namely this: any abstract economic theory, static or dynamic, is built on a certain general background of assumptions regarding the whole institutional setting of the problem. This background we could call the *milieu-type* of the theory. For instance, the economic theory that attempts to explain the barter between two aboriginal tribes (that is to say, that part of the price theory that is sometimes called the theory of isolated exchange) is of an entirely different milieu-type from the theory that tries to explain the relation between the progress velocity of inflation and the deficit in the state budget in a modern country in wartime. Most frequently historical dynamics will be concerned with the evolution of these general phenomena that characterize this milieu-type of the abstract static, or dynamic, economic theory, that is to say, those phenomena characterizing the institutional framework of general assumptions within which the abstract theoretical speculations are worked out.

But historical dynamics is not always concerned with this general background. Sometimes it has as its object a more particular phenomenon which is such that we have not yet succeeded in bringing the analysis of it into rigorous theoretical formulation. For instance, the classical economists showed how an increasing population makes it necessary to take less fertile land under cultivation, or what in this connection amounts to the same, intensify the cultivation on the land already in use. They first showed how this fact became a determining factor in the fixation of the wage rate and the rent of land. In its main traits the theory as it was developed by the classical economists is a static theory. The scheme of thought according to which the analysis is conceived is of the same nature as the scheme of thought that is at the basis of, say, an ordinary demand curve. The argument is: *if* the population is large then the rent of land will be high (provided, of course, that a certain set of underlying factors, for instance, the technique of production, is kept unchanged). However, the theory of rent also contains a truly dynamic side that was touched upon already by the classical economists and which in the future will certainly be taken up to a more penetrating analysis. The theory is dynamic to the extent to which it tries to explain the time order and the velocity of the various phases of the process by which an increasing (respectively decreasing) population entails an increasing (respectively decreasing) rent of land. If the underlying factors (for instance, the technique of production) is assumed constant during this process, it will be possible to give the theory a precise abstract formulation, that is to say, the theory will become an analytical dynamic, not only a historical, theory.

On the other hand, that tendency which counteracts the law of the diminishing return from land and therefore also counteracts the increase in the rent of land, namely, the development of the technique of production, must, at any rate at the present stage of theory be considered as a tendency that is not susceptible of an analytical dynamic analysis. It has, namely, not been possible to formulate exact laws or principles that determine the evolution velocity of the technique of production, its acceleration, etc. One of those things that hastens the development of the technique of production is, no doubt, the very pressure of the population on the soil. In this sense there certainly exists a mutual influence between the rent of land and the stage of the production technique. A high rent of land creates through its inciting influence on the evolution of the technique of production a tendency that in turn will counteract the high rent from land.

If we succeed in bringing this mutual tendency into an abstract dynamic formulation, then we would have made a start to an analytical dynamic (not only a historical dynamic) theory for the development of the technique of production.

Thus at the present stage of economic theory we may say that the development in the technique of agriculture represents a tendency, the theoretical analysis of which in point of principle does not exemplify the distinction between statics and dynamics but the distinction between analytical and historical dynamics.

1.4 The notion of an equilibrium: assumption-equilibrium and situation-equilibrium

The word equilibrium is used in economics in two different senses, sometimes confused; one is equilibrium in the sense of a fulfilment of a certain set of *assumptions*, the other is equilibrium in the sense of a certain kind of *situation*. The first we shall call assumption-equilibrium and the second we shall call situation-equilibrium. The most fundamental difference between these two notions is that an assumption-equilibrium is something of which it has no sense to say that it is fulfilled or that it is not fulfilled. On the other hand, a situation-equilibrium is something that may or may not be fulfilled. The situation is further complicated by the fact that sometimes the distinction between statics and dynamics is confused with the distinction between the case where 'equilibrium is realized' and the case where 'equilibrium is not realized'. In the present section we shall try to untangle these different notions and see what their true meanings are.

1.4.1 Assumption-equilibrium

In any analysis, static or dynamic, we must start by defining the object system within our model world, that is to say, we define *the system of magnitudes or phenomena, the mutual dependency of which we want to analyse*. As an example, let us take the static theory of exchange (without production). Suppose that there is in the market m individuals and n commodities. In this case the object system consists of $(mn+n-1)$ magnitudes, namely, first the n quantities that individual no. 1 trades (sells or buys), next the n quantities that individual no. 2 trades, and so on; in all, mn quantities. To this must be added the $(n-1)$ relative prices. As is well known, in the static theory of exchange it is only a question of the relative, not of the absolute, prices, and we may therefore imagine that all the prices are expressed in relation to one of them, which give $(n-1)$ relative numbers. These $(mn+n-1)$ magnitudes should in point of principle be looked upon as the object system in the theory of exchange (without production). This theory, namely, has as its object to find out how the $(mn+n-1)$ magnitudes considered mutually depend on each other. They form, so to speak, a closed system.

In the above definition of the object system each one of the magnitudes onsidered has so far been defined only as a *variable*. We have not defined any *particular* set of values of these variables. This is what we shall now do.

First we consider the *initial system* (the initial conditions). This is a description of the constellation in which the object system (or a part thereof) found itself when the analysis started. For instance, the initial system in the exchange market (without production) is the set of commodity quantities that the various individuals possessed before the exchange transactions started. This initial system is a set of information that belongs to the data of the problem.

Another special constellation within the object system is the *final system* (the final situation). This is the situation in the object system that will emerge as a result of the exchange transaction. It is just this situation that it is the object of the theory to explain. It is the quaesitum of the problem.

The means by which it is possible to pass from the initial system to the final system are the *equilibrium assumptions* (equilibrium conditions). An equilibrium assumption is a law that tells something about the *way* in which the magnitudes in the object system depend on each other. It is a relation that includes all or some of the magnitudes in the object system. And it must be fulfilled according to the very nature of the problem. It may simply be looked upon as *a definition of the character of our model world*. It is a condition which is such that if it were not complied with then our model world would be upset. Hence, the name equilibrium assumptions. As an example of such an equilibrium assumption we may cite the equation in the exchange market expressing that for any of the commodities, say, commodity j, the sum of the quantities sold must be equal to the sum of the commodities bought. This equation is simply a way of stating that the market in question is isolated, that is to say, that no 'international' trade takes place. Another example in the exchange market is the equation expressing that for any individual, for instance, individual i, the exchange value of the commodities sold must be equal to the exchange value of the commodities bought. This is the budget equation for individual i. It expresses the assumption that in our model world no credit transactions take place. A third example is the relations that express how individual i values the various commodities.

In the definition of the equilibrium assumptions there will, as a rule, explicitly or implicitly, be contained a certain system of magnitudes that could be called the *parameter system*. These are magnitudes that influence the shape of the equilibrium assumptions, and therefore will also have an effect on the final system, but which must, according to the very nature of the problem, be looked upon as not themselves being influenced by the magnitudes in the final system. For instance, the number of children which the individual i has will influence his comparative valuation of the various commodities and therefore also exert some influence on the magnitude which he will buy of commodity j. On the contrary, the quantity bought of commodity j has to be considered as having no influence on the number of children; at any rate, that is what we assume in the setting of the exchange problem here considered. Thus the parameter system is a system of magnitudes whose determination is outside of the scope of the analysis as it is here conceived. They belong to the data of the problem considered.

Which quantities shall be looked upon as belonging to the final system, and which to the initial system or the parameter system, depends on how inclusive the theoretical analysis is conceived. The more inclusive the theory is made the larger the number of magnitudes that are transferred from the parameter and initial system to the final system. Those magnitudes that occur as initial magnitudes in the theory of the exchange market without production will occur in the final system in the theory of the exchange market with production.

The general static problem in the theory of the exchange market without production is, as stated above, to determine the situation that will emerge as a consequence of given initial conditions and given equilibrium assumptions. To formulate one or a few of the equilibrium assumptions does not in itself contain the solution of the whole problem, but it is a step on the road towards such a solution. For every equilibrium condition that we succeed in formulating we reduce the *degrees of freedom* of the system by one. It is only when the number of mutually independent equilibrium conditions has become equal to the number of magnitudes in the object system that the problem is definitely solved. For instance, in order to solve the problem of the exchange market (without production), we need $(mn+n-1)$ mutually independent equilibrium conditions.

This is one of the senses in which we use the expression *equilibrium*. More precisely expressed, it is the assumption-equilibrium. The characteristic features of this manner of attacking this problem are that all the variables are considered simultaneously as mutually determining each other and determined by each other. In this case we may say that the problem is attacked as an *equilibrium problem*. In contradistinction to this way to attacking the problem, we have the scholastic way of thinking based on the 'chain of cause' idea: A is the 'cause' of B, B is the 'cause' of C, and so on.

The following is an example of the pitfalls which are avoided when we attack the problem as an equilibrium problem. If we attempt to explain the rent of land as the part of total product that is left when labour, capital and the entrepreneur have got their parts, and then explain the profit of the entrepreneur as the part that is left when land, labour and capital have got their parts, and so on, we have not given any solution at all of that which is the essential problem in distribution. In the way in which we have here formulated the problem there are, namely, several variables but only one equation, namely, the equation expressing that the whole product is distributed amongst the factors of production. The above-mentioned theories therefore do not in reality contain anything more than *chasing the variables one at a time in turn on the left-hand side of the equation*. It is only when we attack the static problem of distribution as an equilibrium problem that we open the way for a real solution of the problem. This solution has to be sought by introducing marginal efficiency considerations or some other considerations *that add more conditions*. And, if these new conditions are added, we will as a rule find that the original equation (namely, the equation expressing that the entire product is distributed amongst the factors of production), far from being a help in the solution of the problem, really introduces a new problem. For instance, if we look upon the problem from a simplified marginal efficiency standpoint, assuming that each factor is remunerated according to its marginal efficiency, it becomes a problem to explain if these assumptions are or are not compatible with the assumption that the entire product is distributed among the factors of production.

The meaning of the word equilibrium as here discussed has nothing to do with the distinction between statics and dynamics. As a matter of fact, the notion of an assumption-equilibrium has a place both within statics and within dynamics. However, there will be some slight difference in the way in which the idea of assumption-equilibrium is applied in the two fields. I now proceed to a discussion of these differences.

Some authors (for instance, Walras, in his *Element d'économie politique pure*, p. 301) has stated that it should be possible to go from the static to the dynamic theory simply by imagining the static equilibrium (in the sense of an assumption-equilibrium) was changing with time.[8] In other words, we should imagine that at any point of time there was realized a static equilibrium (in the sense of an assumption-equilibrium). This, however, is completely to misunderstand the nature of the dynamic equilibrium (in the sense of assumption-equilibrium). The putting together of a series of static equilibria can never give the explanation of a flux of events which it is the object of the dynamic theory to give. The dynamic theory shall, as mentioned above, show how *one situation grows out of the foregoing*. If the theory only shows that one situation is different from the foregoing because certain data are different on the two points of time, then the theory is still static. The dynamic equilibrium introduces some new idea which is much more fundamental than the idea that the equilibrium changes with time.

It is true that the dynamic equilibrium (in the sense of an assumption-equilibrium) is a certain kind of mutual relationship, a certain set of conditions that are fulfilled *in any moment of time*. But this equilibrium is fundamentally different from the static equilibrium (in the sense of assumption-equilibrium). *There are other things that keep each other in equilibrium by these momentary dynamic equilibria than by the static equilibria*. In the static equilibrium, as mentioned above $(mn+n-1)$, different quantities keep each other in equilibrium (namely, the quantities traded and the prices). In the momentary dynamic equilibrium there is a *greater number of magnitudes* that keep each other in equilibrium, namely, the above-mentioned $(mn+n-1)$ magnitudes and furthermore the *velocities with respect to time of these same magnitudes* (may be also the velocities of higher order, perhaps also other variables). The essential feature in the dynamic point of view is just this fact that the group of things that keep each other in equilibrium is extended to include also the velocities.

Furthermore, there is this difference between the static and the (momentary) dynamic equilibrium that the magnitudes that enter into the latter equilibrium are not, as the magnitudes entering into the static equilibrium, identical with the 'unknown things' of the problem. Regarding what shall be considered as the unknown things, there is, namely, a fundamental difference between statics and dynamics. In statics an unknown thing is simply an unknown *magnitude*. In the static exchange market (without production) there is, for instance, $(mn+n-1)$ unknown magnitudes to be determined. The problem is solved when these $(mn+n-1)$ magnitudes are determined by the $(mn+n-1)$ static equations of equilibrium. On the contrary, in dynamics an unknown thing is the same as an unknown *curve*, precisely expressed: an unknown time curve.

For instance, the dynamic problem of the exchange market is not to 'find' the above-mentioned $(mn+n-1)$ magnitudes, and their velocities with respect to time, by using a set of $2(mn+n-1)$ equations, but to show how the unknown time series of the problem will be determined. In order to do this we do not need as many equations as there are unknown magnitudes entering into the momentary dynamic equilibrium. When the system moves on from one moment of time to the next, we namely have in each new moment of time the situation that not all the magnitudes entering into the momentary dynamic equilibrium are unknown. Some of them may be looked upon as known from the situation existing in the foregoing moment of time. Or we may express the same thing in another way by saying that apart from the particular set of conditions imposed upon the momentary dynamic equilibrium by the nature of the problem at hand, we also have a certain set of conditions that, no matter what the particular problem is, must be fulfilled by the very definition of the rate of change with respect to time. How many particular conditions regarding the momentary dynamic equilibrium do we need then in order to make the problem determinate? We need just as many such equations as there are unknown time curves. Also within dynamics we namely have the rule that one condition is not sufficient to determine several unknown things. We must have just as many (mutually independent) conditions as there are unknown things, neither more nor less. When we want to find out if the dynamic problem is determinate, we therefore have to count on the one hand the number of unknown time curves, and on the other hand the number of equations expressing a condition regarding the momentary dynamic equilibrium. If the number of unknown time curves is N and the problem is formulated in such a way that it involves the rates of change up to the order k, then the number of *magnitudes* entering into the momentary dynamic equilibrium is $(N + kN)$ while the number of *unknown things* is only N.

The initial conditions in the dynamic model world are a set of conditions giving information about how much the variables involved and their velocities with respect to time were in the moment of time when the analysis started. We shall later discuss some examples of how the unknown time curves of such dynamic problems are derived from the momentary dynamic equilibrium conditions and from the initial conditions. As I see it, the further development of this type of analysis will be of considerable importance for the development of a more significant theory of rhythmic changes in the economic system. In the great variety of cycle 'explanations' which we have had in the course of time, there are very few which really attack the cycle problem as an *equilibrium* problem in the sense here envisaged. The great bulk of cycle theories have not yet emerged from the stage where the static theory was before the static equilibrium theories were developed: many of the current cycle 'explanations' consist merely in chasing one unknown at a time in turn on the left-hand side of the equation.

From this discussion we see that the notion of equilibrium taken in the sense of assumption-equilibrium is something which must necessarily always be fulfilled. If by equilibrium we mean an assumption-equilibrium, it has no meaning at all to say 'equilibrium is fulfilled' or 'equilibrium is not fulfilled'. The very distinction between an equilibrium that is fulfilled and an equilibrium that is not does not exist in the case of an assumption-equilibrium. Furthermore, the assumption-equilibrium may be either static or dynamic. We now proceed to the discussion of a different notion of equilibrium, namely the situation-equilibrium. An assumption-equilibrium can be static or dynamic, a situation-equilibrium can be stationary or moving.

1.4.2 *Situation-equilibrium*

The notion of equilibrium which we shall now discuss is a notion which does not arise out of an attempt to characterize a way of thinking (as the assumption-equilibrium does), but arises when we want to characterize a type of situation. The situation-equilibrium stands in the same relation to the notion of assumption-equilibrium as a rainstorm stands to meteorology. The situation-equilibrium is one of those things that are analysed by assumption-equilibria, just as a rainstorm is analysed by meteorology. There are two kinds of situation equilibria, namely, *stationary* and *moving equilibria*. A stationary equilibrium is not the same as a static equilibrium, not any more than a rainstorm is the same as that part of meteorology which is concerned with rainfall. The stationary equilibrium is something characterized by a particular kind of situation that might arise under certain circumstances, the emergence of which is the object of theory to explain, and this explanation may be attempted either by a static theory (involving the idea of static assumption-equilibria) or by a dynamic theory (involving the idea of dynamic assumption-equilibria).

What features then are there in the situation which makes it represent a stationary or a moving equilibrium? We shall first answer this question so far as the stationary equilibrium is concerned.

We have already in Section 1.2 defined what we mean by a stationary state, when we take this conception in the purely descriptive sense. It simply means that the phenomenon in question, as revealed by observation, is actually non-changing. We shall now ask a further question, namely: why is it that the situation is actually non-changing? We now look upon the phenomenon or the situation in a different light: we ask what particular features in the situation will account for the fact that the situation is non-changing? *If a situation has such characteristics as will account for its non-change, then we say that this situation represents a stationary equilibrium.*

The following might serve as an example. If we take a pendulum and hold it in a position different from the vertical position, the pendulum would immediately start moving if we let it loose. Therefore, such a situation from the viewpoint of the theory of the pendulum does not represent a stationary equilibrium from the viewpoint of the theory of the free pendulum. And the same would be true if we did not 'hold' the pendulum but took any situation and looked upon it as one of those situations that are realized during a continuous swing of the pendulum. On the other hand, if we leave the pendulum at rest in a vertical position, then there are no forces at work which would tend to produce a movement. The pendulum would be hanging still (provided, of course, that there are no distur-bances, such as a draught, vibration, or something of that sort). This situation therefore would represent a stationary equilibrium. Similarly, let us take the ordinary static demand and supply construction for a given commodity, and assume that this construction gives a sufficiently true picture of some actual market. Further let us assume that in this market the quantity brought to the market is equal to that quantity which is determined by the intersection of the demand and supply curve, and also that the prevailing price is equal to the price determined by the intersection of the curves. If this is the situation, then there will be no tendency to change the situation; in other words, this is a situation representing a stationary equilibrium. Or again, let us take a dynamic demand relation of the form $x=g(p, \dot{p})$. If we have a situation where $\dot{p}=0$ and where further x and p have such magnitudes as will satisfy the above demand relation for $\dot{p}=0$, and will satisfy also the supply relation (which may be static or dynamic), then the situation considered will represent a stationary equilibrium.

Thus we see that the notion of a stationary equilibrium is intimately con-nected with the characterization of a situation. But, on the other hand, it is not purely descriptive. It also has some features in it connected with the theoretical aspect. That is to say, the type of situation by which we defined the notion of a stationary equilibrium *cannot be described without making a reference to theory*; i.e. to a way of thinking. The fundamental characteristic of the stationary equi-librium is the notion of a situation, but it has a secondary characteristic con-nected with a way of thinking. We may say that the stationary equilibrium is defined by a situation, but this situation is of a particular sort, namely, one which under certain circumstanced appears *in a theoretical analysis*. When we take a situation as defining a stationary equilibrium, we look upon it not only as an empirical fact, but as something occurring in a theoretical analysis. Before we can define our stationary equilibrium we must therefore construct a theoretical analysis which amongst others would explain if a change would occur in a certain phenomenon under certain circumstances. Then we take an actual situ-ation which is such that, according to the theory developed, it would not entail a change. This situation then is taken as defining a stationary equilibrium.

As a rule, the most penetrating analysis of why a given situation represents a stationary equilibrium in this sense will be made by a dynamic theory, but this need not always be the case. In point of principle the theory by which we define the stationary situation may be either static or dynamic. If the theory is such that it explains the velocity with which a system evolves towards a certain asymp-totic situation, then this asymptotic situation represents a stationary equilibrium, and the way in which the system approaches this goal is analysed by a dynamic theory. Otherwise the theory is static. Take, for instance, the example in Section 1.2 regarding the way in which the price adapts itself to a new, ultimately sta-tionary, level, when the quantity brought to the market jumps from one station-ary level to another. If the analysis in this example centres upon the manner in which the ultimate level is approached, then the analysis is dynamic. But if no regard is taken of the way in which the ultimate level is approached, then the analysis is static. But in both cases it would (by a different sort of theoretical assumptions) give an explanation of why the asymptotic level, when reached, would be stationary.

It should be noticed that when the stationary equilibrium is analysed by a dynamic theory it must necessarily appear *as a limiting case* in such a theory, namely, the case where all the velocities with respect to time are equal to 0. No situation where some of the variables with respect to time differ from 0 can be a stationary equilibrium. Similarly, all the higher order velocities must, of course, also be equal to 0.

It will be seen that equilibrium taken in the sense of a stationary equilibrium here described, is something which may or may not exist according to the particular circumstances in each case. In this respect the notion of a stationary equilibrium is fundamentally different from the notion of an assumption-equilibrium (static or dynamic) discussed under Section 1.4.1 above.

I now proceed to a discussion of the meaning of a *moving equilibrium*. In point of principle a moving equilibrium is just as the notion of a stationary equilibrium, something which characterizes a situation that may, under certain circumstances, present itself in a theoretical analysis. The only difference is that when we introduce the notion of a moving equilibrium, we think of the phenomenon as something more *complex*, or more precisely expressed as something made up of *several time components*. Suppose, for instance, that we have the phenomenon composed of a short time and a long time component. Conceivably we may first assume that the long time component is maintained at a stationary level and, under this assumption, we may analyse what happens to the short time component. By a static or a dynamic analysis we may, for instance, explain that it will approach a stationary equilibrium. When the first component has reached this stationary equilibrium, the composite phenomenon will continue in a stationary fashion, because we have assumed the longer component to be maintained stationary. Now let us assume that we enlarge the theoretical analysis by dropping the assumption that the long time component is maintained at a stationary level. Let us, for instance, assume that the long time component is slowly increasing. Also, in this case we may develop a theory regarding the short time component similar to the theory we developed in the first case. The only difference will be that the level towards which the composite phenomenon tends is now not a fixed level any more, but is itself changing. If we look upon the phenomenon from this angle we may say that analysis now consists in explaining that (and possibly also how) the phenomenon will tend to approach a constantly shifting goal. We look upon the first component as tending towards an equilibrium but this equilibrium is not stationary but a moving equilibrium. (The difference between explaining *that* and explaining *how* the first component tends towards its equilibrium, would be a distinction between a static and a dynamic explanation.) In this analysis we may consider the long time component as a datum, as one of those things which shall itself be explained. We might, for instance, try to explain each component by a static theory. Or we might analyse each component by a dynamic theory. Or again we may consider the long time component as a datum and try to explain the short time component by a static theory.[9] Thus we see that the distinction between a stationary and a moving equilibrium has nothing to do with the distinction between statics and dynamics.

It should be noticed that the idea of a moving equilibrium is intimately connected with the idea that the second component moves *more slowly in time* than the first component. If the second component should change nearly as rapidly as the first component, it should have no sense at all to say that the level which the second component has at a given moment of time represents an 'equilibrium' around which the first component fluctuates. In this case the breaking up of the problem into two time components may still be a useful procedure. But it would be rather artificial to speak of one as representing the 'equilibrium level' for the other.

Professor Robbins, in his article in the *Economic Journal*, June, 1930, discusses a distinction which, if it is properly interpreted, comes down to our distinction between an assumption-equilibrium and a situation-equilibrium.[10] His point is that in the Clarkian construction the constancy of the various magnitudes considered is a condition of equilibrium while in the classical construction this constancy is one of the resultants of the equilibrating processes. This distinction, it seems to me, is quite sound. But it must be clearly recognized that Robbins's statement contains two different ideas that must not be mixed up: on one hand we have the distinction between an 'assumption' and a 'resulting situation'. On the other hand, we have the distinction between something which is constant over time and something which is changing. The first distinction is the one which is fundamental in contrasting Clark and the classicists, and I take this as being the main idea of Robbins. However, Robbins's article also contains some other statements which seem to show that he does not clearly distinguish between the two ideas involved in his statement. For instance, he does not seem to distinguish between a 'situation' (which is something to which the distinction between stationary and changing applies) and a 'way of thinking' (which is something to which the distinction between static and dynamic applies). He seems to be taking the two terms, 'stationary' and 'static', as synonymous.[11]

The notion of an equilibrium is sometimes attached to the distinction between a *stable* and an *unstable* equilibrium. This distinction is a distinction applicable to the notion of equilibrium taken in the sense of a situation-equilibrium. This way of splitting the notion of a situation-equilibrium is also different from the distinction between stationary and moving equilibria.

The general notion of situation-equilibrium is defined by reference to certain properties of the situation existing at a given point of time. The subdivision into stable and unstable is effectuated by taking account not only of *the* situation which represents an equilibrium in the above sense, but also taking account of situations *in the vicinity* of this equilibrium situation. That is to say, situations that differ only slightly from the equilibrium situation. If all the situations in the vicinity of an equilibrium-situation are such that they entail a movement directed *towards* the equilibrium situation, then the equilibrium situation in question is called *stable*. If all the situations in the vicinity of the equilibrium situation are such that they entail a movement directed *away from* the equilibrium situation, then we have an *unstable* equilibrium; more precisely addressed, we have a *properly* unstable equilibrium. Conceivably there might be some situations in the vicinity of the equilibrium-situation which entail a movement away from the equilibrium-situation while others entail a movement towards it and still others do not entail any movement at all. In this case the equilibrium is called *improperly* unstable. The distinction of the various cases here considered is perfectly analogous to the various situations which may arise in the study of maxima and minima of functions of several variables.

1.5 Structural, confluent and artificial relations in economic theory

We shall now discuss a distinction between three sorts of mathematical relations, that it is of the utmost importance to recognize clearly when we analyse theoretical economic problems. We shall first by a simplified example illustrate the nature of the distinction.

Let us consider any rectangle. Let the length of the base line be x and the height y. Then according to an elementary formula of geometry, the area of the rectangle is equal to

$$A = x \cdot y \tag{4}$$

This formula has two characteristic features:

I   It holds good identically in the variables involved in the right member. That is to say, the formula holds good whatever the magnitude of x and y. We may, for instance, choose $x=3$ inches, and when this choice is made, we may choose $y=7$ inches. Even if x is chosen we are at liberty to assign any value whatsoever to y. The fact that we have chosen x does not entail any restriction of the further choice of y. That is to say, the two variables are independent.

II In order to insure the validity of formula (4) we do not need to assume that any other relation is fulfilled. (Of course, we assume that all the areas considered are rectangular but that is only a general assumption underlying our whole discussion. It is not any particular relation.)

If we consider the set of all possible rectangles, then we know that the formula (4) holds good for any rectangle in this set. Now let us pick out a sub-set of rectangles, namely, the set consisting of all those rectangles where

$$x = y \tag{5}$$

In this particular sub-set the area A of a rectangle may be expressed by another formula than (1), namely,

$$A = x^2 \tag{6}$$

The last formula has one characteristic feature in common with formula (4), namely, that we may attribute any value to the magnitudes occurring in the right member. In (4) we may attribute any value to x and y. And in (6) we may attribute any value to x. Of course, there is this difference, that in (4) we had two variables in the right member and in (6) we only have one, but this is a minor point in this connection. The essential point is that in each of the two cases those variables that *are* involved in the right member may be varied freely. We may perhaps make the point clearer by thinking that we had originally considered not a rectangle but a rectangular parallelepipedon, that is a rectangular box with width$=x$, length$=y$ and height$=z$. The volume of this box is equal to

$$V = x \cdot y \cdot z \tag{7}$$

This formula holds good for any box, no matter what x, y and z are. If we limit the consideration to a particular sub-set of such boxes, namely, those for which

$$y = z \tag{8}$$

then the volume of the box in this sub-set would be equal to

$$V = x \cdot y^2 \tag{9}$$

And we see that the last formula is similar to (7) with respect to the characteristic of holding good identically in the variables involved in the right member. In (7) there are three variables involved in the right member and the formula holds good identically in all these. In (9) there are only two variables involved in the right member, namely, x and y, but the formula holds good identically in these two variables. That is, we may choose x equal to anything we like and this choice being made, we may further choose y equal to any other magnitude we like.

We now revert to the simpler example of the rectangle. While the formulae (4) and (6) are similar with respect to the characteristic (I), they are different with respect to the characteristic (II). Formula (4) holds good even if we don't make any assumptions regarding the fulfilment of any other relation. On the contrary, formula (6) only holds good if we assume that a particular *side relation* is fulfilled, namely relation (5).

We now proceed to discuss a third kind of formula. In the case where the side relation (5) holds good, the area of our rectangle many also be expressed by another formula, namely,

$$A = \frac{1}{3}x^2 + \frac{2}{3}y^2 \qquad\qquad (10a)$$

or it may be expressed by this formula

$$A = \frac{1}{27}x^2 + \frac{24}{27}y^2 + \frac{2}{27}x \cdot y \qquad\qquad (10b)$$

These two formulae look rather strange, but on examination we see, of course, that they are always fulfilled in the case we have $x=y$. In this case both the last formulae reduce to (6). More generally, we even see that we could put up the formula

$$A = ax^2 + by^2 + cxy \qquad\qquad (11)$$

where a, b and c are three constants that we may choose *arbitrarily*, provided only that their sum is equal to unit, that is,

$$a+b+c=1 \qquad\qquad (12)$$

Now let us compare (10a) with (6) and with (4). We see that (10a) is different from (4) both with regard to the characteristic (I) and with regard to the characteristic (II). (10a) namely holds good only provided the side relation (5) is fulfilled. And furthermore, even if this relation is fulfilled (10a) does not hold good identically in the variables that occur in its right member. On the other hand (10a) and (6) are similar with respect to the characteristic (II), but dissimilar with respect to the characteristic (I). That is to say, both (10a) and (6) assume the same side relation, namely (5), but while (6) holds good identically in the variables in its right member, (10a) does not hold good identically in the variables in its right member.

From this example it is easy to formulate a general definition: A *structural relation* is a relation with the following two properties:

I   it holds good identically in the variables involved;
II it holds good even though we do not assume any particular side relation to be fulfilled (although there will, of course, be some general assumptions underlying the formula, but these are only assumptions underlying the whole problem; they are assumptions that do not change from one point to another in the chain of reasoning before us).

A *confluent relation* is a relation that has the property (I) but not the property (II).

An *artificial relation* is a relation that has neither of the properties (I) or (II).

The existence of artificial relations involves a great danger element both in the purely theoretical analysis and even more so in the attempt at determining the nature of theoretical relations by studying empirical data. The following simplified example will immediately make this clear. Suppose that we have observed a great number of cardboard pieces of rectangular form. Theoretical considerations have probably led us to assume that the area is of the second dimension with respect to the dimension of the sides. That is to say, we will probably look upon the area as being of the same dimension as any of the terms x^2, y^2 or xy. Therefore, a natural and rather plausible hypothesis would be to assume that the area A can be expressed in the form (11) where a, b and c are three constants to be determined. As a matter of fact, this hypothesis is also correct. If, for a moment, we assume that we really have a complete knowledge of the geometrical rule involved, we see immediately that the formula (11) is correct as a structural relation if we put $a=b=0$, $c=1$. But it would involve the greatest danger if we would attempt to determine the coefficients a, b and c by regression methods utilising an empirical material. *If this empirical material has emerged under such circumstance that there is a particular side relation that is fulfilled*, for instance (5), *then the attempt at determining a, b and c by regression would be complete nonsense.* In this case the magnitudes of the three coefficients have, namely, no significance at all. *The three coefficients may now be chosen arbitrarily.* The only significant thing now is the sum of these coefficients, the sum being equal to unity.

However, if the empirical material at our disposal was such as to have the side relation (5) fulfilled, but only fulfilled approximately, a little erratic element giving a slight departure from the fulfilment of the side relation in some or all of the observations, then the ordinary regression methods would furnish three uniquely defined coefficients, a, b and c, making it appear as if there now existed one significant relation of the form (11) with three well-determined coefficients.

Is there any chance of running into pitfalls of this kind when attempting to verify the laws of economic theory by utilizing statistical data? *The answer is that the road is just paved with such pitfalls.* The situation is, namely, that economic theory considers *several* structural relations that are assumed fulfilled simultaneously. Any such structural relation may then be looked upon as a side relation with respect to any of the other structural relations. Sometimes theory even goes so far as to put up just as many structural relations as there are variables involved. However, we need not go to this extreme case in order to illustrate the danger of the pitfalls involved. Let us only assume that the theory involves n variables $z_1,\ldots,z_n$, and only k structural relations, k being less than n. The variables $z_1,\ldots,z_n$ may here stand for any sort of economic magnitudes, quantities, prices, etc. The k relations involved may be written in the form

$$S_1(z_1,\ldots,z_n)=0$$
$$S_2(z_1,\ldots,z_n)=0$$
$$\ldots\ldots$$
$$S_k(z_1,\ldots,z_n)=0$$

(13)

These relations we here assume to be structural. That is to say, any of them, say the relation $S_1 = 0$, will hold good no matter whether the other relations are fulfilled or not. And it holds good identically in all the variables involved.

Now suppose that we have a great number of observations of the variable set $(z_1, \ldots, z_n)$. If these observations are such that all the relations in (13) are actually fulfilled in each observation, then we have a situation which is perfectly analogous to the situation where we tried to determine the constants a, b and c of the rectangular formula (11) from a set of data where only approximate squares were represented. For instance, let us take the structural relation $S_1 = 0$. From theoretical considerations we may very well know the analytical character of S_1. It may, for instance, be of the form

$$A_1(z_1, \ldots, z_n; a_{11}, a_{12}, \ldots) = 0 \qquad (14)$$

where a_{11}, $a_{12}, \ldots$ are constants. This, however, will not help us actually to determine the structural relation $S_1 = 0$. If we attempted to determine from the material the constants a_{11}, $a_{12}, \ldots$ in (14) the result would be complete nonsense, just as it would be nonsense to determine the constants a, b and c in the case of our rectangles. The situation is that if the material conforms to our theory, that is the relations in (13) are approximately fulfilled in our observations and we try to determine the character of S_1, the other relations, namely $S_2 = 0, \ldots, S_k = 0$, must be looked upon as side relations. And similarly if we try to determine the character of S_2, then $S_1 = 0$, $S_3 = 0, \ldots, S_k = 0$ must be considered as side relations, and so on.

Thus we see that if we have *several* structural relations the material does not reveal the character of these relations. It only reveals the character of the confluent relations. These confluent relations are a set of relations obtained from system (13) through elimination and combination, in such a way that the variables involved in each of the new equations are independent variables. It may be that such a system can be obtained simply by eliminating the $(k-1)$ variables $z_{n-k+2}, \ldots, z_n$, thus leaving the variables $z_1, \ldots, z_{n-k+1}$. Such a confluent relation may be written in the form

$$C(z_1, \ldots, z_{n-k+1}) = 0 \qquad (15)$$

and this relation it will be possible to determine from the empirical material at hand.

The following might serve as an economic example of the situation that may arise when we try to determine a structural relation in a case where the material is such that it is only possible to determine confluent relations. Suppose that we have a statistical material consisting of a time series of the price p_t of a certain commodity and the quantity traded x_t, and also a time series P_t of the price level, t designating time. Suppose that from this material we want to determine how x depends on p and P. We may perhaps look upon this as an expression for the 'demand function'. We may even think that we have adopted a rather general and invulnerable hypothesis by admitting into this demand function not only the price of the commodity in question, but also the general price level P. For simplicity we may take the relation in the simple linear form

$$x = h + cp + CP \tag{16}$$

where h, c and C are constants. The assumption of a *linear* relation might in itself be questioned, but that is not the essential point in this connection. What we are driving at would appear in essentially the same form whether we assumed the linear relationship or not, only the development is simpler in the case of a linear relationship.

Let us assume that the data at our disposal are such that both p and P considered as time series *evolve in cycles*. We may even assume that the periods of the two cycles are the same. Of course we assume that the trend and eventually higher cycles have been taken out of our series, so that x, p and P designate not actual data but deviations from these other components. For simplicity let us consider that the time series representing p and P are rigorous sine curves. In an actual case, this would not, of course, be the situation but we might have something similar to it. If p and P are sine curves with the same period *and also the same phase*, then p and P taken in their variation over time *will simply be proportional*. That is to say, we will have

$$p = aP \tag{17}$$

This is easily verified by drawing a historical curve in (p, P) coordinates. If p and P are sine curves of time, with the same period and the same phase, it will easily be seen that this historical curve in (p, P) coordinates is a straight line through the origin. Therefore, attempting from this material to determine the constants c and C in relation (16) would be nonsense. (17) is namely a side relation with respect to the structural relation (16). To determine the regression of x on p and P only has sense provided the material at hand is not such that in it p and P are proportional. In this case the inclusion of P besides p *does not really introduce anything new*. Or rather, it introduces something very bad: it blows up our whole system.

If we assumed only that p and P had the same period but not the same phase, then it would have sense to determine the coefficients of the relation (16) by regression method. But if we now would add one more variable, say, the price q of some other commodity, then our whole system would again blow to pieces if p, q and P evolved with the same period, although they might be out of phase with each other. In this case there namely exists a linear relationship between p, q and P so that it would be nonsense to determine the regression of x on the set p, q and P. This would only have sense provided the material at our disposal was such that the three variables p, q and P were not linearly related.

The following is another economic example. Consider an entrepreneur manufacturing a certain commodity according to the cost curve

$$b = b(x) \tag{18}$$

b being the total cost involved in the production of the quantity x of the commodity in question. The marginal cost in this case will be

$$b'(x) = \frac{db(x)}{dx} \qquad (19)$$

and the average cost will be

$$c(x) = \frac{b(x)}{x} \qquad (20)$$

Total profit r will be a function of the product price p, and the output x. The nature of this function is

$$r = f(x, p) = (p - c(x))x \qquad (21)$$

If the cost curve is given then the function $c(x)$ is known. Therefore the function $f(x, p)$ is also known. And furthermore, the relation $r=f(x, p)$ is a *structural relation*. It holds good no matter what x and p are, and it also holds good without any assumption as to the fulfilment of any side relation.

Now let us assume that we introduce the condition expressing the fact that the entrepreneur tries to make his total net profit as large as possible on the assumption that the price is not appreciably influenced by the quantity x which he produces. The condition for this maximum is that his marginal cost shall be equal to the price of the product. That is, the condition can be written

$$p = b'(x) \qquad (22)$$

This relation we may now consider as a side relation. We may imagine that the relation is solved with respect to x instead of with respect to p. Suppose that if this is done, our side relation takes the form

$$x = h(p) \qquad (23)$$

If this side relation is fulfilled, then the expression for total profit might be written in a different form, namely:

$$r = (p - c(x)) \cdot h(p) \qquad (24)$$

There namely now corresponds to every magnitude of p, a certain magnitude of x is given by (23). Equation (24) is simply the one obtained from (21) by inserting for the last factor of (21) namely, x, the expression taken from (23). We could have gone one step further and introduced this expression for x also in the other place in the right member of (21) where x occurs. That is to say, in the function $c(x)$. If we do this, we get

$$r = [p - c(h(p))] \cdot h(p) \tag{25}$$

Now let us compare the three equations (21), (24) and (25). Equation (21) is a structural relation according to our definition, because it holds good identically in those variables that are involved in the right member (namely x and p) and furthermore, it holds good without assuming any side relation to be fulfilled. Equation (25) is a confluent relation because it only holds good if a certain side relation is fulfilled, namely, the side relation (22), or, which amounts to the same, (23). But if this side relation is fulfilled (25) holds good identically in the variable involved in the right member (there is only one variable in the right member now, namely p). On the contrary, (24) is an artificial relation because it does not hold good identically in the variables involved in the right member (namely, x and p). The two variables involved in the right member are not independent but subjected to satisfying the side relation (22). That is to say, we cannot choose an arbitrary magnitude of p and an arbitrary magnitude of x and use (24) to determine what the profit will be when p and x have the chosen magnitudes. Such a thing we can only do by employing the structural equation (21). If the side relation is fulfilled we can choose, say, p arbitrarily, then deduce the corresponding magnitude of x and insert this set of (p, x) magnitudes into the equation (24). But that is only another way of expressing that we do not use (24) as it stands but we use the confluent equation (25), considering p as an independent variable.

Notes

1 Editors' note: a marginal comment pencilled in by Frisch states that the introduction has been 'stimulated by Kant, Vaihinger and Poincaré'.
2 From a more general point of view the rules of formal logic can themselves in turn be considered as relations in a model world created by ourselves.
3 This example has been suggested to me by my friend and colleague, Professor [Oskar] Jaeger of the University of Oslo.
4 The inverse is not true, because it is, of course, possible also to conceive a model world with contingent (stochastic) laws (i.e. laws of probability or frequency) instead of necessary (unbreakable) laws. Compare the remarks on probability at the end of the present section.
5 The expression: quantity traded at the point of time t' should, rigorously speaking, be conceived of as the average quantity traded per unit time over a very small *interval* of time in the vicinity of t'. However, this is unessential in this connection. We may simply think that the quantity in question is traded in the *point* of time t'.
6 The slope is defined as the angular coefficient of the tangent, that is to say, approximately as the angular coefficient for the secant for a very short interval.
7 In the following we designate quantity produced by u instead of v.
8 Editors' note: the reference is to Walras, L. (1874) *Éléments d'économie politique pure, ou théorie de la richesse sociale*, Lausanne: Corbaz
9 This is essentially the character of H.L. Moore's approach. His 'moving equilibrium' does not make the analysis dynamic, but is an attempt to separate the effect of two different components.
10 Editors' note: the reference is to Robbins, L. (1930) 'On a certain ambiguity in the concept of stationary equilibrium', *Economic Journal*, 40: 194–214.

11 The views of the present writer on the conceptions of statics and dynamics, amongst others the points raised in this section, was first published (in Norwegian) in *Nationalokonomisk Tidsskrift*, Copenhagen, 1929. Editors' note: see Frisch, R. (1929b) 'Statikk og dynamikk i den økonomiske teori', *Nationaløkonomisk Tidsskrift*, 67: 321–79; translated (sections 1–3) as 'Statics and dynamics in economic theory', *Structural Change and Economic Dynamics*, 3 (1992): 391–401.

2 Dynamic formulation of some parts of economic theory

2.1 A dynamic analysis of marginal utility

I now proceed to an analysis of the notion of utility, in particular marginal utility, from the dynamic point of view. I shall first make some remarks on the quantitative definition of utility.

2.1.1 The psychological and the behaviouristic approach to utility measurement

The chain of reasoning by which the founders of the Austrian School in economics reached the notion of marginal utility was somewhat like this: they took as a starting point the empirical fact that when a man gets more of a certain good there is a certain feature in his state of mind that *changes*. In precise objective terms, it is difficult to explain what this change really consists of. But everybody has many times lived through such a process himself. Therefore it is possible to give some kind of description of the process, simply by referring to this internal experience and, so to speak, leave it to the reader or listener himself to supply the concrete meaning of the words. If, on this basis, we want a verbal definition of the process, we can say that the *want* or the *craving* for the good in question diminishes as one gets more of it. The satisfaction that is obtained by the consumption of the *last* unit of the good or, if one prefers, the utility created by this satisfaction, may be called the 'marginal utility'.

This definition has none of the objective criteria that we are accustomed to look for in the definitions of the natural sciences. It has a sense and is understood by other people only because these people themselves have had an internal experience, a want satisfaction, that corresponds to the definition given. It is a definition of the same kind as one we would obtain, say, by defining 'force' as 'the strain exerted when heavy things are lifted'. In particular it should be noticed that this primitive utility definition does not establish marginal utility as a quantitative notion.

Nevertheless, in the earlier days of marginal utility theory the notion was often handled as if it should have been quantitatively defined. It is easy to understand why it was handled this way. If marginal utility shall be of any use at all in the theoretical structure of economics, it must be drawn into a quantitative reasoning. Those phenomena which marginal utility shall explain are, indeed, by their very nature quantitative. For instance: in some way or another one has to introduce the idea that when equilibrium is reached the prices are *proportional* to the marginal utility. Such an idea evidently implies that marginal utility is quantitatively defined. Something which shall be *proportional* to something else must necessarily be quantitatively defined.

This procedure of drawing a non-quantitatively defined notion into a quantitative argument is, of course, entirely illegitimate. It really amounts to giving the notion a meaning by appealing to a certain mental association process in the reader or the listener, and then when a certain number of steps in the reasoning are passed and the attention of the reader or listener is dulled, to use the notion in a different meaning, to attribute to it features which do not lie in the given definition.

As a matter of fact, this point was just one of those where the marginal utility theory in its original form was justly criticized. These criticisms started a series of attempts at rigorously defining utility in a quantitative way. These attempts proceed on two different lines which we may term the *psychological* and the *behaviouristic*. These terms are here used in a special economic-technical sense. One should not read into them the far-reaching implications of the controversy between the psychological and the behaviouristic schools in psychology, although the distinction here made is, of course, somewhat related to the point at issue in psychology. The exponents of the psychological and the behaviouristic approach to a quantitative definition of economic utility are Edgeworth and Fisher, respectively.

Edgeworth believed that he could make the notion of marginal utility more precise by an appeal to experimental psychology.[1] This was a natural avenue of approach if one would follow as closely as possible the original idea of the Austrian School. As a unit of utility, Edgeworth adopts the smallest additional utility that the individual can perceive. And on this basis he builds his hedonistic calculus. In this theory the individuals appear as essentially passive beings, rejoicing or suffering.

Fisher's point of view is different.[2] He considers the individuals as active and acting. Fisher objects rightly against Edgeworth that Edgeworth's theory is psychological, not economic. One could say that Edgeworth represents the psychological, Fisher the anti-psychological point of view. Fisher says:

> The truth is, most persons, not excepting professed economists, are satisfied with very hazy notions. How few scholars of the literary and historical type retain from their study of mechanics an adequate notion of force! Muscular experience supplies a concrete and practical conception but gives no inkling of the complicated dependence on space, time, and mass. Only patient mathematical analysis can do that. This natural aversion to elaborate and intricate analysis exists in Economics and especially in the theory of value. The very foundations of the subject require new analysis and definition.
>
> (Fisher 1892, p. v)

Fisher himself takes the *choice acts* of the individuals as the basis for a quantitative definition of utility. And this basis has been adopted by most of the modern theorists who have gone into the utility problem to any extent. Pareto gave a special name to the theory developed on this basis: he called it *the theory of choice* ('la théorie des choix'). And the choice point of view in the analysis of utility is perhaps best known in connection with Pareto's name. However, the theory of choice was, in fact, first introduced and developed with great consistency by Fisher.

Incidentally the reason why Pareto introduced the particular name for this theory was probably that he wanted to point out the fundamental difference which, according to him, shall exist between the Austrian theory and his own. However, if one has a sense for the continuity in the historical developments of the ideas, it seems to me more correct to consider the theory of choice as a correction and further development of the Austrian marginal theory than a new theory in opposition to the Austrian theory.

The question may arise: have not the Austrians themselves adopted the idea of taking the choice acts of the individuals as a basis for the definition of utility? It is true that in several places in the works of Austrian economists we find extensive studies of the choice acts of the individuals. This is particularly true of Böhm-Bawerk, the great dialectician of the School.[3]

Böhm-Bawerk gives a whole series of arguments showing that in particular there exist certain definite regularities in the way in which people make up their minds about their choice acts. But this in itself is not sufficient to make his theory a behaviouristic theory of choice. There is one essential thing which is characteristic for the behaviouristic theory of choice and which we do not find in Böhm-Bawerk's approach, namely to take the observable regularities in the choice behaviouristic theory as a matter of fact, as something given, without digging very deeply into the psychological *motivation* which led to these regularities. In the behaviouristic theory of choice it is on the choice acts themselves that the utility definition is based and this point of view was never taken by Böhm-Bawerk or the other Austrians. On the contrary, for them the psychological motivation behind the choice acts was always a main point. When Böhm-Bawerk studies the observable choice regularities it is only in order *to use them as a tool in his motivation theory*.

Incidentally Böhm-Bawerk's use of the observable choice regularities as an argument in favour of his motivation theory was not very successful. His whole analysis is rather a proof of the very difficulty of drawing conclusions from the observable choice regularities back to the psychological motivation mechanisms. In a penetrating study of this question, Eugen Slutsky says:

> The fact that people economize rationally, weighing benefits and detriments against one another, and so forth, is no proof that they do so in no other way than by measuring the intensities of sensation, or, respectively, by their summation. What Böhm-Bawerk presents to us is a theory of motivation, though what he endeavours to present to us for its justification, as a fact of

the summation of intensities of sensations (to the extent that it really is a fact), is the fact of motivation itself, whose sheer facticity as such can speak no more for his than for any other theory of motivation.[4]

The behaviouristic approach avoids these difficulties by confining the analysis to the observable choice regularities. It is a sort of short-cut through a field which does not yet seem to be accessible to rigorous quantitative methods. By this short-cut a point is reached where it is possible to get down to positive work both in the sense of an abstract theory and in the sense of empirical verifications. By this short-cut we also avoid the difficulty which arises out of the fact that human behaviour is not built on abstract rational motives as was assumed in the earlier days of the Hedonistic School. As a matter of fact, modern psychology has conclusively proved that if we want to explain human behaviour we have to take account of a whole series of irrational elements. The existence of such irrational elements makes it impossible to arrive at a rigorous quantitative utility definition on the old hedonistic and 'psychological' lines, but it does not prevent the possibility of arriving at a quantitative utility definition by a behaviouristic approach to the problem. The utility definition along these lines must be based on *an axiomatic foundation*. We shall later intimate how this can be done.

The behaviouristic approach to utility definition is not quite equivalent to reducing the utility definition to a definition of the individual demand schedules. The utility definition contains a feature which cannot be expressed simply by reference to individual demand schedules. The individual demand schedules are namely expressed in terms of actual money prices. The connection between utility and demand schedules therefore involves a certain factor of proportionality, namely, the marginal utility of money (or of the income). And this is a notion that cannot itself be directly expressed in terms of ordinary demand schedules. The utility notion therefore involves something more than the notion of individual demand schedules. This distinction is intimately connected with the distinction between what might be called *local* and *interlocal* transactions for a given individual. These notions will be further explained below.

So far as the rigorous definition of utility as a quantity is concerned, the behaviouristic point of view is the one which will be adopted in the present study.

2.1.2 *Internal and external price analysis*

The behaviouristic approach to utility theory should not be confused with the attempt at analysing the pricing process by introducing only observable *market* phenomena into the analysis, for instance, introducing the fact that a market will absorb more of a commodity the lower the price (the static market demand curve), and the like. This approach we may call the *external* approach to the pricing process. It represents an attempt to simplify the pricing problem still more than the behaviouristic utility theory. It avoids the notion of utility altogether and takes as its basis the observable choice acts of the *market* as such without attempting to explain these acts by an analysis of their constituent elements, namely, the *individual* choice acts. This approach leads to the type of price analysis which was first developed by *Cournot* and which in the modern literature has a typical representative in *Cassel*. In distinction to this external type of price analysis we may call a price analysis based on the notion of utility an *internal* price analysis. Many economic problems are such that they lend themselves naturally to an external analysis, at any rate, as a first approximation. But other problems are such that the very questions in which we are interested are essentially of an internal character, the external analysis leading only to a very superficial understanding of the problem. To adopt as a dogma that the pricing process should be studied exclusively by external notions, strictly avoiding the notion of utility, is therefore barring the way to a real significant analysis in a great many problems.

Thus the behaviouristic utility theory draws a dividing line: on one side against the superficiality of the external price analysis and on the other side against the empty metaphysical speculations that resulted when the orthodox marginal utility theory was turned into its own caricature. Unlike the orthodox marginal utility theory, the behaviouristic utility theory endeavours to carry the theoretical constructions in the spirit that the ultimate goal of this theory must be to make way for a significant *statistical attack*. The aim of the behaviouristic theory is to create a rational background by which the statistical price and consumption study can be raised from a blind and busy collection of data into the dignity and significance of a scientific investigation.

Many examples may be given showing how a stubborn observance of the external principle often stops the price analysis at that point where the real significant question arises. We shall give a few simple examples.

The static law of demand states that a given market will, as a rule, absorb more of a commodity the lower the price. To be sure, this in itself is an interesting and important thing to take account of. But we have gained much more of a real insight into the pricing mechanism when we have penetrated to the determining factors behind this law. These determining factors may be classified under the following three headings:

1   the virtually universal law expressing that *each individual* will react in a way similar to the market itself: the lower the price the more the individual will buy;
2   the phenomenon which we call the diminishing marginal utility of money, the effect of which is that the individual at a given price will buy all the more the larger his income;
3   the income distribution in that part of the society which constitutes the market in question.

The way in which these facts work together to determine the shape of the market demand curve can be illustrated thus: let us assume for simplicity that all the individuals have the same marginal utility curve for money. Let this curve be

$$w=f(r) \tag{1}$$

where w is the money utility and r the income (the price level being assumed constant). If we further assume that the dispositions of all the individuals are the same with respect to the commodity in question, the demand function for an individual of income r will be of the form

$$x=G(pf(r)) \tag{2}$$

where x is the quantity demanded by the individual, p the market price, and

$$x=G(u) \tag{3}$$

the function representing the relation between quantity consumed x and the marginal utility u of the commodity in question.

If $h(r)$ is the function representing the income distribution, that is, if there are $h(r) \cdot dr$ individuals with an income between h and $h+dr$, then this income group will at the price p demand a quantity

$$h(r) \cdot G(pf(r)) \cdot dr \tag{4}$$

The total quantity demanded in the market at the price p will consequently be

$$X=K(x)= \int_{r=0}^{\infty} h(r) \cdot G(pf(r)) \cdot dr \tag{5}$$

If we split the market demand phenomenon up in this way we get an opportunity of studying, for instance, *separately the effect which a change in the income distribution will exert on the shape of the market demand function*. Formula (5) shows, for instance, that if the population as a whole becomes richer, that is, if the magnitudes of $h(r)$ for large r are increased at the sacrifice of the magnitudes of $h(r)$ for small r, then X will increase for virtually all magnitudes of p. A large r namely means a small $f(r)$ (the diminishing marginal utility of money), and consequently also a small $pf(r)$ (when p is given). A small $pf(r)$, however, means a large G (the diminishing marginal utility of the commodity in question). That is to say, the effect of the change considered is that under the sign of integration the large magnitudes of G are weighted more heavily than before, and the smaller magnitudes weighted lighter than before. The integral (5) must consequently increase. A further study of formula (5) will reveal many other interesting propositions regarding the effect which a change in the income distribution exerts on the shape of the market demand function.

I do not believe that any economist will deny that these are interesting and important questions. But none of these questions can be raised if one only allows external notions in the analysis of the pricing mechanism.

Another example is the following. The quantity supplied x of a certain kind of labour measured in hours (of a certain average efficiency) per day can as a first approximation be considered as a function $x = g(p)$ of the price of labour, that is, of the wage per hour, p. I shall here not enter upon the controversial question as to what extent and in what sense the individual wage earner under the wage system of our days based upon collective bargaining has a possibility to vary the amount of labour, supplied by him. Quite regardless of this possibility, it is certain that the way in which hours of work and wage per hour is valued *on the average* in the group of workers included in the collective wage agreement plays an important role in the fixation of the collective wage agreement itself. The function $g(p)$ must be looked upon as an expression for this average or typical valuation.

There is reason to believe that the course of the function $g(p)$ will be as indicated in Figure 2.1. This figure does not give the shape of the curve for very large magnitudes of p. It may be that the curve here turns back again so that the entire curve gets a shape like a reverse S. But this is altogether uncertain. What is certain, and what can be subject to a rigorous theoretical analysis is the shape of the curve over the lower part of the p scale, as indicated in Figure 2.1.

The essential feature of this figure is, that if the wage per hour p first is very low and then increases, the amount of labour supplied x will decrease until a certain point x_0 from which point the amount of labour supplied begins to increase if the wage per hour increases further. The entire curve will, of course, be situated to the left of the vertical $x = 24$ hours per day.

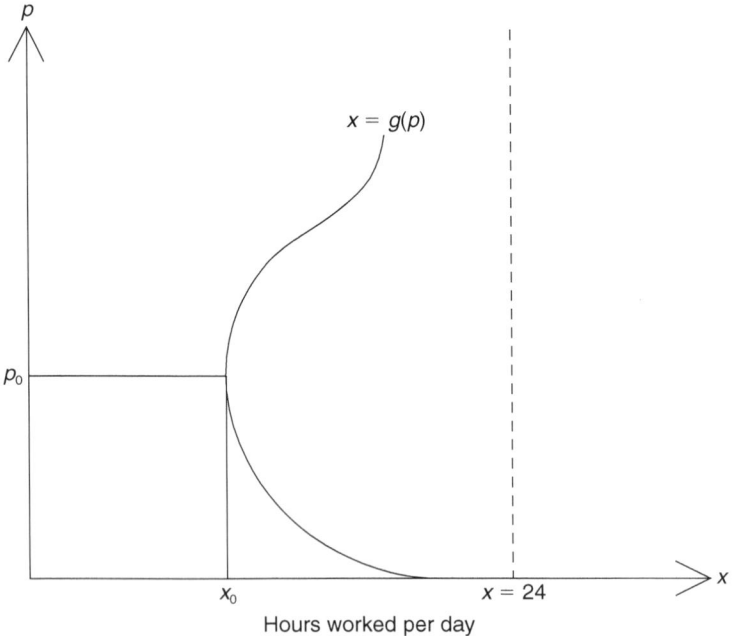

Figure 2.1 The supply curve for labour in hours worked per day.

The external theory of prices would limit itself to accepting this form of the supply curve as a fact, a fact that could enter as an assumption in a further argument but which should itself not be the object for a further analysis.[5]

Marginal utility theory goes one step further. It wants to investigate *why* the supply curve for labour has this characteristic shape. If possible it wants to locate the point where the change takes place. This can be done by assuming the following data.

First the marginal disutility of labour being given as a function $y = c(x)$ that after a certain point x_1 is positive and increasing with increasing hours of work per day, see Figure 2.2.

Second, the marginal utility of money (under a constant price level) as a function $y = f(r)$ which from a certain point r_1 (the minimum of existence) is positive and decreasing with increasing income per day r, see Figure 2.3.

In any point, i.e. for any magnitude of income, the rate of change of the marginal utility of money is characterized by the *flexibility* of the money utility curve. This is the ratio between the percentage increment in marginal utility and the corresponding percentage increment in income, when the increments are very small (strictly speaking, infinitesimal). Let us denote the flexibility of the marginal utility of money by f^*. This notion may be defined with respect to small variations in the vicinity of *any* point of the income scale, that is to say, f^* is just as f itself a function of the income r. Since the marginal utility of money is decreasing as income increases, f^* will be a negative quantity.

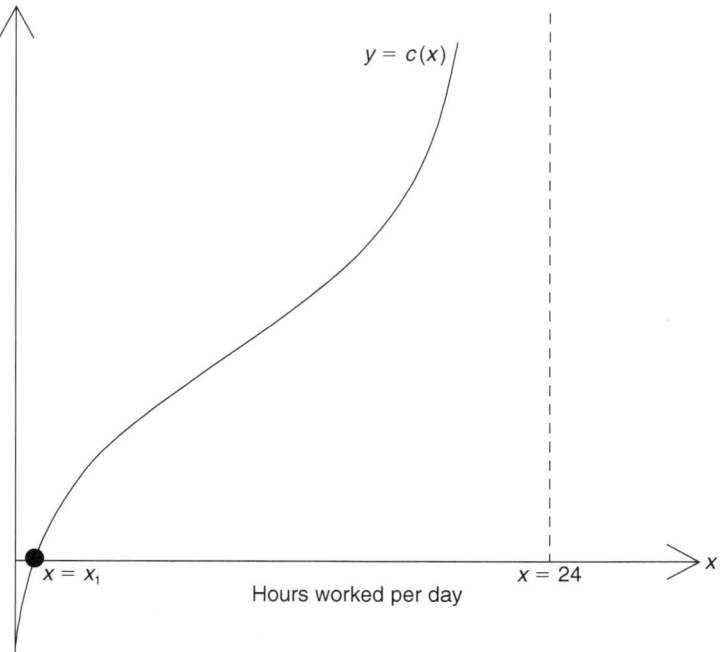

Figure 2.2 The marginal disutility of labour.

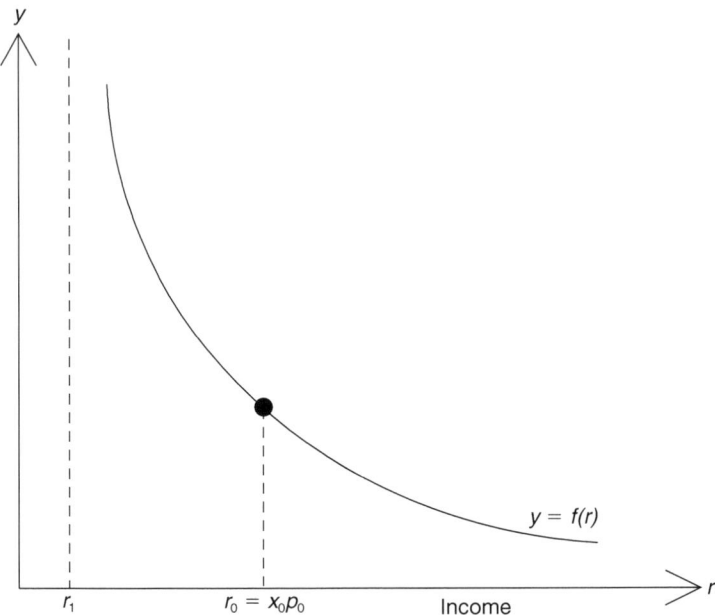

Figure 2.3 The marginal utility of income.

In the same way can we consider the flexibility of the marginal disutility of labour for that part of the curve in Figure 2.2 where the disutility is positive, that is for x is greater than x_1. Let us denote this flexibility by c^*. In real life it is only the part of the labour disutility curve where the disutility is positive that we need to take account of. It is easy to prove and for the rest nearly evident without proof, that the magnitudes of x (hours of work per day) that occur on the supply curve in Figure 2.1 (for positive p) must all be larger than x_1, that is, larger than that number of hours of work per day from which the marginal disutility of labour becomes negative by a further decrease in hours of work per day. For shorter hours per day than x_1 an increase in the number of hours worked will be wanted on account of the enjoyment which is connected with the work (that is p would be negative).

In the same way, we can consider the flexibility of hours worked as a function of the wage per hour, see Figure 2.1. Let us as denote its flexibility g^*. The curve in Figure 2.1 is increasing in a given point if g^* in this point is positive and vice versa.

Now in the equilibrium point the money utility $f(r)$ times the wage rate p must be equal to the labour disutility $c(x)$. That is, we must have

$$f(r) \cdot p = c(x) \tag{6}$$

but the income r (which for convenience we measure in dollars per day) is equal to hours worked per day x times the wage per hour p. In other words, we have

$$r=xp \tag{7}$$

Introducing this in (6) we get

$$f(xp) \cdot p = c(x) \tag{8}$$

Since the function f and c are supposed to be given, (8) defines x as a function of p, and this function is just the labour supply function $x = g(p)$ of Figure 2.1. From equation (8) we can therefore determine how $g^* = \dfrac{dx}{dp} \dfrac{p}{x}$ depends on $f^* = \dfrac{df}{dr} \dfrac{r}{f}$, and on $c^* = \dfrac{dc}{dp} \dfrac{p}{c}$. In fact, differentiating (8) totally with respect to p, under the assumption that x is a function of p, we get

$$f + p \frac{df}{dr} \cdot \left(x + p \frac{dx}{dp} \right) = \frac{dc}{dx} \frac{dx}{dp}$$

that is,

$$\frac{dx}{dp} = \frac{f + px \dfrac{df}{dr}}{\dfrac{dc}{dx} - p^2 \dfrac{df}{dr}}$$

and by introducing $px = r$ and $f = \dfrac{c}{p}$, we get

$$\frac{dx}{dp} = \frac{x}{p} \cdot \frac{1 + \dfrac{df}{dr} \cdot \dfrac{r}{f}}{\dfrac{dc}{dx} \cdot \dfrac{x}{c} - \dfrac{df}{dr} \cdot \dfrac{r}{f}}$$

and consequently

$$g^* = \frac{1 - (-f^*)}{c^* + (-f^*)} \tag{9}$$

In the last formula both c^* and $(-f^*)$ are positive. Consequently g^* will be positive or negative accordingly as $(-f^*)$ is less than or larger than unity. In other words: *the supply curve for labour will be decreasing or increasing accordingly as the flexibility of the marginal utility of money in the income point in question is less than or larger than unity in absolute value.*[6]

The point x_0 (see Figure 2.1) where the change takes place is characterized by the fact that the area of the rectangle $x_0 p_0$ is equal to that income r_0 where the absolute value of the flexibility of marginal utility of money (see Figure 2.3) passes unity.

The result of an investigation I made in 1923 regarding the money utility curve for the group consisting of customers in the Union des Cooperateures, Paris, seems to indicate that the absolute value of the flexibility of the money utility is larger than unity for the entire income interval of the ordinary wage earners in the Paris region.[7] This means that the wage equilibrium will be realized in some point on the lower branch of the curve in Figure 2.1, and the situation will probably be similar for most of the European markets.

In an article published in 1926 I suggested that the situation in the United States is probably different and this suggestion has recently been supported by the results of a joint study made by Professor Irving Fisher and myself regarding the money utility curve for the working class in various parts of the United States.[8] These results, which will soon be published, indicate a flexibility of the money utility decidedly less than unity. If these results are verified by other extensive investigations we have here a fact that throws an interesting light on the collective bargaining fight. So long as the equilibrium occurs in a point on the lower branch of the curve in Figure 2.1 (where the flexibility of the money utility is larger than unity) this fight must namely be particularly violent from the labourers' point of view. Here the labourers must try either to get status quo or simultaneously to obtain both a wage increase and shorter hours. On the upper branch this does not hold good.

It is not improbable that one of the reasons why the US labour market is more peaceful than the European one is to be found in the fact we have found that the average labourer has in United States reached an income interval where the absolute value of the flexibility of the money utility is less than unity as indicated by the results of [Part III,] Section 7.[9] That is to say, the collective bargaining fight in America should take place in some point on the upper branch of the curve in Figure 2.1 while in Europe it is still going on in the lower branch of the curve. If this is true, we should here have an example of the opposite extreme of the situation that was realized under the development of the factory system in England about the end of the eighteenth century when a very low wage per hour forced the labourers to work 14–16 hours a day, that is to say, when the wage equilibrium was realized at some point very low on the lower branch of the curve in Figure 2.1.

It seems to me that there should be attached a very real interest to a theoretical analysis of this question. But the possibility of such an analysis is barred if one wants strictly to observe the principle of the external approach to the pricing problem, namely, to adopt as the only datum for the analysis the various market reaction functions (the market supply and demand functions) and to avoid any utility analysis that attempts to find out what is behind these market functions.

If, forced by the economic realities, one modifies the principle in such a way as to permit a closer analysis of what is behind the market consumption functions, or the labour supply functions, etc., one has given up the external principle. It will only be in name then that a pricing theory elaborated on such a basis will differ from a marginal utility theory.

These examples tend to show that the external approach, while interesting in certain cases, will not always lead to the ultimate solution of the problems in which we are interested in price analysis. That does not mean that the internal approach always leads to the ultimate solution of the problems. There are also problems which are of such a kind that the ultimate solution cannot be built up exclusively on an analysis of the reactions of the individuals. Or, more precisely expressed, there are certain phases of the behavior of the individuals that cannot be explained by considering each individual separately. We also have to take account of the fact that sometimes the behaviour of human beings changes when they get together and form a crowd.

2.1.3 Some remarks on the axiomatic foundation of utility definition

2.1.3.1 Axiomatic and actual observations

The axiomatic definition of utility as a quantity is based on a system of fictitious *interrogation experiments* performed on an individual. We invent, so to speak, a series of situations, and imagine that we ask the individual questions as to what he would do in these various situations. These questions we may call the *choice-questions*. From the description of the situations involved in the choice-questions and from the answers given we try then to formulate the rigorous utility definition.

The choice-questions must, of course, be such that both the situations and the answers can be formulated in objective terms. Sometimes it may even be necessary to require that they can be formulated in quantitative terms. But, if we only have the *definition* of utility in mind, it is not necessary that the interrogation experiments shall be actually possible in a technical and practical sense. It does not matter if the cost of, or the practical difficulties involved in, an actual statistical survey would be prohibitive. It is sufficient that the experiments are possible in principle.

The point may perhaps be made clear by a comparison with some of the axiomatic 'experiments' of physics. Take, for instance, the light signals of relativity axiomatics. These are not actually 'possible' in a technical sense. Strictly speaking, they are only a way of thinking. They are only a theoretical tool used in order to give a precise and concrete significance to our ideas. When we look upon them and talk about them as 'experiments' it is just because this similarity with actual experiments furnishes the preciseness and clearness of thought that are necessary in the logical construction of the science. A similar role is played by the interrogation experiments of utility theory.

Thus we have to distinguish clearly between an *axiomatic* experiment (or observation) and an *actual* experiment (or observation). Sometimes in economics it is possible to construct an actual interrogation scheme that is very nearly a true copy of an axiomatic interrogation scheme. I shall later give some examples of this. But, as a rule, the actual observations have a technique of their own and involve a series of practical experiments quite different from those involved in the axiomatic procedure.

There is also this difference between an axiomatic and an actual interrogation experiment, that the latter must always be made on some living individual (or on a concrete group of individuals that are guided by some sort of joint action), while the former can be conceived of as made on some average or *typical* individual. In this latter case we have to adopt some general assumptions or *choice-axioms* regarding the way in which our typical individual will react when subjected to our 'experiments'. Otherwise our 'experiments' would be a complete chaos without any meaning. It is on a set of such choice-axioms that the utility definition of the following sections is based.

From a formal point of view we are at liberty to choose any set of choice-axioms that we may favour, but in reality we are under a very severe restriction, namely that of adopting a set of axioms that will lead to a really fruitful theory fitting the facts, that is, a theory which will be able to 'explain' the results of actual observations or actual experiments.

2.1.3.2 Direct and indirect utility

When we ask a choice-axiom we must take care to specify if the assumption is that the transaction involved in the choice-question shall be the only one which the individual is allowed to make, or if the assumption is that the individual, after having made this transaction, shall be allowed to make *other* transactions which a possible third party may offer him. It is obvious that his answer to the choice-question may be different in the two cases. Suppose for instance that a passionate smoker is asked if he wants 50 good Havana cigars or a carload of Californian peaches as a present. If it is understood that he may accept the peaches and *afterwards sell them*, he will, of course, choose the peaches, because the sale of these will bring money enough to buy both Havana cigars and many other things. But if it is understood that he must actually keep and consume the thing he chooses, then he would probably choose the cigars. In the example cited here, the 'transaction' allowed consists in accepting the present.

Since the answer to a choice-question may differ accordingly as we assume the transaction involved in the question to be the only transaction allowed or not, the notion of utility which is defined by such question will, of course, also be different in the two cases. The kind of utility which is defined by assuming, in each choice question, that the transaction involved in the question is the only transaction allowed, we shall call a *direct* utility. The other kind we shall call an *indirect* utility. This definition is equivalent to saying that a direct utility is the utility of a good which is actually wanted by the individual for consumption purposes, while an indirect utility is the utility of a good that the individual does not want to consume but only wants to dispose of in exchange for other goods. The direct utility could therefore also be called a *utility-in-use*; and the indirect utility a *utility-in-exchange*.

From an axiomatic point of view the fundamental difference between a direct and indirect utility lies in the fact that the choice-question by which the latter is established *has no sense unless the whole set of exchange possibilities in the market (prices, etc.) are given*, while these data in general are irrelevant to the choice-question establishing the direct utility. In other words, direct utility can be defined without reference to the market situation but indirect utility cannot. The notion of direct utility therefore offers itself as a more fundamental tool of analysis than indirect utility.

This fundamental character of direct utility is emphasized by the fact that the notion of indirect utility can be derived from an analysis of the exchange mechanism based on the notion of direct utility. A good which has direct utility we shall call direct good. And a good which has no direct utility, but which may under certain market situations have an indirect utility to the individual, we shall call an indirect good.

The marginal utility of money is essentially an indirect utility when the good serving as money is only a medium of exchange without any intrinsic usefulness to the individual. The definition of money utility therefore demands special care. So far as the utility definition is concerned, money cannot be treated in exactly the same way as the direct goods. Therefore the procedure used by Pareto and his followers, that is to take any commodity as a 'numéraire' and by convention put its price equal to unit, breaks down when the money is not a direct good. Pareto himself does not seem to have been aware of this fact. This question will be analysed in more detail in one of the later sections.

2.1.3.3 Choice-object and delivery-situation

When we formulate a choice-question there are two things that must be specified in order that the choice-question shall have a definite meaning, namely:

1   those alternative transactions between which the individual has an option; these we may call the *choice-objects*;
2   to each of the alternatives specified under (1) there must be associated a description of the complete economic situation in which it is assumed that the individual will find himself just before the transaction in question is to be effectuated. This we may call the *delivery-situation*.

At first glance the distinction between choice-objects and delivery-situations seems so obvious that one would not think it necessary to insist upon it. However, intricate problems arise in the building up of a strict axiomatic foundation of utility, and the definition may easily be lost sight of and this may give rise to serious errors. It will therefore be worthwhile here to elaborate somewhat on the distinction.

The fundamental distinction between the two notions here considered is that the *choice-objects are something which are subject to choice, while a delivery-situation is not subject to choice*. A delivery-situation is a *datum* in the formulation of the choice-question. It is a given economic background which the individual cannot alter. It will exist just in the specified way *regardless of which one of the alternative choice-objects he might choose*.

It is largely on the nature of the given delivery-situation (or situations) involved in the choice-question that the answer will depend. The answer may change if the delivery-situation (or situations) change, even though the choice-objects are the same.

We could therefore also formulate the definition of the delivery-situation by saying that it is the entirety of all those things which must be specified (in addition to the description of the choice-objects) in order that the individual considered shall be able to make up his mind regarding the answer to be made to the choice-question.

Let us take some examples. Suppose we have a typical working man's family with a certain household budget for the year: certain specified items of food, of clothing, of entertainment, etc. Let us imagine that all these items are planned in detail for the year and let us assume that the expenses are provided for by the salary of the head of the family (the 'breadwinner'), and that we have reason to believe that everything in the economic life of the family in this year is going to happen just as it is planned. We are here only concerned with this single year and do not take into account what is going to happen in the future. This being so, let us assume that we offer to the family as a present, *in addition to the specified budget*, either one of the following two things:

1   one pound of ham per month for the coming year;
2   36 talkie admissions for the year.

The family can choose either one of these two things, but when the choice is made it must actually consume the chosen thing. It is not allowed to sell it and instead buy something else. Nor is it allowed, after the choice is made, to make any modifications in the previously specified budget. In this example, the specified budget for this year is the delivery-situation and the ham and the talkie admissions represent two choice-objects.

The choice-question appears in its clearest form when the choice-objects are put up as alternative *presents*, but in point of principle this is not necessary. Suppose, for instance, that ham is included in the specified budget, but no talkie admissions, because up to now there has been no talkie in the town. Then to the family's surprise a talkie is opened. We may now ask the question: in case the family had an offer to give up 12 pounds of ham in exchange for 36 admissions, would it accept it or not? In a concrete situation there may perhaps be other alternatives, for instance, to give up just a few pounds of ham and to receive three admissions for each of the pounds given up. The family may even consider other and more far-reaching rearrangements of the budget. But all this we now assume to be excluded. The question is only: if an exchange of 12 pounds of ham for 36 tickets, without any other change in the budget, is the only offer made, will the family accept it or not? There is only one choice-object now, namely, the transaction consisting in exchanging 12 pounds for 36 tickets, and this object may be accepted or declined. The delivery-situation is the same as before, namely, the one defined by the specified budget.

In the above examples the delivery-situation had reference to a *whole period of time*, one that was so long that it contained a great number of consumption cycles. This is expressed by the fact that the various items in the budget describing the situation were measured in quantities *per unit of time*. In other cases the delivery-situation may be defined as a situation referring to a single consumption act. In this case the items characterizing the situation will not have the denomination 'per unit of time' but simply be measured in pounds, yards, etc. Besides quantitative parameters characterizing the delivery-situation similar to those involved in the above examples there may, of course, also occur a number of other characteristics of a more or less qualitative character.

2.1.3.4 *Local and interlocal transactions*

In the choice-questions of the above example there only occurs one delivery-situation. In more complicated choice-questions there might occur two or more such situations. The question may, for instance, be this: let it be *given* that our working man's family on one occasion (for instance, this year), will have a certain specified budget *P*, and on another occasion (for instance, next year) another specified budget *Q*. The budgets *P* and *Q* are given in the same sense as the single budget of the previous example was given. Now let us assume that we offer the family as a present either one of the following two things:

1   12 pounds of ham in addition to the budget *P*;
2   36 talkie admissions in addition to the budget *Q*.

Or we may offer the family to give up ham from the budget *P* and instead receive tickets in addition to the budget *Q*. In any of these cases *P* and *Q* are two given delivery-situations. There is no choice about these situations themselves. Whatever the family might decide regarding the choice-objects (1) and (2) it is certain that the family will be on the one occasion in the situation *P* and on the other occasion in the situation *Q*. Such a transaction we shall call an *interlocal transaction* as distinguished from a *local transaction* only involving one delivery-situation. Correspondingly we may speak of interlocal and local choice-questions.

The distinction between local and interlocal transactions (choice-questions) plays an important role in utility axiomatics and will be further studied in some of the later sections.

2.1.3.5 *Decision-situation and the corresponding choice-constitution.* *Mediate and intermediate choice-acts*

The delivery-situation should not be confused with the situation that exists when the choice-question is asked and the answer given. This latter situation might be called the decision-situation. For example, this year when my economic situation is *J* I may be fairly certain that next year my situation will be *P* and the year after next *Q*. This being so, somebody may, this year, offer me a choice between either a present *a* to be given to me next year, or a present *b* to be given to me the year after that. Here *a* and *b* are choice-objects. *P* and *Q* are delivery-situations and *J* the decision-situation.

The time sequence between the various situations in this example should not be looked upon as something essential. It is not the time sequence but the dissimilarity between the situations considered that is the main point here. The time sequence in the example is only a more or less accidental feature due to the fact that in real life we cannot get different situations other than by taking different points of time.

Sometimes we may have the simple case where the choice-question only involves one delivery-situation and where furthermore this single delivery-situation involved coincides with the decision-situation. In this case the choice-question is a question as to how the individual would react if he had an offer to make a local transaction in that situation in which he actually finds himself at the time of the offer. Such a choice-question we shall call an *immediate* choice-question. And the decision of the individual in this case we shall call an immediate choice-act.

A choice-question involving at least one delivery-situation that is different from the decision-situation we shall call a *mediate* choice-question. Thus an immediate choice-question is a question only involving an actual situation while a mediate choice-question involves at least one hypothetical situation. Obviously it is only a local choice-question that can be immediate. All interlocal questions must necessarily be mediate because they involve at least two delivery situations and, of course, both cannot be identical with the decision-situation. On the other hand, there evidently exist local questions that are mediate.

In a concrete case the individual will, of course, find it easier to make up his mind regarding an immediate rather than a mediate choice-question. And if the hypothetical situations occurring in the mediate question become too different from the actual situation or from what the individual is used to, the question somewhat loses its reality. To ask a Chinese peddler what he would choose, either a new country home or a yacht, if he were in the economic situation of a well-to-do New York banker, is a rather too abstract question. But it is also a question without any great economic significance. We do not need to take such extreme questions into account in order to lay the foundations of a theory of utility. It will presently appear that we only need to take account of situations that are *somewhat* but not exceedingly different from the actual situation. And such questions certainly have a very definite meaning. The best proof of this is that most of us actually do calculate with such hypothetical situations each time when we make decisions that will be of consequence for our future economic situation. Furthermore, for such mediated choice-questions we need not even take account of the whole range of possible choice-objects. It is sufficient to select a few standard objects for comparison purposes as we shall presently see.

The notion of a decision-situation is intimately connected with the notion of a *choice-constitution*. This is the entirety, the sum total, of all the answers which an individual has made or would have made to a certain set of choice-questions.

The set of choice-questions considered may be more or less complete, thus establishing a more or less complete choice-constitution. And there may also be differences in the nature of the questions. We may, for instance, consider the sum total of all answers which an individual will make if in a certain decision-situation he is asked choice-questions for all possible delivery-situations of interest for this individual, and for all possible choice-objects in each of these delivery-situations. Such a constitution we may call a *complete mediate constitution* established from a given decision-situation. Another constitution is the one obtained by imagining that the individual successively finds himself in a series of situations and in each such situation is asked all possible immediate choice-questions. Such a constitution we may call an immediate constitution. Such a constitution must always be incomplete in the sense that it does not give any information about the disposition of the individual towards interlocal transactions. We shall, however, later see that it is possible to supplement this set of immediate questions in a certain way by interlocal (and consequently mediate) questions so as to obtain a constitution that may be called *quasi-immediate*. The complete mediate, the immediate, and the quasi-immediate are the three main types of choice-constitutions we shall consider.

The fact that two individuals have the *same* immediate choice-constitution (assumed unchanging with time) does not mean that they always actually behave in the same way. It only seems that they would behave in the same way if they were in the same situation.

Evidently any actual situation may be considered as a decision-situation. In every actual situation we may imagine that we formulate a whole system of choice-questions, both mediate and immediate questions. In this way we may imagine that we construct a mediate choice-constitution in each instance of the life history of the individual. This being done we may proceed to a comparison between these constitutions. There are two main groups of problems which arise out of such a comparison.

First we may investigate if the decision-situation and its remoteness in time from other situations of the choice-constitution should have any systematic effect on the nature of the constitution. In other words, we may imagine that we take a great number of constitutions, single out in each constitution the delivery-situation that is identical with the situation actually existing when the constitution was constructed (the decision-situation of the constitution considered), and then compare all the constitutions in order to find out if there is any systematic variation in the nature of the constitutions that can be correlated with the variation in the decision-situation.

If actual interrogation experiments were to be carried out on an individual, we would, of course, find that in each constitution it would only be for those situations that are not too different from the decision-situation that the nature of the constitution would be distinctly determined. The other and more remote parts of the constitution would, so to speak, lose themselves in the haze. Other significant effects of the decision-situation would also be very likely to be discovered, for instance, systematic effects due to time preference. All these problems of investigating the effect of the decision-situation we may classify under the heading of *perspective* problems in the choice analysis.

The second group of problems in the comparison of the mediate choice-constitution of an individual is to find out if there is any systematic variation in the nature of the constitution apart from the variation due to the decision-situation. These problems we may call *evolution* problems of the choice-constitution.

2.1.3.6 *Object-continuum and situation-continuum*

In the utility analysis the choice-objects are those things the utility of which we want to find and the delivery-situation is the sum total of all those things, the change of which (even though the decision-situation is given) may cause a change in the utility considered. Strictly speaking, there is no limit to the sort of things that might be drawn into the analysis and looked upon as constituent parts of the delivery-situation. The satisfaction which an individual gets out of a certain piece of a good that he consumes at a certain moment of time will, if we look sufficiently minutely into the matter, depend on the whole life history of the individual up to that moment, on his relation to other individuals, etc. Such an absolutely general point of view, however, leads nowhere. It may appeal to the pure empiricist who delights in minute recording and description of facts, but it is useless in a constructive theoretical analysis. In some way or another we must simplify the problem by specialization. So we select a certain number of things which we look upon as the only *relevant* determining factors, and the sum total of these things we consider as the delivery-situation. The group of things we select will, of course, depend on the nature of the particular problem at hand and may vary from one case to another. Furthermore, in one and the same problem we may consider a series of successive approximations by including an increasing number of things into the definition of the delivery-situation.

Similar remarks may be made about the definition of the choice-objects. In each case there is a certain degree of minuteness in the description of the objects beyond which it is useless to go. There is also a certain connection between the nature of the choice-objects and the kind of feature which it is necessary to take account of in the definition of the delivery-situation. For instance, if the problem at hand involves foodstuff as choice-objects it will as a rule not be necessary to introduce as features of the delivery-situation such things as the nature and quality of the furniture which the individual has, or the character of the housing, etc. In this case we may say that the utility of food is independent of the situation with respect to furniture, housing, etc.

Of particular interest is the case where either the delivery-situation or the choice-objects, or both, can be described by a certain number of *quantitative parameters*. The following is an illustration of such a case.

Let us suppose that the thing the utility of which is to be defined is a complex consisting of n goods, nos. 1, 2 ... n. Each of these goods is supposed to be such that its *quantity* can be measured in some sort of technical units, say by counting pieces, by weighing, by measuring length or duration, etc. In this case we may look upon a choice-object as a complex consisting of certain amounts ΔX_1, $\Delta X_2, \ldots, \Delta X_n$ of the n goods. These magnitudes we shall call the *object-parameters*.

This being so, the idea naturally presents itself to consider the n magnitudes ΔX_i as rectangular coordinates of a point ΔX in an n-dimensional continuum, and to take the point as the *image* of the choice-object. The continuum we may call the object-continuum and the point the object-point.

For $n=2$ we would have a plane representation as in Figure 2.4.

Any point ΔX in the plane of Figure 2.4 represents a choice-object. In particular, if $\Delta X_1 = 0$ the object only consists of a certain amount of good no. 2, and if $\Delta X_2 = 0$ it only consists of a certain amount of no. 1. The object-parameters ΔX_1 and ΔX_2 may be either positive or negative. A positive parameter indicates that the choice-question considered involves a *receipt* of a certain amount of the good in question, and a negative parameter indicates that the choice-question involves the *giving up* of a certain amount of this good.

Now for a graphical representation of the delivery-situation. We shall first, for simplicity, assume that the only features of the delivery-situation which we need to take account of are the amounts $X_1, X_2, \ldots, X_n$ of the n goods which the individual had assigned for consumption before the question about the choice-object came up. We shall here assume that these amounts are amounts to be consumed in one single consumption act at one particular occasion, not to be spread out over several consumption acts. In other words $X_1, X_2 \ldots X_n$ are quantities measured in pounds, yards, etc., not in pounds, yards, etc., per unit of time. Further we shall assume that

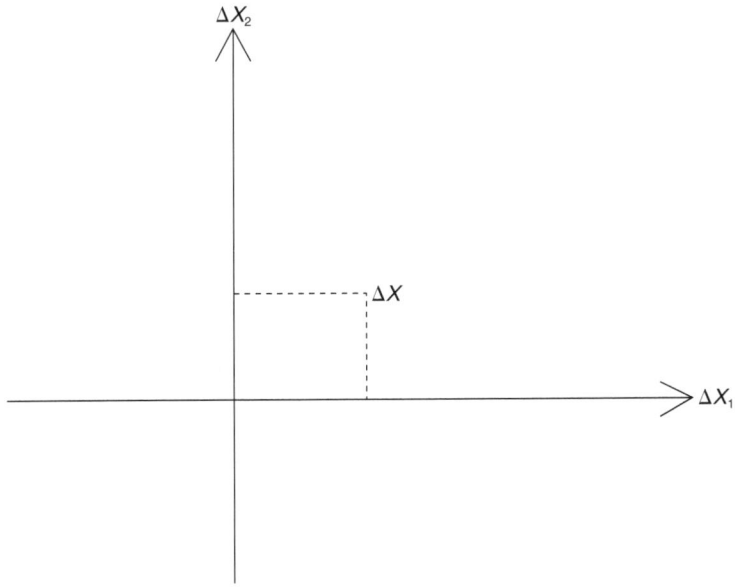

Figure 2.4 Object-continuum.

these amounts are amounts that actually must be consumed, not only amounts which the individual has at his disposal. In this case all the quantities X_i must be non-negative. In the case here considered the delivery-situation is, just as the choice-object, uniquely defined by a set of n parameters. And the parameters defining the delivery-situation are just the n quantities X_i. These we shall call the *situation parameters*. If we look upon the n magnitudes X_i as the n rectangular coordinates of a point X in an n-dimensional continuum, we get an image of the delivery-situation. This point we shall call the *situation-point*, or, more precisely, the *delivery-point*. The X continuum itself we shall call the situation-continuum. There is one point in the situation-continuum that is of particular interest, namely, the point J representing the decision-situation. This point we shall call the *decision point*. Figure 2.5 represents a situation-continuum in the case $n=2$. J in Figure 2.5 is the decision point. So long as we maintain the assumption that the magnitudes X_1 represent quantities actually consumed, it is only the quadrant generated by the positive parts of the axes that is of any interest.

The notions of object-continuum and situation-continuum are of great help in handling the problems of utility theory. In the simplest cases the notion of marginal utility turns out to be something that from a formal point of view is identical with the notion of *force*, or *field intensity* in physical space. It can consequently be handled by the same mathematical apparatus: vectors, matrices, etc., by which the physical field is analysed. It will therefore be natural to call the situation-continuum a *choice field*. If the choice-situations become more complicated the analogy with a physical field cannot be maintained literally. But

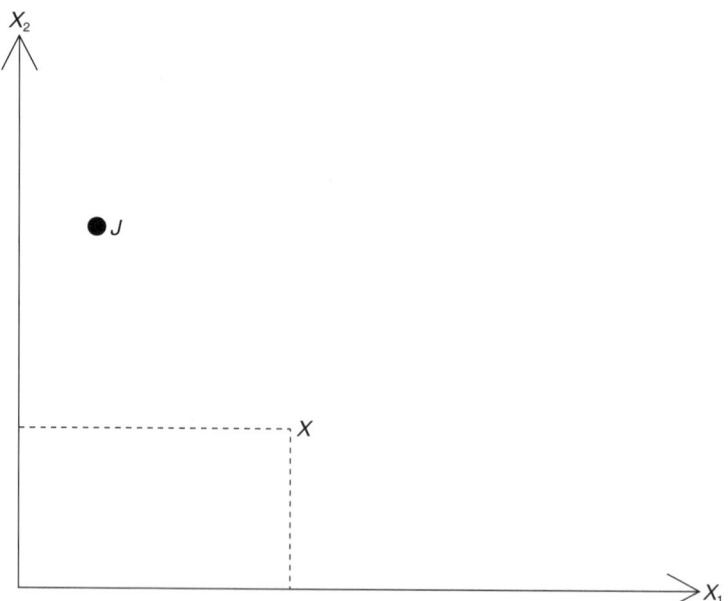

Figure 2.5 The situation-continuum.

by some generalization of the representation it may be maintained in a symbolic way, which is also a great help in the analysis and the exposition. We shall consider some examples of these more complicated situations.

First suppose we have a mediate choice-constitution where it is sufficient to characterize each delivery-situation by the n parameters X_i of the preceding example and by one more parameter, namely, the length of time τ which is assumed to elapse between the instant of the choice-question and the future instant where the hypothetical delivery-situation is laid. Thus the choice-question is now of the form: 'If τ years (or months, weeks, etc.) from now you were in the situation $X=(X_1, X_2,\ldots, X_n)$, and you were offered…'. The delivery-point P is now a point in the $(n+1)$ dimensional space $(X_1, X_2,\ldots, X_n, \tau)$.

Figure 2.6 represents the case $n=2$. The point J in Figure 2.6 is the image of the decision point. For this point we evidently have $\tau=0$. The parameter τ may be called the *futurity* parameter and we may say that the magnitude of τ indicates the futurity of the delivery-point.

We may go a step further and consider different decision-points, namely, one such point for each moment of historical time. We designate by T the point of time where the decision was made, and we call this parameter T the decision parameter. Evidently T may be measured from an arbitrary origin. The characteristic features of the decision are now not represented by a point J in the n-dimensional subspace $(X_1, X_2,\ldots, X_n)$, as in the previous case, but by a whole empirical curve (J, J') in this subspace. This curve is the curve indicating how the situation of the individual has actually changed with time. Figure 2.7 represents the case $n=1$ (one good only). (J, J') in Figure 2.7 is the historical situation curve for the individual.

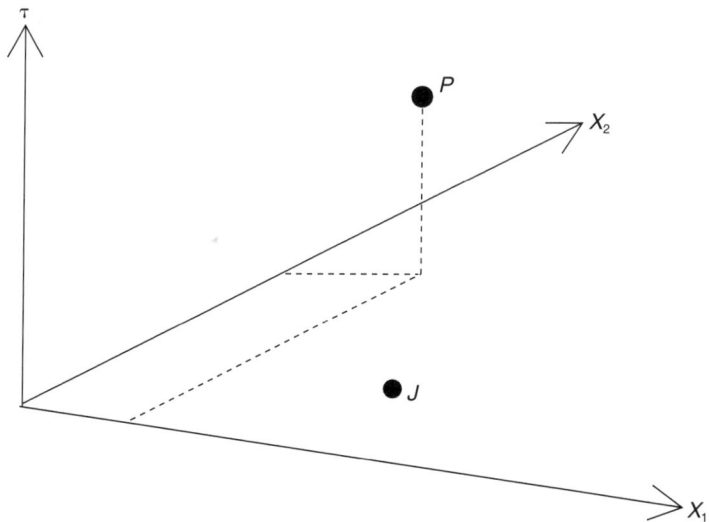

Figure 2.6 The situation-continuum with futurity axis.

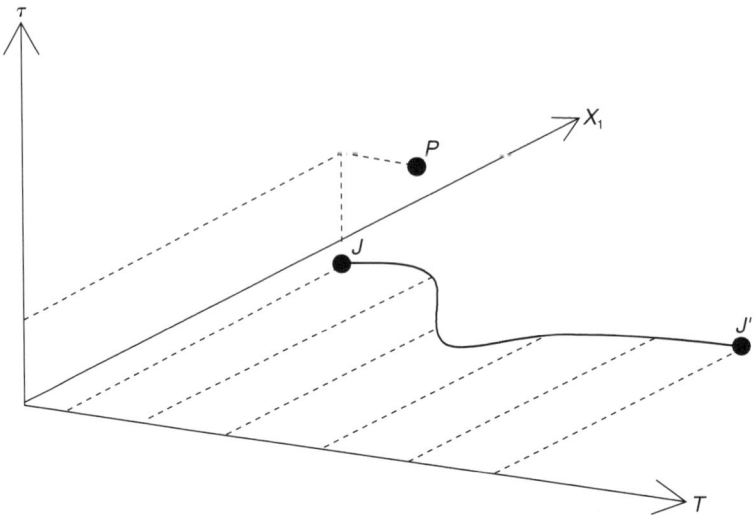

Figure 2.7 The situation-continuum with futurity axis and decision axis.

So far as the nature of the choice-constitution goes, the case now considered is not essentially different from the foregoing. The present case is in reality only an accumulation of a whole series of choice-constitutions, each such constitution existing at a given instant, and being of the kind indicated in the previous example.

The following is an example of a more fundamental generalization. Let us suppose that the utility of the choice-object depends not only on the situation $(X_1, X_2, \ldots, X_n)$ that exists at the moment of time t when the object is delivered to the individual for consumption (or taken away from him), but on the whole course which the consumption of the individual has followed in the interval of time previous to t. This course would be described by considering each of the quantities $(X_1, X_2, \ldots, X_n)$ as a function of time. Thus $X_1(t)$ would indicate how much the individual had consumed of good no. 1 up to and including the point of time t (time being measured from an arbitrary moment taken as origin). Similarly $X_2(t)$ would indicate how much he had consumed of good no. 2, etc. The functions $X_1(t), X_2(t), \ldots, X_n(t)$ may be called the consumption functions. In real life consumption usually takes place at certain isolated points of time separated by periods of non-consumption. If the problem at hand is such that it is necessary to take account of these discontinuities, each of the functions $X_i(t)$ must be considered as a non-decreasing step function of time (see Figure 2.8). Otherwise the consumption function may be considered as continuous. In this case it will even as a rule be plausible to assume that they have continuous derivatives with respect to time:

$$x_i(t) = \dot{X}_i(t) = \frac{dX(t)}{dt}$$

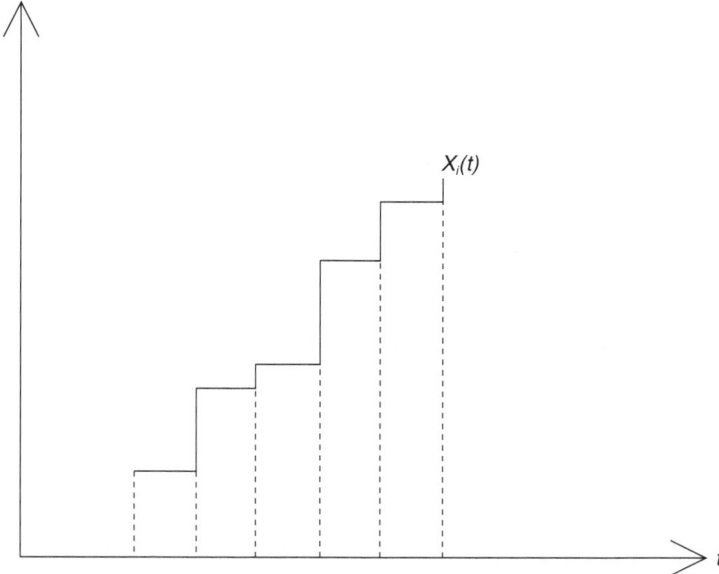

Figure 2.8 X_i as a step function.

In the case where the choice depends on the whole course of the consumption functions up to the point of time *t*, the delivery-situation to be considered is a situation which is characterized not by *n* magnitudes $(X_1, X_2, \ldots, X_n)$ but by the time-shape of *n* curves $(X_1(t), X_2(t), \ldots, X_n(t))$. If any one of these curves changes its form (over the whole or a part of its range), the delivery situation is changed. In this case the delivery situation cannot be represented as a point in an ordinary *n*-dimensional continuum. We must have recourse to the symbolic representation by a 'point' in a 'function-space'. From a mathematical point of view the theory of such function-spaces has been developed to a certain extent, the notions of 'distance', 'angle', etc., being built up in analogy with these notions for ordinary spaces. In the following we shall, however, not use these several notions of the function-space to any large extent. We shall primarily use only the simple notion of a 'point' *P* in this abstract space in order to have a convenient way of expressing the entirety of all the things on which the delivery-situation depends. Since we shall not use any of the more complicated 'geometric' properties of the function space we can just as well make our space notion still more general, and let it stand to represent *any* of the things on which it may be plausible to assume that the delivery situation depends, whether these things are expressible in quantitative form as magnitudes, curves, etc., or not. In the general axiomatic analysis of the following sections, it is such an abstract situation space which we shall use. In each particular case to which this general notion is applied, it becomes a special problem to find out to what extent it is possible to formulate the characteristic features of the delivery-situation and of the choice-objects in a quantitative way.

2.1.3.7   The system of choice-axioms for a given decision-situation

The French mathematician, Hadamard, has said something to the effect that in the attempt at building up a rigorous logical foundation of the notion of numbers and of mathematics in general, we have to behave like a person who knows about a *secret* which is the guidance of his actions, but which he must never make any reference to in his conversation with other people. His society manners must be such as not to arouse the slightest suspicion about his greatest secret. From a formal point of view he must act as if the secret did not exist. This remark is very much to the point: in some way or another we have actually got some suspicion as to what sort of arithmetics, algebra or geometry will be most useful to us. The problem is only to find a basis from which this sort of mathematics can be deduced by a rigorous, logical structure. And in the erection of such a structure it is of course essential not to allow the slightest element of our secret to mix with the strictly logical building materials. Such a mixture will at once spoil the logical water-tightness of the structure. Formally, we therefore have to behave as if the secret did not exist at all.

In the attempt at constructing a scientific notion of utility the situation is very much the same. Here the role played by the secret is perhaps even more important than in mathematics, because in the case of utility we have ourselves really lived through the thing which we try to objectivize into a rigorous scientific notion. This is a help, but at the same time a great danger. It creates a nearly irresistible temptation to mix elements of the secret into the logical structure. In a rigorous analysis of utility it is therefore of the utmost importance to be on guard against such slips of thought at every step. In this respect it will be found very useful to formulate the whole discussion in terms of certain *choice-axioms*. The rigorous statement and systematic use of such axioms is a powerful tool in keeping the mind from getting off the track. The axioms used in the foundation of utility can be more or less general in character according to the point of view adopted. In the present section we shall state the various axioms in a very general form to show their nature and the logical inter-relationships between them. In the following sections we shall show how the adoption of certain combinations of these axioms, or certain special cases of them, makes it possible to give a more or less complete definition of utility as a quantity. The completeness of the definition will, of course, depend on how far-reaching a set of axioms we assume. Each special feature of the utility notion is, as a rule, connected with some particular axiom.

When we formulate and use the choice-axioms we shall always assume that there exists a certain relation between the choice objects and the delivery-situations in the sense that the *acceptance* of a certain object leads over from the delivery situation where this object was received to a new situation, this new situation being uniquely determined by the original situation and the object in question. Thus, if the working man's family from our previous example *decides* on one of the choice-objects, say decides to accept the 12 pounds of ham, the family is no longer in the original situation determined by the specified budget but in a new situation where the 12 pounds of ham is included in the budget. And this new situation is the one which must be taken as the delivery situation if a *further* choice-question is asked. In this simple example the connection between objects and delivery-situation is *mutual* in the sense that not only does the acceptance of a given choice-object in a given situation lead over to a uniquely determined new situation, but inversely if the original situation is given and also the final situation, this determines uniquely the choice-object. There is only one choice-object that leads from the former to the latter situation. This, however, is only a special feature of our simple example and will not be put up as a general assumption regarding the choice-objects and the delivery-situation. We shall presently see examples of cases where there is not only one but an infinity of objects leading from one situation to another. The only general assumption which we shall adopt in the following is the assumption that the original situation, together with a given choice-object, determine uniquely the final situation. This assumption we shall call the *connectivity* assumption. We do not consider this assumption as one of our axioms but rather as an element of the definition of those things which are involved in the axioms. But, of course, this is only a formal question and there would not have been any logical objection against listing the connectivity assumption as one of our axioms. We now proceed to a statement and discussion of axioms.

Notes

1 Edgeworth, Francis Y. (1891) *Mathematical Psychics*, London.
2 Fisher, Irving (1892) *Mathematical Investigations into the Theory of Value and Prices*, New Haven, Connecticut.
3 Eugen von Böhm-Bawerk (1886) 'Grundzüge der Theorie des wirtschaftlichen Güterwerts', *Jahrbücher für Nationalökonomi und Statistik*, 47: 1–82, 477–541; Eugen von Böhm-Bawerk (1912) *Kapital und Kapitalzins*, 3rd edition, Vol. II.2, Exkurs VIII and X.
4 Editors' note: here quoted from Slutsky, E. (2004) 'A critique of Böhm-Bawerk's concept of value and his theory of the measurability of value', *Structural Change and Economic Dynamics*, 15: 357–369, which is a translation and and reissue of Slutsky, E. (1927) 'Zur Kritik des Böhm-Bawerkschen Wertbegriff und seiner Lehre von der messbarkeit des Wertes', *Schmollers Jahrbuch für Gesetzgebung, Verwaltung und Volkswirtschaft im Deutschen Reich*, 51: 37–52. Frisch quoted the original article: 'Jene Tatsache, das Leute vernünftig wirtschaften, Vorteile und Nachteile gegeneinander abwägen usw. ist *kein* Beweis dafür, das sie es in keiner anderen Weise wie durch die Messung der Befühlsintensitäten bzw. durch deren Summieren ausführen. Was uns E. v. Böhm-Bawerk vortragt, ist eine Motivationstheorie, was er uns aber zu ihrer Begründung als eine Tatsache des Summierens der Gefühlsintensitäten anzugenben trachtet (insofern es wirklich eine Tatsache ist), ist die Tatsache der Motivation selbst, dessen blosse Faktizität an sich so wenig für seine, wie für irgendeine andere Motivationstheorie sprechen kann.'
5 Cassel's remark (in Cassel, G. (1918) *Theoretische Sozialökonomie*, Leipzig: Wintersche Verlagshaltung, p. 314) is in this respect characteristic 'können wir als normalen Zug der Entwicklung feststellen das mit steigendem Arbeitslohn die Anspruche auf Verkürzung der Arbeitszeit immer starker hervortreten'. It is only a question of 'feststellen', not a question of a theoretical explanation of the phenomenon. In this same

connection Cassel speaks about the disutility theory in a way which would be interpreted to the effect that a monotonously increasing supply curve follows from the disutility theory. As shown above, the reverse is true. The disutility theory has as its objective first to explain why one part of the supply curve has the shape indicated by Cassel, and second to investigate in which point the change takes place.

6 Editors' note: Frisch made a trivial mistake here, it should be 'increasing or decreasing'.

7 Frisch, R. (1926a) 'Sur un problème d'économie pure', *Norsk Matematisk Forenings Skrifter*, Oslo, Series 1, No. 16, 1–40.

8 Frisch, R. (1926b) 'Kvantitativ formulering av den teoretiske økonomikks lover' ['Quantitative formulation of the laws of economic theory'], *Statsøkonomisk Tidsskrift*, 40: 299–334.

9 The originally planned section 7 of Part III was entitled 'A statistical analysis of selected groups of data by the methods developed in the presenet course', but omitted in the lecture notes, see Editors' introduction.

3 Statistical verification of the laws of economic theory

3.1 A short statement of some of the classical formulae in correlation and linear regression analysis

In this section we shall give some of the classical formulae in correlation and regression analysis that will be useful in the following. For simplicity we shall first consider the case of two variables.

Suppose that we have made a large number of observations, each observation being characterized by the magnitude of two quantitative attributes X_1 and X_2. Thus each of our observations consists of two measurements, namely, the measurement of X_1 and the measurement of X_2. Any number of examples may be given. Our observation may, for instance, consist of the measurements of X_1 = height and X_2 = weight of a recruit. The measurement of the first recruit may be designated $(_1X_1, _1X_2)$, the measurement of the second recruit may be designated $(_2X_1, _2X_2)$, and so on. Again X_1 and X_2 may be represented, say, by the quantity traded of a commodity and the price of this same commodity. Or X_1 may represent pig iron production and X_2 represent the interest rate, and so on.

If we pick out any of the observations we shall generally denote it by the 'frontscript' t, thus $_tX_1$, $_tX_2$. The last of the observations we shall designate by the frontscript N, that is to say, the number of observations is equal to N. If the two variables considered represent magnitudes varying in time, then the variable t in our notation would actually designate time. But if the variables considered are not time series but variables in any statistical distribution, then t would only be a number designating the particular observation considered. And in this case the succession of the various observations will as a rule be unessential for the problem at hand, while in the first case, namely, when t actually designates time, the succession of the observations might be essential.

The result of such a set of observations may be represented graphically by a *scatter diagram*. This is constructed in the following way: we draw a system of axes (X_1, X_2). In this diagram we mark off a point that has the coordinates $(_1X_1, _1X_2)$, that is to say, a point whose abscissa is equal to $_1X_1$ and whose ordinate is equal to $_1X_2$. This point represents the first observation. For shortness we may represent this point itself by the symbol $_1X$. We shall call it the first observation point. Similarly, the second observation $(_2X_1, _2X_2)$ is represented by a point whose abscissa is equal to $_2X_1$ and whose ordinate is equal to $_2X_2$. This point we designate $_2X$ and we call it the second observation point. Similarly the following observations are represented by a set of points $_3X$, $_4X$,..., $_NX$. If the number of observations is N there will be in all N points (see Figure 3.1). This set of points will form a 'swarm' or a 'cluster', the nature of which is characteristic for the observations. *All the information obtained by the observations at hand is represented in this scatter diagram.* Studying the result of our observations is therefore equivalent to studying the nature of the scatter diagram. The problem of analysing the result of observations may therefore be looked upon as a problem of studying the various characteristics of the scatter diagram.

To give a few examples: one of the essential properties of the scatter diagram is its *centre of gravity.* Another feature is the density with which the points cluster around this centre. In this regard we may speak of the concentration in the vertical or in the horizontal direction. And another feature is whether or not the cluster is *organized* in the sense that if we increase one of the variables then we will on the average also increase the other. This latter problem, namely the problem of the organization of the cluster, contains in itself two separate problems, namely:

1   The problem regarding the nature of the relationship which is exhibited by the scatter diagram. That is to say, what is the nature of underlying trend in the cluster, is it linear, curvilinear, etc.?

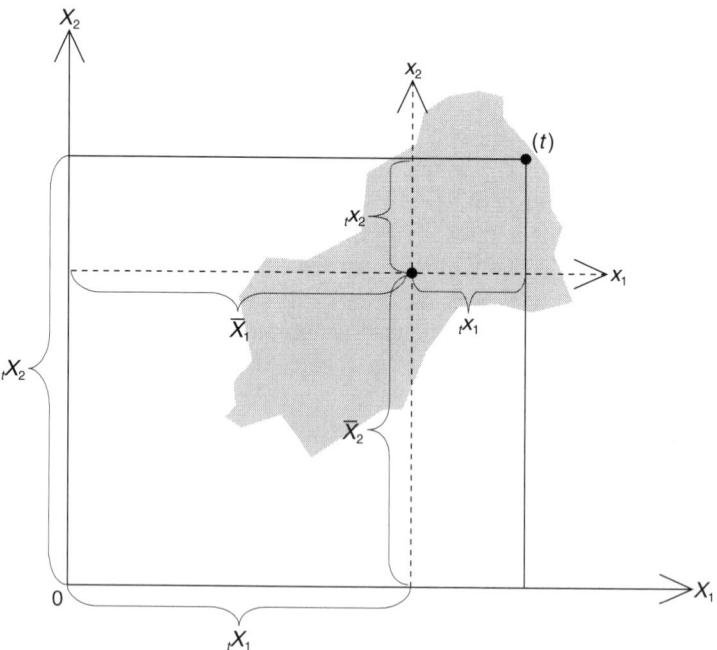

Figure 3.1 The scatter diagram.

2   What is the amount of deviation from the underlying trend which is exhib-
    ited in the scatter diagram? In other words, do the points of the scatter
    diagram cluster very densely around that underlying trend or do the points
    of the scatter diagram come very far from showing a dense clustering
    around this trend? Figure 3.2 is an example of a dense clustering around the
    trend. Figure 3.3 is an example of the opposite.

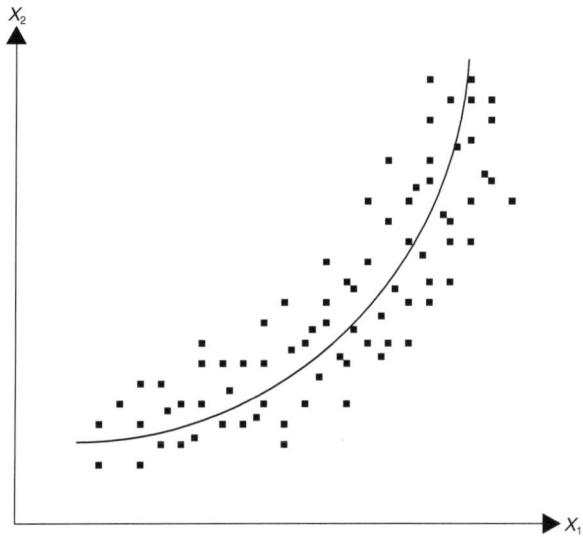

Figure 3.2 Dense clustering around the trend.

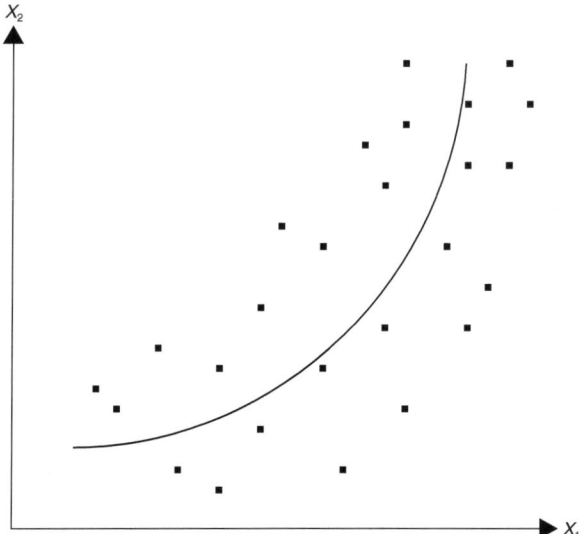

Figure 3.3 Sparse clustering around the trend.

We now proceed to define a set of parameters by which we may express in a numerical form some of the properties of the scatter diagram in which we are interested.

First we define the mean $\bar{X}_1$ of the variable no. 1. This mean is equal to

$$\bar{X}_1 = \frac{1}{N}({}_1X_1 + {}_2X_1 + \dots {}_NX_1) \tag{1}$$

For shortness we shall in the following write the sum which is in the right member of (1) in one of the following three forms:

$${}_1X_1 + {}_2X_1 + \dots {}_NX_1 = \sum_{t=1}^{t=N} {}_tX_1 = \sum_t {}_tX_1 = \sum X_1 \tag{2}$$

The relations in (2) express three different ways of writing the sum which is indicated in the left member of (2). The first sum to the right in (2) may be looked upon as the most explicit form. The second expression is still more abbreviated and the third expression is further simplified. Most of the time we shall use the simplified expression to the extreme right in (2).

In exactly the same form, we may define the mean $\bar{X}_2$ of the variable no. 2. That is to say, we have by definition

$$\bar{X}_1 = \frac{1}{N} \sum X_1$$
$$\bar{X}_2 = \frac{1}{N} \sum X_2 \tag{3}$$

The set of variables (X_1, X_2) we shall designate the *origin* set. This is a set of variables which are measured from the origin that is given by the nature of the observations. In distinction to the origin set we shall designate, under the name of the *reduced* set, the set of variables which we obtained by subtracting from our observation the mean of the variable in question. The reduced set we shall designate (x_1, x_2). That is to say, the two variables x_1, x_2 are defined by the equation

$${}_tx_1 = {}_tX_1 - \bar{X}_1$$
$${}_tx_2 = {}_tX_2 - \bar{X}_2 \tag{4}$$

If in Figure 3.1 we take any point (t) and measure its coordinates with respect to the origin 0 we obtain the quantities ${}_tX_1$ and ${}_tX_2$. And if we measure the coordinates of the point t with respect to the system of axes which is obtained by translating the original system of axes to the point whose coordinates in the original system is $(\bar{X}_1, \bar{X}_2)$, then we obtain the two quantities ${}_tx_1$ and ${}_tx_2$.

Further we shall define the *moments* of the statistical distribution considered. Let i and j be any two of the numbers 1 and 2, for instance $i=1, j=1$, or $i=1, j=2$ or $i=2, j=1$, or $i=2, j=2$. Then we put up the following definition:

$$M_{ij} = \sum X_i X_j = {}_1X_i \cdot {}_1X_j + {}_2X_i \cdot {}_2X_j + \ldots + {}_NX_i \cdot {}_NX_j \tag{5}$$

The quantity M_{ij} is the (i,j)-th moment taken about the origin, or, shorter, the origin moment no. (ij).

Similarly, we define the *reduced* moments

$$m_{ij} = \sum x_i x_j = {}_1x_i \cdot {}_1x_j + {}_2x_i \cdot {}_2x_j + \ldots + {}_Nx_i \cdot {}_Nx_j \tag{6}$$

The moments M_{ij} and m_{ij} are called *straight square* moments if $i=j$, and *cross* moments if $i \neq j$. In either case the moments are called square moments to distinguish them from other sorts of moments which we shall consider later.

Further, we define the *standard ordinate* of the variable no. i.

$$S_i = +\sqrt{M_{ii}/N} = +\sqrt{\Sigma X_i^2 / N} \tag{7}$$

and the *standard deviation* of variable no. i.

$$\sigma_i = +\sqrt{m_{ii}/N} = +\sqrt{\Sigma x_i^2 / N} \tag{8}$$

By definition we choose the positive magnitude of the square root both in (7) and in (8). In order to remind us of this definition we have written a plus sign in $\sqrt{}$ (7) and (8).

Both the origin moments M_{ij} and the reduced moments m_{ij} depend upon the units of measurement. If we divide each variable by the standard ordinate before we proceed to determining the origin moments, then we still obtain an origin moment which is independent of the units of measurement. The origin moment no. (ij) thus obtained will be equal to

$$R_{ij} = \frac{M_{ij}}{+\sqrt{M_{ii}M_{jj}}} \tag{9}$$

Similarly if we divide each of the reduced variables by its standard deviation before we construct the reduced moment then we also obtain moments that are independent of the units of measurement. These moments will be equal to

$$r_{ij} = \frac{m_{ij}}{+\sqrt{m_{ii}m_{jj}}} \tag{10}$$

The four quantities R_{ij} are called the *origin correlations* and the quantities r_{ij} the *reduced correlations* in the set of variables no. (1, 2). In practice, it is only one of the four quantities R_{ij} that is characteristic. We namely have $R_{ii}=R_{jj}=1$ and $R_{ij}=R_{ji}$. This follows immediately from the definition (9). Therefore it is in reality only the quantity R_{12} that is characteristic. Similarly, if we consider the reduced correlations r_{ij} we will find that it is only the quantity r_{12} that contains any characteristic information. This quantity r_{12} is the classical Pearsonian coefficient of correlation.

We shall later discuss the significance of this parameter as a means of characterizing the distribution. At present we only give the formal definitions.

If we compare the four sets of quantities

$$M_{ij} \ m_{ij} \ R_{ij} \ r_{ij}$$

we see that the Ms are not invariant either for a change of the origin of the variables or for a change in units of measurement. The ms are invariant for a change in origin but not for a change in units of measurement. The Rs are invariant for a change in the units of measurement but not for a change in the origin. And finally, the rs are invariant both for a change in origin and for a change in the units of measurement.

The ratio between the standard deviation and the standard ordinate of the variable no. i we shall call the *coefficient of variability* for the variable no. 1. We designate it m_i so that we have by definition

$$m_i = \frac{\sigma_i}{S_i} = \frac{\sqrt{m_{ii}}}{\sqrt{M_{ii}}} \tag{11}$$

This definition of the coefficient of variability differs from the usual definition which consists of defining the coefficient of variability as equal to the ratio between the standard deviation and the mean of the variable in question. That is to say, if this usual coefficient of variability is designated v_i we have

$$v_i = \frac{\sigma_i}{\overline{X}_i} \tag{12}$$

The reason for introducing the coefficient of variability defined by (11) instead of the coefficient defined by (12) is that the coefficient defined by (12) only has a definite sense in the particular case where the variable no. i is such that it is always positive by the very nature of the problem at hand. In case the variable no. i is not essentially positive, then positive and negative terms will cancel out in the definition of the mean, so that the mean may become 0 or even negative. But it is obvious that if the mean becomes equal to 0, then the coefficient defined by (12) becomes infinite. That is to say v_i is a magnitude to which there is no limit. It may be any number between $-\infty$ and $+\infty$. Therefore if we are given any such quantity we have no convenient means at all to judge whether it is 'large' or 'small'. Furthermore the fact that v_i may become infinite introduces a troublesome complication in the handling of the formulae. In both these respects the coefficient of variability m_i is more advantageous. Namely, it always is a positive quantity situated between 0 and 1. This will follow from one of the formulas given below. Furthermore, the coefficient of variability m_i is the natural tool to apply when we consider time series components. A time series component that moves cyclically through positive and negative quantities will, namely, most of the time have a mean which is close to 0 or even rigorously equal to 0 and in that case the coefficient of variability defined by (12) has no sense.

We now proceed to give a set of formulae expressing certain relations between the magnitudes here defined. First we see that the mean of any of the reduced variables is equal to 0. That is to say, we have

$$\bar{x}_i = 0 \tag{13}$$

or, which amounts to the same,

$$\Sigma x_i = 0 \tag{14}$$

In order to prove the last formula, we simply notice that we have

$$\Sigma x_i = \Sigma(X_i - \bar{X}_i) = \Sigma X_i - N\bar{X}_i = N(\bar{X}_i - \bar{X}_i) = 0$$

The reduced moments may be expressed in terms of the origin moments by the following formula:

$$m_{ij} = M_{ij} - N \cdot \bar{X}_i \cdot \bar{X}_j \tag{15}$$

The last formula is proved as follows:

$$m_{ij} = \sum (X_i - \bar{X}_i).(X_j - \bar{X}_j) = \sum (X_i X_j - \bar{X}_i X_j - X_i \bar{X}_j + \bar{X}_i \bar{X}_j)$$
$$= M_{ij} - N \cdot \bar{X}_i \bar{X}_j - N \cdot \bar{X}_i \bar{X}_j + N \cdot \bar{X}_i \bar{X}_j = M_{ij} - N \cdot \bar{X}_i \bar{X}_j$$

Between the standard ordinate and the standard deviation we have the following relation:

$$S_i^2 = \sigma_i^2 + \bar{X}_i^2 \tag{16}$$

This formula follows by putting $i=j$ in (15). Since $\bar{X}_i^2$ is a non-negative quantity, (16) shows immediately that S_i is not less than σ_i. Furthermore, both σ_i and S_i are by definition non-negative quantities. Therefore, the coefficient of variability m_i defined by (11) must always be a quantity between 0 and 1.

By the last equation we can obtain a simple formula expressing the relation between the coefficient of variability m_i defined by (11) and the coefficient v_i defined by (12). If we divide (16) by S_i^2 we obtain $1 = m_i^2 + (\bar{X}/S_i)^2$ and if we divide (16) by $\bar{X}_i^2$ we obtain $(S_i/\bar{X}_i)^2 = v_i^2 + 1$.

Introducing in the first equation the expression for $(\bar{X}_i/S_i)^2$ taken from the last equation, we obtain

$$1 - m_i^2 = \frac{1}{1 + v_i^2} \tag{17}$$

The last equation may be solved with respect to either m_i^2 or v_i^2, thus giving either m_i^2 in terms of v_i^2 or vice versa. It is worthy of note that the relation between the two coefficients of variability is a relation between the two *squares* m_i^2 and v_i^2.

From (16) we immediately deduce a formula expressing the mean of the variable no. i in terms of the standard ordinate of this variable. We get

$$\bar{X}_i = (\text{sgn } X_i) \cdot S_i \cdot \sqrt{1 - m_i^2} \tag{18}$$

where the symbol $(\text{sgn } \bar{X}_i)$ means 'the sign of $\bar{X}_i$'. That is to say, the symbol $(\text{sgn } \bar{X}_i)$ is equal to either $+1$ or -1 or 0 accordingly as $\bar{X}_i$ is positive, negative or 0. This sign being introduced in (18) the square root itself is taken positive.

Between the origin correlations R_{ij} and the reduced correlations r_{ij} we have the following relation:

$$R_{ij} = m_i m_j r_{ij} + \text{sgn } \bar{X}_i \bar{X}_j \sqrt{(1 - m_i^2)(1 - m_j^2)} \tag{19}$$

In order to prove this formula we notice that from the definition (11) and the formula (18) we have

$$\frac{\sqrt{m_{ii} m_{jj}}}{m_i m_j} = \sqrt{M_{ii} M_{jj}} = \frac{\text{sgn } \bar{X}_i \bar{X}_j \cdot N \cdot \bar{X}_i \bar{X}_j}{\sqrt{(1 - m_i^2)(1 - m_j^2)}} \tag{20}$$

Therefore we may divide the left member of (15) by the expression to the extreme left in (20) and divide the first term in the right member of (15) by the expression in the middle of (20) and finally divide the last term in (15) by the expression to the extreme right in (20). If this is done, we get formula (19).

We now proceed to derive a formula which is a very powerful tool in analysing the relationships between moments. It may, for instance, be used for an immediate proof of the important fact that the origin correlation coefficient R_{12} (and also the reduced correlation coefficient r_{12}) is always lying between -1 and $+1$. The formula in question is:

$$M_{11} M_{22} - M_{12}^2 = \frac{1}{2} \sum_{pq} ({}_p X_1 \cdot {}_q X_2 - {}_q X_1 \cdot {}_p X_2)^2 \tag{21}$$

where

$$\sum_{pq} \text{ denotes the double summation } \sum_{p=1}^{N} \sum_{q=1}^{N} \tag{22}$$

This formula we shall call the *fundamental moment formula* (for two variables). In order to prove it we simply carry out the summation $\sum_{pq}$ separately on each term obtained by multiplying out the expression in the right member of (21). This gives

$$\frac{1}{2} \sum_{pq} ({}_p X_1^2 \, {}_q X_2^2 - 2 \, {}_p X_1 \, {}_q X_2 \, {}_q X_1 \cdot {}_p X_2 + {}_q X_1^2 \cdot {}_p X_2^2) =$$

$$\frac{1}{2} (M_{11} M_{22} - 2 M_{12}^2 + M_{11} M_{22}) = M_{11} M_{22} - M_{12}^2$$

From the fundamental moment formula we immediately deduce that

$$0 \le R_{12}^2 \le 1 \tag{23}$$

and

$$0 \le r_{12}^2 \le 1 \tag{24}$$

Formula (23) follows immediately from the fundamental moment formula. The right member of this formula namely consists of a number of terms, each of which is a square and therefore non-negative. The entire right member of (21) must therefore also be non-negative, that is to say, we have $0 \le M_{11}M_{22} - M_{12}^2$ and dividing this inequality by the quantity $M_{11}M_{22}$ (which is positive, not 0, if both the variable no. 1 and the variable no. 2 really show any change at all in the material at hand), we obtain immediately formula (23). And from (23) follows (24). (24) may namely be looked upon as a special case of (23). (23) holds good for *any* set of two observational variables, and the set of variables (x_1, x_2), that is to say, the set of variables measured from the mean, is, of course, also a set of observational variables.

* * *

In the presentation of a subject like correlation we may distinguish between three different tasks.

1   *The algebraic definitions.*
    This consists of an exact definition of those quantities which are contained in the theory, for instance, defining the moments, the correlation coefficients, etc. This is what we have done in the preceding lines, for the case of two variables.
2   *The interpretation of the notions involved.*
    In order fully to grasp what the theory involves, it is not sufficient only to understand each step of the formal algebraic definitions. We must also arrive at a more or less intuitive understanding of the significance of the various notions involved. For instance, when we speak of a correlation coefficient it is not sufficient to be able to read the algebraic definition of the coefficient. We must also understand what particular property of the scatter diagram the correlation coefficient expresses. Does a high correlation coefficient mean that the scatter diagram is highly organized in the sense that the scatter points come close to lying on some well defined curve? Or does a high correlation coefficient mean that the underlying curve, around which the scatter points cluster, is of some particular form?
3   *Practical rules of computation.*
    If we have a full understanding of the first two points then we may proceed to the actual application of these notions to a practical case. This involves a

computation work which may be more or less laborious according to the nature of the data involved. In this computation work there are many practical labour-saving devices which may be applied advantageously.

In the present lecture we shall not go into any details regarding the practical computation rules which may be found useful in correlation analysis. In addition to the development of the algebraic definitions given above, we shall only discuss some points which may help in giving a better understanding of the significance of what is involved in some of the notions defined, and particularly in the notion of correlation coefficient. In order to do so we need a set of lemmas to which we now proceed.

Let us consider a (x_1, x_2) diagram. Any direction in this diagram, say, the direction from the point R to the point P may be represented by the ratio between the vertical and horizontal coordinate of P measured from the point R as origin. In Figure 3.4 the vertical coordinate of P measured from R is a_2 and horizontal coordinate a_1. The ratio expressing the direction of the straight line from R to P is therefore equal to a_2/a_1. Similarly, the direction of the straight line from R to the point Q is measured by the ratio b_2/b_1.

In Figure 3.4, a_1, a_2 and b are positive magnitudes while b_2 is a negative quantity. Now let us consider the point of intersection M between the vertical a_2 and the horizontal a_1, and further the point of intersection N between the horizontal b_1 and the vertical b_2. If the two directions (R, P) and (R, Q) are *perpendicular* to each other, then the two triangles (R, M, P) and (Q, N, R) are similar, and vice

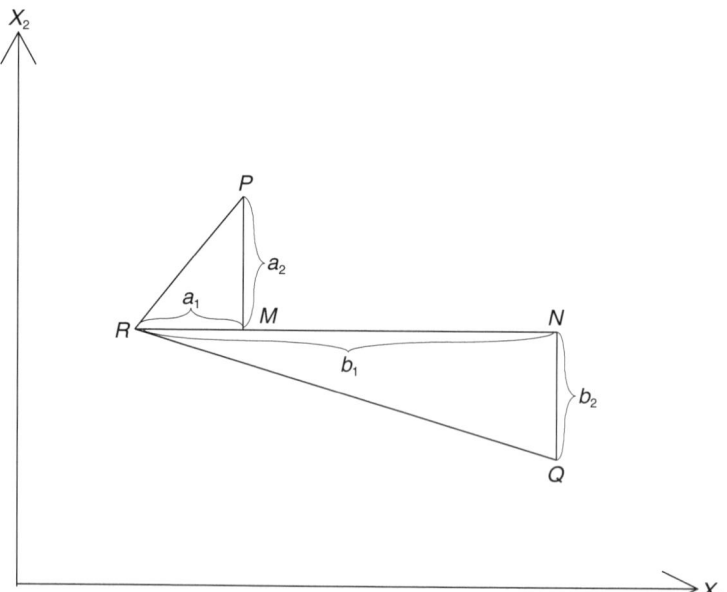

Figure 3.4 Direction ratios.

versa. That is to say, if we only take account of the length of the sides of these triangles (disregarding the sign of these lengths) we have

$$a_1/a_2 = -b_2/b_1 \qquad (25)$$

This can also be written

$$a_1 b_1 + a_2 b_2 = 0 \qquad (26)$$

Thus we see that we have the following proposition: if (a_1, a_2) and (b_1, b_2) are two sets of direction numbers, the two directions in question will be perpendicular to each other when, and only when, we have equation (25).

Now let us consider a straight line in (x_1, x_2) coordinates. Any such line has the equation

$$a_0 + a_1 x_1 + a_2 x_2 = 0 \qquad (27)$$

The direction or slope of this line is given by the ratio $-a_1/a_2$. This coefficient, expressing the slope of the straight line, is the coefficient which appears before x_1 when equation (27) is solved with respect to x_2.

If we impose on the line to go through a given point (x_1', x_2') then the equation of the straight line takes on the form

$$x_2 - x_2' = -\frac{a_1}{a_2}(x_1 - x_1') \qquad (28)$$

We see that in this new form the constant term a_0 has disappeared. We may therefore say that imposing on this straight line to go through a given point is equivalent to disposing of the constant term in the equation. But the condition imposed does not contain any restriction on the slope.

If we know the equation of a straight line and also know the coordinates of a given point (x_1', x_2') in the plane we can easily determine *the distance from the point to the line*. This distance is equal to

$$\pm \frac{a_0 + a_1 x_1' + a_2 x_2'}{\sqrt{a_1^2 + a_2^2}} \qquad (29)$$

This formula is general and holds good no matter what the concrete significance of the coordinates (x_1', x_2') are. Thus the formula would hold good for the variables (X_1, X_2) previously defined. In order to prove formula (29) we introduce the point $(x_1'', (x_2''))$ where the perpendicular from the point (x_1', x_2') to the straight line considered intersects this straight line. The coordinates of this point of intersection must satisfy two conditions, namely, first the direction between the point x' and the point x'' must be perpendicular to the slope of the straight line considered. That is to say, we must have, by virtue of (26)

$$a_2(x_1'' - x_1') - a_1(x_2'' - x_2') = 0 \tag{30}$$

Next the coordinates of the point x'' must lie on the straight line. That is to say, the coordinates of x'' must satisfy equation (27). We must consequently have

$$a_1(x_1'' - x_1') + a_2(x_2'' - x_2') = -(a_0 + a_1 x_1' + a_2 x_2') \tag{31}$$

If we solve the two equations (30) and (31) for $(x_1'' - x_1')$ and $(x_2'' - x_2')$ we obtain

$$x_1'' - x_1' = \frac{-a_1(a_0 + a_1 x_1' + a_2 x_2')}{a_1^2 + a_2^2} \tag{32}$$

$$x_2'' - x_2' = \frac{-a_2(a_0 + a_1 x_1' + a_2 x_2')}{a_1^2 + a_2^2} \tag{33}$$

From (32) and (33) follows immediately

$$\sqrt{(x_1'' - x_1')^2 + (x_2'' - x_2')^2} = \pm \frac{a_0 + a_1 x_1' + a_2 x_2'}{\sqrt{a_1^2 + a_2^2}} \tag{34}$$

This proves (29).

We next proceed to develop a very useful formula for the area of a triangle. Let us consider a system of (X_1, X_2) axes as indicated in Figure 3.5.

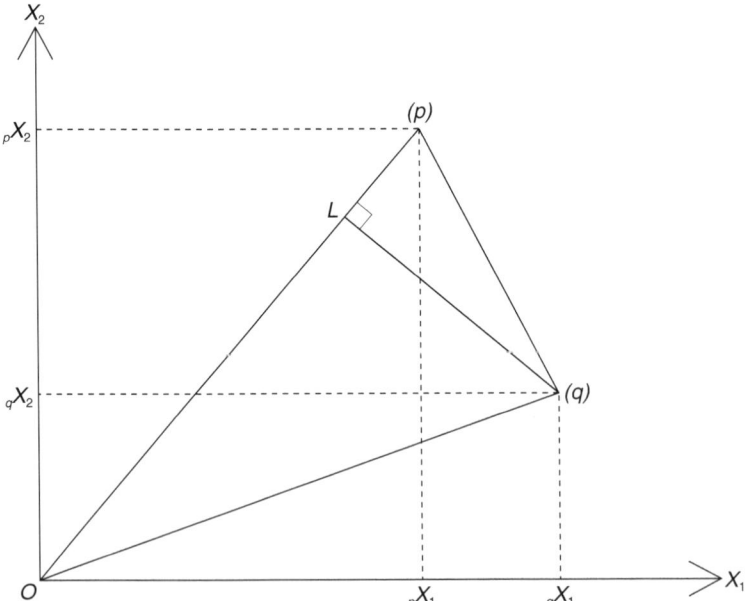

Figure 3.5 The area of a triangle.

Let (p) and (q) be two arbitrary points in the plane and let us consider the triangle whose three corners are formed by the origin 0, (q) and (p). We want to express the area of this triangle in terms of the coordinates $(_pX_1, _pX_2)$ and $(_qX_1, _qX_2)$ of the points (p) and (q) respectively.

Let L be the point where the perpendicular from (q) on the line from 0 to (p) intersects this line. The area of the triangle in question is then 0.5 times the length $(0p)$ times the length (Lq). Now the equation of the line $(0p)$ is

$$_pX_2 \cdot X_1 - _pX_1 \cdot X_2 = 0 \tag{35}$$

By (29) the distance (Lq) is consequently equal to

$$\frac{_pX_1 \cdot _qX_2 - _qX_1 \cdot _pX_2}{\pm\sqrt{_pX_1^2 + _pX_2^2}} \tag{36}$$

The denominator of (36) is the length of $(0p)$. The area of the triangle, namely 0.5 times the length of $(0p)$ times the length of (Lq) is consequently

$$\frac{1}{2}(_pX_1 \cdot _qX_2 - _qX_1 \cdot _pX_2) \tag{37}$$

We notice that the magnitude defined by (37) will change sign if we interchange the points (p) and (q). That is to say, the area expressed by (37) is defined in such a way that it might be either positive or negative, and whether it shall be one or the other will depend on a convention regarding the order of succession in which we take the corners.

We now have all the tools we need in order to give an interpretation of the significance of the correlation coefficient. Let us consider a scatter diagram. Let us pick out two arbitrary observation points (p) and (q), and let us construct the triangle whose three corners are formed by the two points selected and the mean point $(\bar{X}_1, \bar{X}_2)$. This triangle can be looked upon as a triangle in the system of reduced coordinates (x_1, x_2) and in this system of coordinates the triangle considered will be a triangle with one corner in the origin. The area of this triangle is therefore by virtue of (37) equal to

$$\frac{1}{2}(_px_1 \cdot _qx_2 - _qx_1 \cdot _px_2) \tag{38}$$

If the two points (p) and (q) which we have selected are collinear with the mean point that is (p), (q) and the mean point lie in a straight line, *then the area defined by (38) will be equal to 0*, and inversely if these three points do not lie in a straight line, then the area is different from 0. Furthermore, we see that the area will be larger the more the three points considered deviate from lying in a straight line. We may therefore simply take the magnitude of the area as a measure of how far the three points are from *average* magnitude of all such triangles formed by selecting in all possible ways the set of two points (p) and (q) in the scatter diagram. If we form such an average we would have to take account of the fact already mentioned in our discussion of formula (37), namely, that the area is affected by a conventional sign. If we extended the average considered to all possible points we would simply obtain 0 as a result, because to every point (p, q) there corresponds another point (q, p) and the two areas defined by these two sets of points would cancel out. In order to get around this difficulty we simply take the *square* mean instead of the ordinary mean. That is to say, we use the same procedure as we used when we introduced the standard ordinate instead of the ordinary arithmetical mean of the variables: we extend the summation to the *square* of those things which are to be averaged, and then afterwards we take the square root of the result obtained. There are N^2 sets of possible points (p, q) which we may select in the scatter diagram, namely the sets we obtain by letting p run through all the observations, that is, putting successively $p = 1, 2, \ldots, N$, and for each such magnitude of p letting q run through all the observations, that is to say, putting successively $q = 1, 2, \ldots, N$. The quantity obtained by averaging the squares in this way would be equal to

$$\frac{1}{4} \cdot \frac{\sum_{pq} (_p x_1 \cdot_q x_2 - _q x_1 \cdot_p x_2)^2}{N^2} \tag{39}$$

and the square root of this quantity would be something of the sort we are looking for. However, it is easily seen that an average as such obtained would depend on the units of measurement. For instance, if we increase the unit of measurement of the variable no. 1 to 100 times what this unit was before, then the average defined as the square root of (39) would be reduced to one-hundredth of what it was before. In order to obtain a coefficient that is independent of the units of measurement, we may compute an expression similar to (39) but introducing the *normalized* variables instead of the variables measured in the original units. That is to say, each variable is divided by its standard deviation. The result would be an expression equal to (39) but only containing the extra factors σ_1^2 and σ_2^2 in the denominator. The square root of such an expression would be an average of the type we need. We shall, however, make still another slight amendment to our definition. Evidently, it would not make any difference if we considered the average as above defined or we considered c times this average, where c is some arbitrary constant different from 0. For instance, whether we consider the average as above defined or whether we consider twice this average, would not make any difference. The magnitude we are defining is to be used for comparisons between different scatter diagrams. And in this comparison the common factor c would not matter. But we might get a more convenient form of our coefficient by attributing some particular magnitude to c. We shall put $c = \sqrt{2}$. The reason for this choice will presently become obvious. If our coefficient is defined in this way it must always be lying between 0 and 1 as we shall presently see. To sum up, then, the coefficient σ expressing the average magnitude of the areas of the triangles which can be formed by picking out in all possible ways two scatter points and combine these two points with the mean point of the cluster as a third point, will be

$$s = {}^{+}\!\sqrt{\frac{\frac{1}{2}\Sigma_{pq}({}_{p}x_{1}\cdot_{q}x_{2}-{}_{q}x_{1}\cdot_{p}x_{2})}{N^{2}\sigma_{1}^{2}\sigma_{2}^{2}}} \qquad (40)$$

The coefficient s as thus determined we shall call the *collective scatter coefficient* in the set of variables (x_{1}, x_{2}) or, shorter, the scatter coefficient. In order to indicate that it is here a question of a scatter coefficient for the *reduced* set of variables (x_{1}, x_{2}), not for the origin set (X_{1}, X_{2}), we may call s the reduced scatter coefficient. The $+$ sign in (40) indicates that by definition the square root in (40) shall be taken positive. By applying the fundamental moment formula (21) we see that the formula for the scatter coefficient s reduces to

$$s = \sqrt{\frac{m_{11}m_{22}-m_{12}^{2}}{m_{11}m_{22}}} = \sqrt{1-r^{2}} \qquad (41)$$

where $r=r_{12}$ is the correlation coefficient previously defined. That is to say, the correlation coefficient r and the scatter coefficient s are related by the formula

$$r^{2}+s^{2}=1 \qquad (42)$$

Now we can see what the meaning of the correlation coefficient r is. *It is a coefficient expressing how close the points in the scatter diagram come to lying in a straight line*. The closer the observation points come to lying in a straight line, the smaller s^{2} will be. That simply follows from the way in which s^{2} is defined. s^{2} *is equal to 0 when, and only when, all the observation points are lying rigorously in a straight line*. And the smaller s^{2} the larger r^{2}, because r^{2} and s^{2} are two quantities such that one is the complement of the other to unity, as shown by (42). (42) shows also that both r and s are quantities, the square of which must be lying between 0 and 1. From this follows again, what we have proved before, that r must be lying between -1 and $+1$. The scatter coefficient which by the definition (40) is essentially a positive quantity must be lying between 0 and $+1$.

In exactly the same way as we have here defined, the scatter coefficient Σ for the set of variables measured from the mean, we may define the scatter coefficient S of the variables measured from the origin. This coefficient would be equal to

$$S = {}^{+}\!\sqrt{\frac{\frac{1}{2}\Sigma_{pq}({}_{p}X_{1}\cdot_{q}X_{2}-{}_{q}X_{1}\cdot_{p}X_{2})^{2}}{N^{2}S_{1}^{2}S_{2}^{2}}} = {}^{+}\!\sqrt{\frac{M_{11}M_{22}-M_{12}^{2}}{M_{11}M_{22}}} = \sqrt{1-R^{2}} \qquad (43)$$

where $R=R_{12}$ is the origin correlation as previously defined. The scatter coefficient S defined by (43) we shall call the *origin* scatter coefficient as distinguished from the *reduced* scatter coefficient s. Between R and S we evidently have the relation

$$R^2 + S^2 = 1 \tag{44}$$

If we remember that S is defined as an average of the triangles formed in the scatter diagram by associating any set of two observation points with the *origin* of the original variables, we see that R is a measure of how close the scatter points come to lying in a straight line *that goes through the origin of the original variables*. This shows the difference in significance between R and r. While r is simple a measure of the linear character of the cluster, R is a measure of how far the cluster comes to lying in a particular sort of straight line, namely a straight line through the origin.

We now proceed to a study of *linear regression lines in two variables*. The equation of any straight line referred to the original coordinates (X_1, X_2) may be written

$$A_0 + A_1 X_1 + A_2 X_2 = 0 \tag{45}$$

where the coefficients A_0, A_1 and A_2 are constants independent of X_1 and X_2.

If we introduce in (45) the expression for X_1 and X_2 in terms of the variables x_1 and x_2 measured from the mean, we obtain a new equation

$$a_0 + a_1 x_1 + a_2 x_2 = 0 \tag{46}$$

where the new coefficients a_0, a_1 and a_2 depend on the coefficients A_0, A_1 and A_2 and the means $\bar{X}_1$ and $\bar{X}_2$ in the following way

$$\begin{aligned} a_1 &= A_1 \\ a_2 &= A_2 \\ a_0 &= A_0 + A_1 \bar{x}_1 + A_2 \bar{x}_2 \end{aligned} \tag{47}$$

Inversely, it is clear that to any equation of the form (46) there corresponds an equation of the form (45). Therefore, it does not make any difference whether we handle the equation of a straight line in the form (45) or in the form (46). Generally it will be found most convenient to handle the form (46), and that is what we shall do in the following lines.

If the equation (46) is solved with respect to x_1 and x_2 respectively, we obtain

$$x_1 = b_{10} + b_{12} x_2 \tag{48}$$

$$x_2 = b_{20} + b_{21} x_1 \tag{49}$$

where

$$\begin{aligned} b_{10} &= -a_0/a_1 \quad \text{and} \quad b_{12} = -a_2/a_1 \\ b_{20} &= -a_0/a_2 \quad \text{and} \quad b_{21} = -a_1/a_2 \end{aligned} \tag{50}$$

Since (48) and (49) are derived from (46), and it is inversely possible to obtain (46) from either (48) or (49), one should prima facie think that all these three equations are equivalent. As a matter of fact they are not. It is only (46) that represents the *perfectly general* straight line. (48) represents *nearly* all possible lines and so does (49). But there are some particular cases which are not covered by (48) and (49) respectively. For instance: it is impossible to choose the constants of (48) in such a way as to make (48) represent a straight line parallel to the x_1-axis. Such a straight line is represented by the equation $x_2=x_2'$, where x_2' is a constant. And similarly it is impossible to choose the constants of (49) in such a way as to make this equation represent a straight line parallel to the x_2-axis. Such a line is $x_1=x_1'$ where x_1' is a constant.

We may test the two last statements by actually trying to determine the constants in (49) in the case referred to. Suppose that we have the straight line $x_1=x_1'$. Let us select two points on this line, one with the coordinate x_2' and the other with the coordinate x_2''. The classical procedure for determining the constants in such a way as to make the equation represent a straight line through two given points is to insert successively in the equation the coordinates of these two points and determine the constants from the two equations thus obtained. If we do that in the present case we obtain the two equations

$$x_2' = b_{20} + b_{21}x_1'$$
$$x_2'' = b_{20} + b_{21}x_1'$$

(52)

It is obvious that if the two points considered do not coincide, that is to say if $x_2' \neq x_2''$, then the two equations in (52) are not compatible because from (52) we obtain $x_2' \neq x_2''$. And if the two points considered coincide, that is to say, if $x_2'=x_2''$ then the two equations in (52) are not independent. More precisely expressed, the two equations in (52) then simply reduce to one single equation. This only expresses the fact that it is possible to construct a straight line of the form (49) going through the point (x_1', x_2'). But it is not possible to have an equation of the form (49) represent the vertical line $x_1=x_1'$

On the other hand, equation (46) is perfectly general and can represent not only any line having a slope different from the vertical or the horizontal, but it can also represent both any vertical and any horizontal straight line. For instance, the vertical straight line $x_1=x_1'$ is represented by (46) when we choose

$a_2=0$, $a_1=$ arbitrary constant $\neq 0$, $a_0=-a_1x_1'$.

The last example shows that if we impose on the coefficients in (46) the conditions that (46) shall represent a given straight line, then this does not determine uniquely the coefficients a_0, a_1, a_2.

The coefficients will only be determined *apart from an arbitrary common factor* $\neq 0$. For instance, if we have found that $a_0=2$, $a_1=-3$, $a_2=1$, represents a certain straight line, then the equation obtained by doubling or tripling, etc., the coefficients would also represent exactly the same straight line. And the same would be true of any equation obtained by multiplying the constants by any common factor that is not equal to 0. We shall refer to this fact as the homogeneity property of the coefficients of equation (46).

We now proceed to discuss how we can determine the coefficients of (46) in such a way as to make the straight line represented by (46) as closely as possible *fit a scatter diagram*. There may be different ways of determining the coefficients accordingly as we define the meaning of 'as closely as possible fit a scatter diagram'. The following are three examples of how we could formulate such a principle of closest fit.

1   *The first elementary regression.* This is the straight line which is obtained by requesting that the sum squares· of the deviations of each observation point measured horizontally from the straight regression line shall be made as small as possible. Measuring the deviations horizontally means measuring the deviation in x_1 direction.

2   *The second elementary regression.* This is a straight line obtained by requesting that the sum squares of the deviations measured vertically (that is in the x_2 direction) shall be rendered as small as possible. It is to be expected that this direction will entail a determination of the coefficient which is different from the determination obtained by measuring the deviations horizontally, and we shall also presently see that the two determinations actually are different.

3   *The orthogonal mean regression.* Both in the determination of the first and in the determination of the second elementary regression, the two variables x_1 and x_2 are treated asymmetrically. In the first case we selected x_1 as the variable in whose direction the deviations are measured and in the second case we select the variable x_2. In most actual problems this asymmetry introduces something artificial in the handling of the problem. Often the nature of the problem is such that we have no a priori reason to select either one of the two variables as the one in whose direction the deviation shall be minimized. If this is the case, we must look for some minimizing principle which treats the two variables symmetrically. Such a principle is the principle of least orthogonal distances. This means that we request the sum squares of the deviations *measured perpendicularly to the regression line* to be as small as possible. The regression line obtained in this way we shall call the *orthogonal mean regression.* We call it orthogonal because it is the perpendicular deviations that are minimized, and we call it mean because it treats the two variables symmetrically. In distinction to such a mean regression the first two of the above defined regressions will be called elementary regressions.

In one of the later sections where we shall attempt to develop a new theory of linear regression, we shall discuss other forms of mean regression, particularly a mean regression, which will be called the *diagonal* mean regression, and a regression which will be called the *composite* mean regression. At present we shall discuss how the coefficients of (46) are determined when we adopt the three principles above specified.

First we notice that when we formulate the principle of the first elementary regression *we have implicitly assumed that the regression line is not a straight line parallel to the x_1-axis.* If the observation points are not lying rigorously in a straight horizontal line then any horizontal line adopted as the regression line would give a horizontal sum square which was infinite. We can therefore immediately draw the conclusion that if the square of the correlation coefficient is not rigorously equal to 1 (that is to say, if we do not have the case where all the observation points are lying rigorously in a straight line) then the first elementary regression cannot be a horizontal line. Similarly we see that if the square of the correlation coefficient is not rigorously equal to 1, the second elementary regression cannot be a straight vertical line. Therefore we get the following expression for the sum squares measured horizontally

$$\Sigma_t \left({}_t x_1 - \left(-\frac{a_0}{a_1} - \frac{a_2}{a_1} {}_t x_2 \right) \right)^2 \tag{53}$$

which can also be written as

$$\frac{1}{a_1^2} \Sigma_t (a_0 + a_1 \cdot {}_t x_1 + a_2 \cdot {}_t x_2)^2 \tag{54}$$

Both these expressions have a definite meaning since we may assume that $a_1 \neq 0$ (i.e. the regression line is not horizontal).

Similarly, the sum square of the deviations measured vertically will be

$$\frac{1}{a_2^2} \Sigma_t (a_0 + a_1 \cdot {}_t x_1 + a_2 \cdot {}_t x_2)^2 \tag{55}$$

If we take the fraction $1/a_1^2$ into the parenthesis in (54) we obtain an expression of the form

$$\Sigma_t (a_0' + a_1' \cdot {}_t x_1 + a_2' \cdot {}_t x_2)^2 \tag{56}$$

where the coefficients a' are equal to the coefficients a apart from the division by a_1. That is to say, we have $a_1' = 1$. Similarly, the vertical sum square (55) may be written in the form (56) where now $a_2' = 1$. But since the coefficients in a linear relation of the form (46) may be multiplied by an arbitrary factor $\neq 0$, without changing the straight line represented by the equation, it does not matter whether we say that the first elementary regression is the one which is obtained by minimizing the sum square (56) by putting $a_1' = 1$ or putting a_1' equal to some other magnitude $\neq 0$. The thing which matters is that a_1' is looked upon as a *constant*, that is to say, as a magnitude *not to be determined by the minimizing conditions*, but to be disposed of by a more or less arbitrary choice.

We may even generalize the problem and say that we reserve the possibility of choosing a_1' equal to any magnitude we like, disregarding the condition that it shall be $\neq 0$. It may happen in certain limiting cases that we will find it convenient to define the first elementary regression by disregarding the condition $a_1' \neq 0$. If we obtain the solution of this generalized problem of the first elementary regression, we will, of course, thereby also have obtained the solution of the restricted problem. The solution of the restricted problem is obtained by choosing $a_1' \neq 0$. Similar consideration may be made regarding the second elementary regression.

This being so, the primes on the coefficients a in (56) are of no avail, because they only stand for unknowns to be determined. Thus we may reformulate the problem of the elementary regression and get it in the following form.

Consider the function of three variables a_0, a_1, a_2

$$G = \Sigma_t (a_0 + a_1 \cdot {}_t x_1 + a_2 \cdot {}_t x_2)^2 \tag{57}$$

The first elementary regression is a regression of the form (46) where the coefficients a are determined by minimizing function (57), keeping a_1 as a constant, not to be determined by the minimizing process but to be given some conveniently chosen magnitude. And similarly, the second elementary regression is a regression of the form (46) where the coefficients a now are determined by the minimizing expression (57), keeping a_2 as a constant, not to be determined by the minimizing process, but to be given some conveniently chosen magnitude. The problem before us then is to determine what the coefficients a, as thus determined, will be.

We shall show that both in the case of the first and in the case of the second elementary regression, the constant term, that is to say, the coefficient a_0 in (46) must be put equal to 0, so that the two elementary regressions may be written in the form

$$a_{11} x_1 + a_{12} x_2 = 0$$
$$a_{21} x_1 + a_{22} x_2 = 0 \tag{58}$$

The coefficients in the first equation of (58), namely, (a_{11}, a_{12}) are the coefficients in the first elementary regression and similarly (a_{21}, a_{22}) are the coefficients in the second elementary regression. We may represent these two sets of coefficients as two lines in a table. Thus

$$[a_{ij}] = \begin{pmatrix} a_{11} & a_{12} \\ a_{21} & a_{22} \end{pmatrix} \tag{59}$$

The table consisting of two lines and two columns we shall call *the elementary regression matrix*. And the problem of determining the two elementary regressions may be formulated by saying that it consists in determining the elementary regression matrix.

We shall show that the elementary regression matrix can be obtained directly from the knowledge of the *moment matrix*

$$[m_{ij}] = \begin{pmatrix} m_{11} & m_{12} \\ m_{21} & m_{22} \end{pmatrix} \tag{60}$$

by a very simple rule.

In order to exhibit this rule we shall introduce the notion of the *adjoint moment matrix*. This is a notion which will also be found useful in a great number of other problems. The adjoint moment matrix

$$[m_{ij}^*] = \begin{pmatrix} m_{11}^* & m_{12}^* \\ m_{21}^* & m_{22}^* \end{pmatrix} \tag{61}$$

is defined in the following way. Its element no. (*ij*), that is m_{ij}^*, is equal to $(-1)^{i+j}$ times the element which is left when the *i*-th line and the *j*-th column are crossed out from the moment matrix. Thus we have

$$\begin{pmatrix} m_{11}^* & m_{12}^* \\ m_{21}^* & m_{22}^* \end{pmatrix} = \begin{pmatrix} m_{22} & -m_{21} \\ -m_{12} & m_{11} \end{pmatrix} \tag{62}$$

We shall show that the regression matrix is simply equal to the adjoint moment matrix, so that from the knowledge of the adjoint moment matrix we may write down immediately the two elementary regressions. In order to show that the first line of regression matrix (59) is equal to the first line of regression matrix (62) we simply have to consider the function G, defined by (57), as a function of the two variables a_0 and a_2 and determine the minimum of this function.

We denote the partial derivatives of the function G with respect to the variables a_0, a_1 and a_2 by G_0, G_1 and G_2 respectively. Now, a necessary condition that G should be a minimum, when a_0 is a variable, is that the partial derivative $G_0 = 0$. But from (57) we see that we have

$$G_0 = 2\sum_t (a_0 + a_1 \cdot {}_t x_1 + a_2 \cdot {}_t x_2) = 2Na_0 \tag{63}$$

Consequently, since N is a number different from 0, we must have $a_0 = 0$. And we see that this must hold good no matter whether we have the first or the second elementary regression in mind. For the purpose of determining the elementary regression we may therefore simplify function (57) by writing it

$$G = \sum_t (a_1 \cdot {}_t x_1 + a_2 \cdot {}_t x_2)^2 = m_{11}a_1^2 + m_{22}a_2^2 + 2m_{12}a_1a_2 \tag{64}$$

From (64) we see that we have

$$\begin{aligned} G_1 &= 2(m_{11}a_1 + m_{12}a_2) \\ G_2 &= 2(m_{22}a_2 + m_{12}a_1) \end{aligned} \tag{65}$$

Consequently, the magnitudes which the two coefficients a_1 and a_2 shall have in the first elementary regression, that is to say, the magnitudes (a_{11}, a_{12}) must be determined by the equation

$$m_{22}a_2 + m_{12}a_1 = 0 \tag{66}$$

But it is obvious that we will satisfy the last equation by putting $a_1 = m_{22}$ and $a_2 = -m_{21}$ which shows that the necessary minimizing for the first elementary regression will be satisfied if we put the first line in the regression matrix equal to the first line in the adjoint moment matrix. In reality (66) only determines the ratio between a_1 and a_2. As above mentioned we can here choose a_1 arbitrarily. Choosing $a_1 = m_{22}$ means that we have performed the minimization process by attributing to the constant a_1 in the function G defined by (64) a particular magnitude characterizing the scatter diagram, namely m_{22}.

This particular choice of the constant a_1 means that in certain cases this constant might become equal to 0, namely, in those cases where the standard deviation of the variable no. 2 is equal to 0. In this case, the first elementary regression as determined by the coefficients in the first line of the moment matrix will strictly speaking be indeterminate, since $m_{22} = 0$ entails $m_{12} = 0$. By convention the regression may now be looked upon as a straight line parallel to the x_1-axis provided $m_{11} \neq 0$. In other words, we have now removed the particular restriction which was put on the first elementary regression in the original formulation of the minimizing problem for the first elementary regression, namely $a_{11} \neq 0$.

Similarly we see that the coefficients of the second elementary regression are determined by the equation

$$m_{11}a_1 + m_{12}a_2 = 0 \tag{67}$$

and this shows that we satisfy the necessary minimum condition for the second elementary regression by putting the second line in the regression matrix equal to the second line in the adjoint moment matrix.

In the above discussion we have only considered necessary conditions for the minima in question. It is, however, possible to prove that the solutions obtained are not only necessary but also sufficient to insure that the function G in the points considered actually attain minima (and, for instance, not maxima). We shall, however, not go into this matter any further here.

We now proceed to the orthogonal mean regression. From formula (29) we see that if we want to determine the coefficients a_0, a_1 and a_2 in the orthogonal mean regression we have to divide expression (57) by $(a_1^2 + a_2^2)$ and then minimize the function thus obtained, considering all the three coefficients a_0, a_1 and a_2 as variables. If we do that we get the following solution of the orthogonal mean regression problem. We define the standard deviation *distance d* by the formula

$$\frac{m_{11} - m_{22}}{+\sqrt{m_{11}m_{22}}} \tag{68}$$

In terms of this quantity and the correlation coefficient $r = r_{12}$ in the set of variables considered, the equation of the orthogonal mean regression can be written in the following form

$$\sqrt{\sqrt{d^2 + 4r^2} - d} \cdot x_1 = \text{sgn}(m_{12}) \cdot \sqrt{\sqrt{d^2 + 4r^2} + d} \cdot x_2 \qquad (69)$$

Formula (69) is very convenient in the actual computation of the orthogonal mean regression in two variables. We shall here only give the formula without proving it. Formula (69) shows that the orthogonal mean regression always goes through the mean of the scatter diagram, equation (69) namely does not contain any constant term.

Further we see that if both d and r are equal to 0, then the orthogonal mean regression is indeterminate. That is to say, if the two variables are uncorrelated and have the same standard deviation, any straight line through the mean of all observations will satisfy the conditions for the orthogonal mean regression.

In any other case the orthogonal mean regression is uniquely determined. In particular, we see that if $r = 0$, that is to say, if the two variables are uncorrelated, the orthogonal mean regression is a straight line parallel to the axis of that variable which has the largest standard deviation.

Thus we can see that the orthogonal mean regression is a regression which depends very essentially on *the units of measurement used*. If we change the units of measurement for one of the variables we will also change the relationship which is expressed by (69). This is a very unsatisfactory situation. We shall later go into the matter of *invariance* of regressions more fully. In particular, we shall introduce the previously mentioned *diagonal* mean regression and show that this regression is invariant for a change in the units of measurement. We shall also indicate a regression which is invariant for a homogeneous linear transformation.

We shall now discuss under what conditions the two elementary regressions coincide. If we draw the two elementary regressions in a system of (x_1, x_2)-axes we get a situation as the one illustrated in Figure 3.6.

The first elementary regression L_1 will form a larger angle with the x_1-axis than the second elementary regression L_2, and similarly L_2 will form a larger angle with the x_2-axis than L_1. This simply follows from the fact that the angular coefficient for the angle between L_1 and the x_1-axis is equal to m_{22}/m_{11} and the angular coefficient for the angle between L_2 and the x_1-axis is equal to m_{12}/m_{11}. Disregarding the sign of these coefficients we see that the condition that we shall have the particular situation described is the following

$$\left(\frac{m_{12}}{m_{11}} \right)^2 \leq \left(\frac{m_{22}}{m_{21}} \right)^2$$

But this condition is nothing other than the condition that the square of the correlation coefficient does not exceed unity. In particular we see that the two elementary regression lines L_1 and L_2 will coincide when, and only when, the correlation coefficient r_{12} is equal to either $+1$ or -1, that is to say, that the scatter

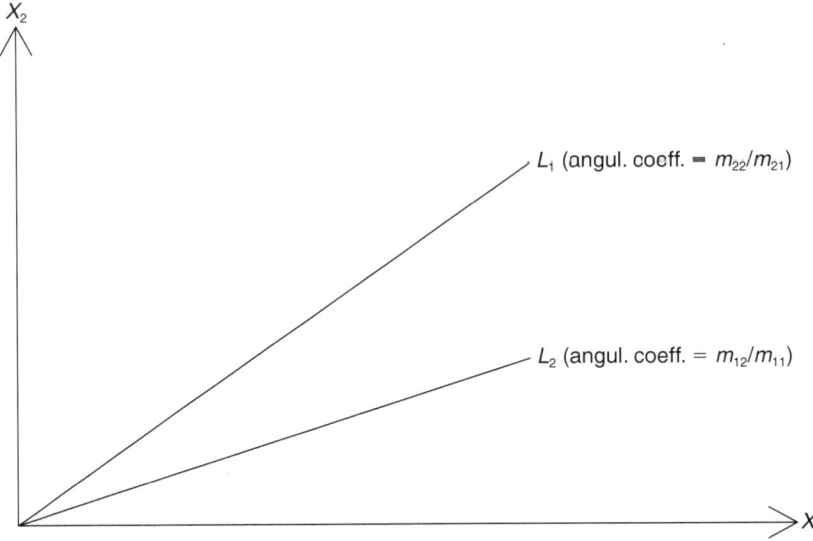

Figure 3.6 The two elementary regressions.

coefficient s_{12} is equal to 0. And they will be perpendicular to each other when, and only when, $r_{12} = 0$.

If we solve the first elementary regression with respect to x_1 and the second elementary regression with respect to x_2, we get two equations of the form

$$x_1 = b_{12}x_2$$
$$x_2 = b_{21}x_1$$

(70)

where $b_{12} = m_{21}/m_{22}$ and $b_{21} = m_{12}/m_{11}$. Comparing the two equations (70) we see that if the two elementary regressions coincide, then b_{21} is equal to $1/b_{12}$, that is to say, we have $b_{12} \cdot b_{21} = 1$. Conversely, if the two lines do not coincide, the product $b_{12} \cdot b_{21}$ is different from 1. This suggests the idea of simply taking the magnitude of this product as an expression of how close the two regressions come to coinciding. This product, however, is nothing other than the square of the correlation coefficient. We therefore have

$$r_{12}^2 = b_{12} \cdot b_{21}$$

(71)

* * *

Correlation coefficients and standard ordinates in the case where each of the two variables correlated contains two (or more) components.

We now proceed to discuss the case where each of the two variables correlated is made up of two (or more) components. That is to say, we consider two variables X_1 and X_2 and we want to find out how the correlation between these two variables will be affected by the fact that X_1 is made up of two components and similarly X_2 is made up of two components. For simplicity we shall only discuss the case of additive components. That is to say, we consider the case where we have

$$X_1 = X_3 + X_5$$
$$X_2 = X_4 + X_6$$
(72)

We have numbered the various quantities in (72) in such a way that the components of X_1 are designated by uneven numbers and the components of X_2 by even numbers.

We shall not enter any discussion as to the concrete significance of the fact that X_1 (or X_2) is made up of two components. In an actual case, say when X_1 is represented by a time series, X_5 might stand for the trend of the series X_1 and X_3 might stand for the cyclical fluctuation. To be more precise we may say that X_3 represents the sub-cycle in X_1, that is to say, a cycle with a duration of somewhere between three and five years. Similarly, we might interpret X_4 as the sub-cycle of X_2 and X_6 as the trend of X_2. Or again, we may think of X_1 not as a time series but simply as representing observations of a certain physical magnitude, X_3 representing accidental errors in this observation and X_5 representing systematic errors in the observation.

In any actual case, the significance of the various components would have to be exactly defined by some criterion outside of those things which are necessary in order to define the magnitude X_1 (or X_2) itself. If we have given any set of observations X_1 (or X_2) we may namely construct an arbitrary fictitious set of observations X_3 (or X_4) and say that this X_3 (or X_4) is the first component in X_1 (or X_2). Any such construction would be compatible with the observations of X_1 (or X_2). We only have to define X_5 (or X_6) as the difference between the actual observations X_1 and the fictitious component X_3 (the difference between X_2 and the fictitious component X_4). The following formulae are general and may be applied to any set of additive components no matter what their concrete significance may be.

We shall first see how the standard ordinate S_1 of X_1 depends on the standard ordinates S_3 and S_5 of the two components X_3 and X_5. A simple application of the definition of the standard ordinate leads to the formula

$$S_1^2 = S_3^2 + S_5^2 + 2S_3 S_5 R_{35}$$
(73)

where R_{35} designates the origin correlation between the variables 3 and 5. Formula (73) shows that if there is no origin correlation between X_3 and X_5 then the square of the standard ordinate of the sum X_1 is equal to the sum of the squares of the standard ordinates of the two terms X_3 and X_5. Furthermore, we notice that by this very definition of the origin correlation we have the formula

$$\sum X_i X_j = N S_i S_j R_{ij}$$
(74)

where N is the number of observations. Applying the last formula to the separate terms of the expression

$$R_{12} = \frac{1}{NS_1S_2} \Sigma(X_3X_4 + X_5X_4 + X_3X_6 + X_5X_6)$$

we get

$$R_{12} = \frac{S_3S_4}{S_1S_2} R_{34} + \frac{S_5S_4}{S_1S_2} R_{54} + \frac{S_3S_6}{S_1S_2} R_{36} + \frac{S_5S_6}{S_1S_2} R_{56} \tag{75}$$

and a similar formula would, of course, hold good if we replaced the capital letters S and R by the small letters σ and r. That is to say if we measure all of the variables from the means. Now let us see what the effect would be if X_5 was the *dominating* component in X_1, and X_6 the *dominating* component in X_2. This means that the standard ordinate of X_5 is very large as compared with the standard ordinate of X_3 and the standard ordinate of X_6 very large when compared with the standard ordinate of X_4. If this is the case, we see from (75) that the standard ordinate of X_3 will only be a small fraction of the standard ordinate of X_1. That is to say that S_3/S_1 will be a small fraction. And similarly, S_4/S_2 will be a small fraction. But S_5/S_1 will be close to unity, and S_6/S_2 will also be close to unity. Therefore we see that in (75) the last term in the right member will be the dominating one. We will even have approximately

$$R_{12} = R_{56} \tag{76}$$

This result we can formulate in the following principle: If the variable X_1 is made up of two components, one of which is dominating over the other (in the sense that its standard ordinate is large as compared to the standard ordinate of the other component), and if the variable X_2 is also made up of two components, one of which is dominating over the other, then the origin correlation R_{12} between X_1 and X_2 will be very close to the origin correlation between the dominating component in X_1 and the dominating component in X_2.

Evidently the whole argument can be repeated also for the set of variables measured from the means. In this case it will not be a question of whether one of the components in X_1 has a large standard ordinate as compared with the other component, but it will be a question of whether it has a large *standard deviation* as compared with the other component. In terms of the variables measured from the means we may re-state the principle thus: *if the variable x_1 is the sum of two components, one of which has a large standard deviation compared with the other, and if similarly the variable x_2 is the sum of two components, one of which has a large standard deviation compared with the other, then the reduced correlation r_{12} (the Pearsonian correlation coefficient) between the variables X_1 and X_2 will be very close to the reduced (Pearsonian) correlation coefficient between the dominating component in X_1 and X_2. This principle is called the principle of correlation domination.*

The principle here formulated is intuitively rather obvious, but it is always safe to check up on the intuition of a relationship by computing an exact formula for it. The exact expression for the principle of correlation domination is contained in formula (75) and the corresponding formula obtained by replacing R by r and S by σ. It would even be possible to utilize (75) for deriving exact upper and lower limits for the correlation coefficients (the origin correlations of the reduced correlations) in terms of the ratios between the standard ordinate (standard deviation) of the dominating components and the corresponding non-dominating components, but we shall not enter upon this here.

The principle of correlation domination has an immediate and interesting application to the correlation between time series. For instance, if there is a pronounced *trend* in X_1 and also a pronounced *trend* in X_2, and if there also is a cyclical component in X_1 and a cyclical component in X_2, however such that the amplitude of the cycle is small as compared with the total change in which the trend ordinate undergoes over the interval of time considered, then the compound correlation between the two time series X_1 and X_2 will come very close to being equal to the correlation between the two trends, that is to say, it will be near (+ or −) unity if the two trends are approximately linear.

We can get more exact information of how close the total correlation between the time series will come to unity by figuring out what the standard ordinates and the standard deviation of an approximately linear trend will be. In order to do this, let us consider a quantity X which is a linear function of time

$$X = A + Bt \tag{77}$$

If we assume that the observations are distributed equally densely over time and furthermore that they are so frequent that we can look upon the observation of the quantity X as being virtually continuous, then the standard ordinate S will be defined by the formula

$$S^2 = \frac{1}{N} \int_{t'}^{t''} (A + Bt)^2 \, dt \tag{78}$$

where $N = t'' - t'$ is the length of the interval over which observation is extended, t' being the first moment of time, and t'' the last moment of time for which observations are available. If we multiply out the square under the sign of integration in (78) we get

$$S_2 = (A + B\bar{t})^2 + B^2 N^2 / 12 \tag{79}$$

where $\bar{t} = (t' + t'')/2$.

In the same way we find that the mean of the observations will be

$$\bar{X} = A + B\bar{t} \tag{80}$$

Therefore by virtue of (16) the standard deviation σ will be equal to

$$\sigma = \pm BN/\sqrt{12} \qquad (81)$$

where the sign is chosen so as to make σ positive.

This shows that if the trend in X_1 and also the trend in X_2 is approximately linear, then the compound correlation between the two time series will be all the closer to (+ or −) unity, the *steeper* the slope of the two trends. The slope is represented by the magnitude of the coefficient B in (81) and the trend correlation exerts the dominating effect if the two trend standard deviations are large. Again, this is a rather obvious result; what the preceding formulae do is only to put the result in a more exact shape.

We thus see that if the correlation we are after is the correlation between the short time component in X_1 and the short time component in X_2, it makes no sense to simply take the compound correlation between X_1 and X_2. Before we can proceed to a significant computation of the correlation we have in mind, we must *decompose* the two time series.

The facts which we have here discussed furnish a simple explanation of the seemingly puzzling problem which Professor Yule has discussed in his paper 'Why do we sometimes get nonsense-correlations between time series?'[1] From Yule's analysis it is obvious that the distinction between 'true' and 'nonsense' correlation which he has in mind is really a distinction between short time component correlation and trend correlation. The point of view which underlies his whole approach is that the trend correlation is not 'true' but the short component correlation is. It is only by adopting this distinction that it is possible to give a coherent interpretation of his analysis. But when this meaning of the distinction between 'true' and 'nonsensical' correlation is revealed, then the whole puzzle which Yule is struggling with disappears − it simply reduces to the fact that if two series both show, roughly speaking, linear trends with considerable slopes, and the fluctuations around these trends are comparatively small in amplitude as compared with the total change in trend ordinate over the interval observed, then, as above explained, the compound correlation between the two time series will be close to (+ or −) unity, *no matter what the correlation between the deviations from trend are.*

We may illustrate this by considering the correlation between $X_1 =$ bank clearings in the United States, and $X_2 =$ liabilities of commercial failures in the United States. The bank clearings and the liabilities *move in opposite directions* during the short cycles, so that if we would compute the correlation between the cyclical component in bank clearings and the cyclical component in liabilities of commercial failures we would obtain a very high *negative* correlation. But if we compute the compound relations between bank clearings and liabilities, we would obtain a very high *positive* correlation, namely, both bank clearings and liabilities show a tremendous secular trend, and it would be the correlation the two trends that would dominate the compound correlation between the two time series.

The fact here discussed is another of these things which point to the necessity of decomposing our time series before analysing their inter-relationships. The decomposition problem of time series shall be taken up in some later section of this course.

In the above discussion of the principle of correlation domination we have assumed that the trends in the two series were approximately linear. We shall now go a little more fully into this matter of linearity. We shall develop formulae showing how a departure from linearity in the two trends will influence the trend correlation (which is equal to + or –1 in the case of linear trend) and also how it will influence the compound correlations. As a result of this analysis we will also find that if we have two continuous functions of time with finite convexity, and a slope different from 0, we can always make the interval of correlation so short that the correlation between the two functions will be practically equal to + or –1.

We shall first show how we can express *any* function of time $X(t)$ as the sum of a linear function and a *remainder* term. The nature of this remainder term will then indicate the departure from linearity which the function $X(t)$ exhibits. That is to say, we express $X(t)$ in the form

$$X(t) = A + Bt + R(t) \tag{82}$$

where A and B are constants and $R(t)$ is the remainder term. The nature of this remainder term will, of course, depend on how the constants A and B are determined. We shall in particular consider the case where the two constants A and B are determined by the following formula

$$A = \frac{t''X(t') - t'X(t'')}{t'' - t'}$$
$$B = \frac{X(t'') - X(t')}{t'' - t'} \tag{83}$$

where t' and t'' designate respectively the first and last points of time observed. If A and B are determined in this way, then the remainder term will be equal to

$$R(t) = -(t - t')(t'' - t)X(t, t', t'') \tag{84}$$

where $X(t, t', t'')$ is the so-called *second order divided difference* of the function $X(t)$ over the set of three points t, t' and t''. This second order divided difference is in turn defined by the first order divided differences, which themselves are defined directly by the function $X(t)$.

The scheme of definition is the following

First order divided differences
$$X(t, t') = \frac{X(t) - X(t')}{t - t'}$$
$$X(t', t'') = \frac{X(t') - X(t'')}{t' - t''} \tag{85}$$

Second order divided differences $X(t,t',t'') = \dfrac{X(t,t') - X(t',t'')}{t - t''}$ (86)

where $X(t, t')$ is the first order divided difference taken over the set of two points t and t'. From definition (85) it is immediately obvious that the first order difference is an expression for the *slope* of the function $X(t)$ over the two sets of points entering into the first order divided difference. And the second order divided difference as defined by (86) is an expression for how the first order divided difference *changes* when we go from one set of two points, say, from the set (t, t') to another set of two points, say, to the set (t', t''). Therefore, the second order divided difference is an expression of the *convexity* (curvature) of the function $X(t)$. If the function $X(t)$ is rigorously linear, then it has no convexity (curvature) and the second order divided difference is equal to 0 for any set of three points (t, t', t'') we may choose. This is immediately verified by assuming that $X(t)$ is of the form $X(t) = A + Bt$, and computing what the first order and the second order divided differences will be in this case. It will be found that the first order differences are constant and the second order differences are all equal to 0.

From (84) we see that the remainder term will vanish both for $t = t'$ and $t = t''$, no matter what the nature of our function $X(t)$ is, provided only that it has a finite second order difference. That is to say, both in the points $t = t'$ and in the point $t = t''$ the function $X(t)$ coincides with the linear function $A + Bt$, provided the coefficients A and B are determined by (83). This shows the significance of determining the coefficients A and B in the linear term of (82) by expression (83): it means that the linear term $A + Bt$ is determined in such a way that the straight line represented by this linear term passes through the observation point in the beginning of the material (that is for $t = t'$) and through the observation point at the end of the interval (namely for $t = t''$). Determining the coefficients A and B by (83) this means determining a particular sort of straight line *trend* through the observations of the function $X(t)$. In practice this sort of trend will usually not be the one which gives the best fit to the observations, but that is not so essential for the present purpose. What we want to do now is only to give some rough upper limits for the convexity of the function $X(t)$.

Such an upper limit we can obtain by using a well-known mean value theorem regarding divided differences. We have the following proposition: if $X(t, t', t'')$ is the second order divided difference of the function $X(t)$, and if $\ddot{X}(t)$ is the second order *derivative* of $X(t)$, then there exists at least one point of time t^* between the earliest and the latest of the three points of time t, t', t'' such that

$X(t,t',t'') = 2\ddot{X}(t^*)$ (87)

Now $\ddot{X}(t)$ is an expression for the convexity of the function $X(t)$. If C is the largest magnitude (regardless of sign) which $\ddot{X}(t)$ assumes in the interval (t', t''), then C is an expression for the maximum convexity of $X(t)$ in this interval. Furthermore, by using (87) we see that we have the following upper limit for the absolute magnitude of the remainder term

$$| R(t) | \le 2(t - t')(t'' - t)C \tag{88}$$

This expression may be further simplified. We namely see that if we consider the expression

$$f(t) = (t - t')(t'' - t) \tag{89}$$

as a function of t, then this function $f(t)$ is equal to 0 for $t = t'$ and for $t = t''t''$. And between these two points $f(t)$ increases monotonically up to a maximum which is reached for $t = (t' + t'')/2$ and from this point it decreases monotonically down to 0 again. In the point $t = (t' + t'')/2$ the function $f(t)$ is equal to $(t'' - t')^2/4 = (N/2)^2$. Therefore the upper limit in (88) for the remainder term $R(t)$ may be simplified to the following

$$| R(t) | \le N^2 C / 2 \tag{90}$$

By the general formula here developed we shall now prove an interesting proposition regarding the correlation between any two functions of time.

Let $X_1(t)$ and $X_2(t)$ be functions of time such that each of them has a finite convexity and a slope different from 0 in any point over a certain interval of time. *Then it is always possible to determine a certain sub-interval such that for this sub-interval the Pearsonian correlation coefficient between X_1 and X_2 comes as near to (+or −) unity as we please.* In order to secure this we only have to make the sub-interval very small. This is proved in the following way.

Let C_1 and C_2 be the upper limit of $\ddot{X}_1(t)$ and $\ddot{X}_2(t)$ respectively over the entire interval considered. Then in any sub-interval we have

$$\begin{aligned} X_1 &= X_3 + X_5 \\ X_2 &= X_4 + X_6 \end{aligned} \tag{91}$$

Where X_5 and X_6 are linear functions

$$\begin{aligned} X_5 &= A_5 + B_5 t \\ X_6 &= A_6 + B_6 t \end{aligned} \tag{92}$$

and X_3 and X_4 are two functions, the ordinates of which (regardless of sign) by virtue of (90) are bounded by the upper limits

$$\begin{aligned} | X_3 | &\le N^2 C_1 / 2 \\ | X_4 | &\le N^2 C_2 / 2 \end{aligned} \tag{93}$$

Therefore a fortiori we must have

$$\sigma_3 \leq N^2 C_1 / 2$$
$$\sigma_4 \leq N^2 C_2 / 2 \tag{94}$$

where σ_3 and σ_4 are the standard deviations of X_3 and X_4 respectively. On the other hand by (81) we have

$$\sigma_5^2 = B_5^2 N^2 / 12$$
$$\sigma_6^2 = B_6^2 N^2 / 12 \tag{95}$$

so that

$$\frac{\sigma_3}{\sigma_5} \leq \sqrt{3} \, \frac{N C_1}{|B_5|}$$
$$\frac{\sigma_4}{\sigma_6} \leq \sqrt{3} \, \frac{N C_2}{|B_6|} \tag{96}$$

where $|B_5|$ and $|B_6|$ designate the absolute magnitudes (regardless of sign) of B_5 and B_6 respectively.

Formula (96) shows that if C_1 is a finite number and furthermore B_5 is different from 0, then it is always possible to make N so small that the ratio σ_3/σ_5 becomes as small as we want it to. Similarly, if C_2 is a finite number B_6 is different from 0, then it is always possible to render the ratio σ_4/σ_6 as small as we want to. Therefore, by making the length of the interval of correlation N sufficiently small, we see, by the principle of correlation domination, that it is possible to make the compound correlation between X_1 and X_2 come as near as we please to the correlation between X_5 and X_6. But the latter correlation is equal to unity, since the two functions X_5 and X_6 defined by (92) are linear functions of time.

We have here only given *sufficient* conditions under which it is possible to make the correlation between two functions come as close to perfection as we want to, by making the interval of correlation small enough. It would be possible to relax considerably on these sufficiency conditions. For instance, we might drop the assumption that the 'trends' X_5 and X_6 are linear with respect to time. This is obviously something which is not necessary for our proof. We have, namely, not utilized this linearity in any other way than by concluding to the linear relationship between X_5 and X_6 and it is evident that such a linear relationship between X_5 and X_6 may exist even though both X_5 and X_6 are extremely nonlinear with respect to time. We would, for instance, have a linear relationship between X_5 and X_6 if both these magnitudes were sine functions of time with the same period and the same phase. But we shall not here go any further into the question of necessary conditions for the approach to perfect correlation between X_1 and X_2.

Similar considerations as the one here developed may be undertaken for the case where each of our functions X_1 and X_2 consists of more than two components, but we shall not go any more fully into this matter here.

* * *

3.1.1   *Preliminary remarks on the phase diagram*

We now proceed to discuss the case where we have two time variables that fluctuate over time in cycles with approximately the same period, but having a different phase (timing). The amplitudes may also be different, or, more precisely expressed, the two ordinates might be incommensurable, one being measured, say in a unit different from the other.

For simplicity we shall consider the case where the fluctuations may be represented by rigorous sine functions, but the essence of our argument will hold good as an approximation even for the case where the fluctuations are not exactly sine functions.

Let $X_1(t)$ and $X_2(t)$ be our two sine functions of time, defined by the formula

$$X_1 = A_1 \sin 2\pi(a_1 + t)/p$$
$$X_2 = A_2 \sin 2\pi(a_2 + t)/p \tag{97}$$

The constant p designates the period (this period being common to the two time functions considered), the two constants A_1 and A_2 designate the *amplitudes* of the two sine functions and the constants a_1 and a_2 designate the *phase*. If $a_2 \le a_1$ then the function X_1 will be *leading*. That is to say, a maximum point in X_2 will occur a time distance equal to $(a_1 - a_2)$ after the point where X_1 passes a maximum. And similarly, for the minimum points. The time distance $(a_1 - a_2)$ we shall call the lead of X_1. It will be convenient to express this lead as a fraction of the common period p. That is to say, we put

$$a_1 - a_2 = hp \tag{98}$$

so that h designates the lead of X_1 expressed as a fraction of the common period p.

We now construct the *phase diagram*. This is an (X_1, X_2) diagram where we mark off the successive points that represent the time observations of X_1 and X_2 (see Figure 3.7). For instance, let the point $_1P$ designate the first observation. That is to say, the abscissa of $_1P$ represents the magnitude which X_1 had in the first observation and the ordinate of this point represents the magnitude which X_1 had in the first observation. In Figure 3.7 both these observations were negative.

Similarly the point $_2P$ represents the second observation, and so on. If we have a whole set of observations, we may join all the observation points by a continuous curve. This curve is the phase diagram. If the two variables X_1 and X_2 are sine functions with same period, that is sine functions of the type defined by (97), then the phase diagram X_1 and X_2 will be an *ellipse* as indicated in Figure 3.7. The characteristic features of this ellipse, for instance, the inclination of its

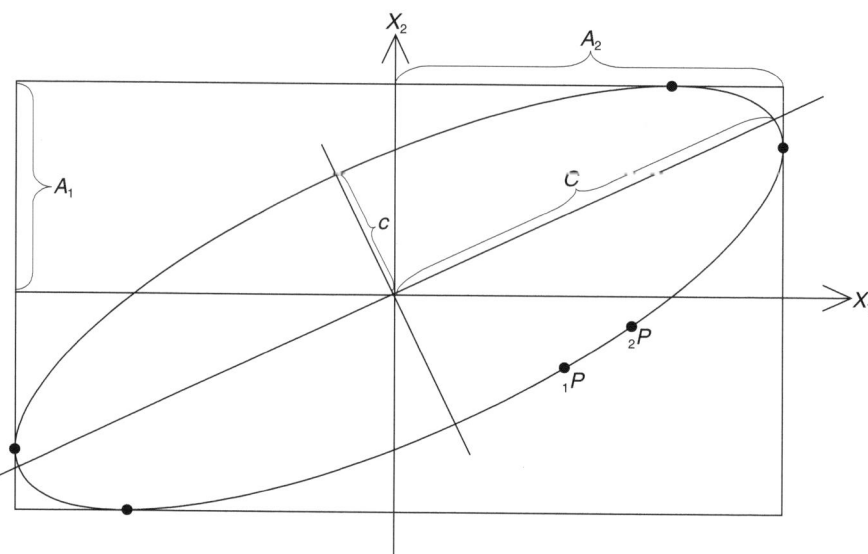

Figure 3.7 The phase diagram.

main axis, the 'thickness' of the ellipse, that is to say, the ratio between the length of the short axis c and the length of the long axis C will be characteristic for the nature of the original sine functions X_1 and X_2.

These features of the phase ellipse will be characteristic for the timing and the amplitude, etc., of sine curves X_1 and X_2. We now proceed to show in what way the characteristics of the phase ellipse are determined by the characteristics of the original sine functions. The formula thus obtained will give us a means of drawing conclusions back from the shape of the phase diagram to the nature of the original sine functions. And this is what we need in practice.

Let us introduce in the first equation of (97) the expression $a_1 = a_2 + hp$ taken from (98). This gives $X_1 = A_1 \sin 2\pi(a_2 + t + hp)/p$. If we develop this formula according to the well known rule from elementary trigonometry $\sin(u+v) = \sin u \cos v + \cos u \sin v$, we get

$$\frac{X_1}{A_1} = \sin 2\pi(a_2 + t)/p \cdot \cos 2\pi h + \cos 2\pi(a_2 + t)/p \cdot \sin 2\pi h$$

Further using the trigonometric formula $\cos v = \pm\sqrt{1 - \sin^2 v}$ we get

$$\frac{X_1}{A_1} = \frac{X_2}{A_2} \cos 2\pi h \pm \sqrt{1 - \left(\frac{X_2}{A_2}\right)^2} \cdot \sin 2\pi h$$

If in the last formula we carry the square root over to one side and then square the equation we get

$$\left(\frac{X_1}{A_1}\right)^2 - 2\frac{X_1 X_2}{A_1 A_2}\cos 2\pi h + \left(\frac{X_2}{A_2}\right)^2 = \sin^2 2\pi h \tag{99}$$

Now from analytical geometry we know that an equation in X_1 and X_2 of the form (99) represents an ellipse with its centre in the origin of the (X_1, X_2) coordinates. From elementary geometry we have the following rule.

If x_1 and x_2 are connected by the equation

$$a_{11}x_1^2 + 2a_{12}x_1 x_2 + a_{22}x_2^2 = H \tag{100}$$

where

$$0 \le a_{11}, \ 0 \le a_{22}, \ 0 \le a_{11}a_{22} - a_{12}^2 \ \text{and} \ 0 \le H \tag{101}$$

then the relation between x_1 and x_2 is represented by an ellipse whose center is at the origin of the (x_1, x_2) coordinates. Furthermore, the characteristics of this ellipse are the following.

If $a_{12} = 0$, the ellipse has axes coinciding with the coordinate axes, that is to say, either the main axis of the ellipse is horizontal and the short axis vertical, or vice versa.

If $a_{12} \ne 0$, then the main (long) axis of the ellipse (and consequently also the short axis) is oblique. The angular coefficient of the slope of the main axis, that is to say, the ratio between the ordinate and the abscissa for a point on the main (long) axis is equal to

$$-\mathrm{sgn}(a_{12})\sqrt{\frac{\sqrt{(a_{11} - a_{22})^2 + 4a_{12}^2} + (a_{11} - a_{22})}{\sqrt{(a_{11} - a_{22})^2 + 4a_{12}^2} - (a_{11} - a_{22})}} \tag{102}$$

Furthermore the ratio between the length of the short axis and the length of the long axis is equal to

$$\sqrt{\frac{a_{11} + a_{22} - \sqrt{(a_{11} - a_{22})^2 + 4a_{12}^2}}{a_{11} + a_{22} + \sqrt{(a_{11} - a_{22})^2 + 4a_{12}^2}}} \tag{103}$$

We may now apply this to equation (99). We see that all the conditions in (101) are fulfilled. The phase curve which the point (X_1, X_2) describes must therefore, as above stated, be an ellipse with origin as center.

As a further characteristic of the phase ellipse we shall introduce the ratio

$$\lambda = c/C \tag{104}$$

between the length of the short axis and the length of the long axis. This ratio must evidently be a number between 0 and 1. Finally, we introduce the ratio

$$\upsilon = A_2 / A_1 \tag{105}$$

between the amplitude of X_2 and the amplitude of X_1. We may always assume that the two constants A_2 and A_1 are positive. For instance if A_1 were not we could simply replace the phase a_1 by $a_1' = a + hp/2$, this would give a sine expression for X which had a positive constant $A_1' = -A_1$. And similarly for X_2. Therefore we may assume that υ is a positive number, but it is not confined to lying between the limits 0 and 1, it may assume any magnitude between 0 and ∞. The ratio λ represents the 'thickness' of the ellipse in Figure 3.7. And the ratio υ represents the ratio between the height and the base of the *rectangle*, which circumscribes the ellipse (see Figure 3.7). These two characteristics may be obtained graphically if we have given empirically a phase ellipse. In an actual case we would, of course, have to determine the phase ellipse by a smoothing process (free hand or otherwise) and it would be from the smooth ellipse as thus obtained that the reading of the two ratios υ and λ would have to be made.

In terms of the two ratios υ and λ the parameters of the original sine curves may be determined as follows.

If we introduce in (103) $a_{11} = 1/A_1^2$, $a_{22} = 1/A_2^2$ and $a_{12} = -(\cos 2\pi h)/A_1 A_2$, we get

$$\lambda^2 = \frac{A_1^2 + A_2^2 - \sqrt{(A_1^2 + A_2^2)^2 - 4A_1^2 A_2^2 \sin^2 2\pi h}}{A_1^2 + A_2^2 + \sqrt{(A_1^2 + A_2^2)^2 - 4A_1^2 A_2^2 \sin^2 2\pi h}} \tag{106}$$

Furthermore we see that by the definition of υ we have

$$\frac{A_1 A_2}{A_1^2 + A_2^2} = \frac{\upsilon}{1 + \upsilon^2} \tag{107}$$

Therefore dividing (106) by $(A_1^2 + A_2^2)$ we obtain

$$\lambda^2 = \frac{1 - \sqrt{1 - (\frac{2\upsilon}{1 + \upsilon^2})^2 - \sin^2 2\pi h}}{1 + \sqrt{1 - (\frac{2\upsilon}{1 + \upsilon^2})^2 - \sin^2 2\pi h}} \tag{108}$$

Now by ordering equation (108) so as to have the square root on one side, and then squaring the equation, we obtain

$$\sin 2\pi h = \frac{\lambda}{\upsilon} \cdot \frac{1 + \upsilon^2}{1 + \lambda^2} \tag{109}$$

The sign of the right member in (109) is uniquely determined since we assume that $0 \le h \le 1$. If we had not made this assumption about h, the sign of the right member in (109) would not have been determined by the reduction of (108) here performed.

Formulae (104), (105) and (109) give the means of determining the original sine functions in terms of the phase ellipse characteristics υ and λ.

We now proceed to show how the characteristics of the original sine curves can be determined also in another way by introducing the straight square moment and the cross moments of the two time functions X_1 and X_2. Let t' and t'' be respectively the first and last point of time for which the two time curves X_1 and X_2 are observed. And let $N = t'' - t'$ be the length of the interval of observation. We assume, for simplicity, that the observations have been virtually continuous so that we can determine the means $\bar{X}_1$ and $\bar{X}_2$ and the moment M_{12} by *integration* instead of by finite summation. By using the elementary integration formulae for trigonometric functions we obtain

$$\bar{X} = \frac{\sin \pi N / p}{\pi N / p} \sin 2\pi(a + \bar{t}) / p \tag{110}$$

where $\bar{t} = (t' + t'')/2$ is the point of time in the middle of the range of observation. In formula (110) we have not put on any subscript, the formula holds good both for the subscript 1 and for the subscript 2.

From (110) we see that if the range of observations covers an exact number of periods, that is to say, if N is equal to kp where k is an integer, then the mean $\bar{X}$ is equal to 0. And furthermore, we see that if the length of the interval of observation is very large, then $\bar{X}$ tends towards 0 regardless of whether or not the observations cover an exact number of periods. In the case where the range of observation is very large we may therefore as a first approximation assume that the mean $\bar{X}$ is equal to 0. This will simplify the formulae considerably.

Similarly, we obtain

$$M_{12} = \frac{A_1 A_2}{2} \cdot \left[t \cos 2\pi h - \frac{p}{4\pi} \sin 2\pi(a_1 + a_2 + 2t) / p \right]_{t=t'}^{t=t''} \tag{111}$$

The last formula means that we shall first put $t' = t''$ in the bracket and then subtract what we obtain by putting $t' = t''$. If we do that we see the first term in the bracket will be the principal term. That is to say, if the range of observations is very large it is only this first term that will count. The contribution to the total expression which comes from the second term will be insignificant. On the same assumption as the one which led to considering the mean $\bar{X}$ as equal to 0, we therefore obtain

$$m_{11} = N A_1^2 / 2$$

$$m_{22} = N A_2^2 / 2$$

$$m_{12} = (N A_1 A_2 \cos 2\pi h) / 2 \quad \text{(approx. when } N \text{ is large)} \tag{112}$$

The expression for m_{11} and m_{22} in (112) are obtained immediately from the expression for m_{12} by putting $h=0$ and replacing both subscripts by 1 and the next two subscripts by 2.

From (112) we immediately obtain

$$r_{12} = \cos 2\pi h \quad \text{(approx. when } N \text{ is large)} \tag{113}$$

This shows that there is an immediate connection between the lag of the two original sine curves and the correlation between them taken over time. *The correlation coefficient is nothing else than an expression for the length of the lag.* Therefore we may change the correlation by advancing one of the two curves. Advancing one of the curves means that we take the correlation between them, not by pairing $_tX_1$ with $_tX_2$, but by pairing $_tX_1$ with $_{t+kp}X_2$ where k is a number conveniently chosen. If we choose $k=-h$, that is to say, if we artificially advance one of the curves just enough to make up for the natural lag between them, then we get a correlation coefficient equal to 1. And furthermore, we see that by attributing successively different values to k we change the correlation coefficient accordingly. *We even see that by a suitable choice of the amount by which one of the curves is advanced we may render the correlation coefficient equal to any magnitude whatsoever between -1 and $+1$.* This shows quite clearly that the correlation coefficient in this case has no significance whatsoever as a measure of whether or not one of the two quantities observed 'determined' the other.

If the natural lag h has a magnitude between 0 and 0.25 then the main axis of the phase ellipse will be positively inclined, and the ellipse will be described counter-clockwise as the observation point moves as a function of time. Similarly, if the natural lag h is lying between 0.25 and 0.5 the main axis of the phase ellipse will be negatively inclined, but still the phase ellipse will be described counter clockwise. If h is lying between 0.25 and 0.75 the main axis will be inclined negatively and the phase ellipse described clockwise. Finally, if h is between 0.75 and 1, the main axis of the phase ellipse will be inclined positively and the phase ellipse described clockwise. In general, we will in the various cases have situations which are exhibited by the scheme in Figure 3.8. This scheme is a rather convenient tool in the analysis of phase diagrams given empirically.

The curves to the left in Figure 3.8 are time curves of X_1 and X_2. The eight alternatives illustrate eight different lags. For convenience in drawing, these time curves are represented with the same amplitude.

To the right in Figure 3.8 are represented the phase diagrams that correspond to each of the eight alternatives. To each lag alternative we have drawn three phase diagrams, namely one representing the case where the amplitude of X_1 is the largest, one where the two amplitudes are equal, and one where the amplitude of X_2 is the largest. Of course there is no other significance to these three cases than what is involved in the choices of units of measurement. A glance at Figure 3.8 also shows that three phase diagrams on a given line in the figure (that is for a given lag alternative) have the same general characteristics.

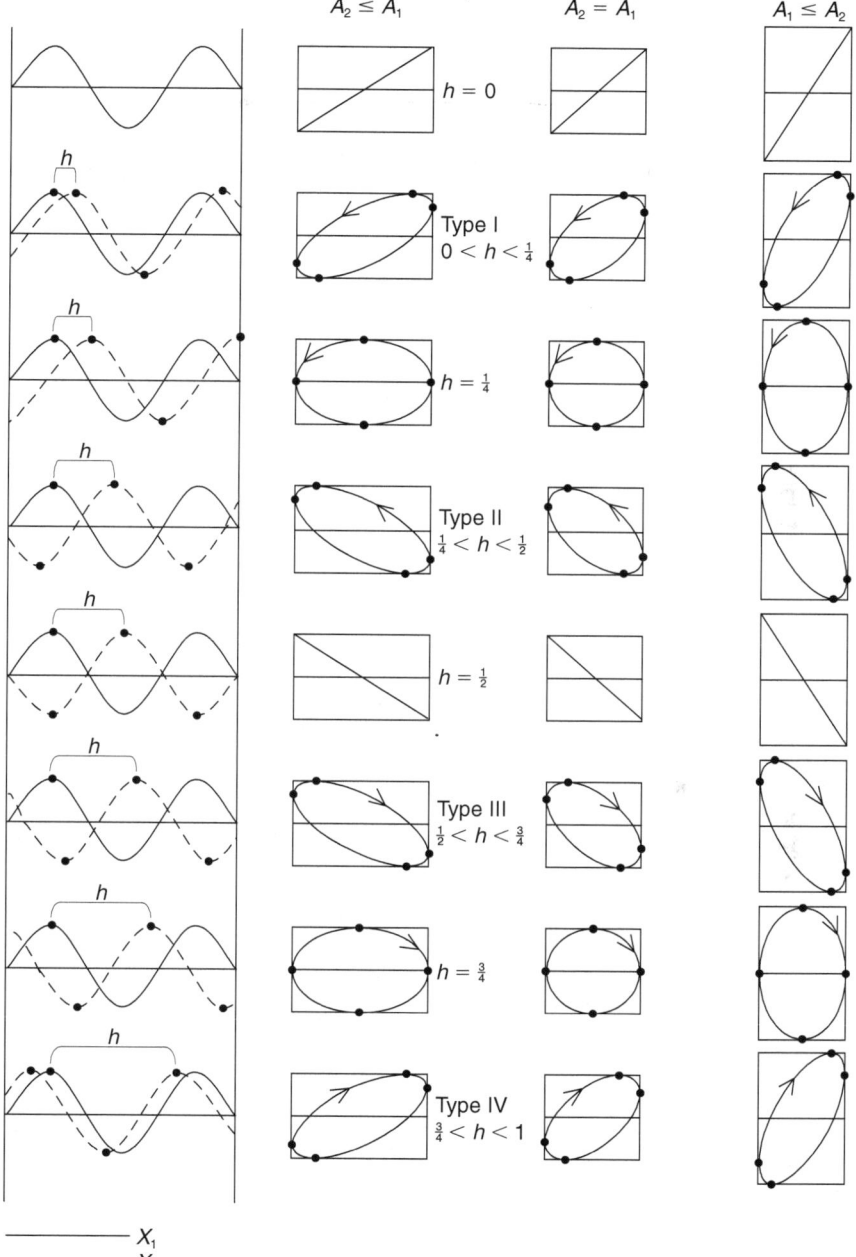

Figure 3.8 Standard types of phase diagrams.

3.1.2   *Linear regression in several variables*

We now proceed to generalize the notions of regression and correlation to several variables. We consider a set of n variables. These variables measured from their origins we denote $X_1, X_2, \ldots, X_n$. When we select an arbitrary of these variables we shall usually denote it X_i. Furthermore, we let $_tX_i$ designate the observation number t of the variable no. i.

For completeness we shall re-state the definitions of means, moments, etc., although these definitions are now quite obvious, being built on analogy with the similar definitions in the case of two variables. The means are defined by

$$\bar{X}_i = \frac{1}{N}\Sigma X_i \tag{114}$$

it being understood that the summation in (114) is a summation over t.

The variables measured from the means we denote

$$_tx_i = {}_tX_i - \bar{X}_i \tag{115}$$

The origin moments and the reduced moments are defined by

$$M_{ij} = \sum X_i X_j \tag{116}$$

$$m_{ij} = \sum x_i x_j \tag{117}$$

The tables of n^2 quantities M_{ij} and m_{ij} respectively

$$[M_{ij}] = \begin{pmatrix} M_{11} & M_{12} & \ldots & M_{1n} \\ M_{21} & M_{22} & \ldots & M_{2n} \\ \ldots & \ldots & \ldots & \ldots \\ M_{n1} & M_{n2} & \ldots & M_{nn} \end{pmatrix} \tag{118}$$

$$[m_{ij}] = \begin{pmatrix} m_{11} & m_{12} & \ldots & m_{1n} \\ m_{21} & m_{22} & \ldots & m_{2n} \\ \ldots & \ldots & \ldots & \ldots \\ m_{n1} & m_{n2} & \ldots & m_{nn} \end{pmatrix} \tag{119}$$

are called the *origin moment matrix* and the *reduced moment matrix*.

The quantities

$$R_{ij} = \frac{M_{ij}}{\sqrt{M_{ii}M_{jj}}} \tag{120}$$

$$r_{ij} = \frac{m_{ij}}{\sqrt{m_{ii}m_{jj}}} \tag{121}$$

are the origin correlation coefficients and the reduced (Pearsonian) correlation coefficients. The matrices

$$[R_{ij}] = \begin{pmatrix} R_{11} & R_{12} & ... & R_{1n} \\ R_{21} & R_{22} & ... & R_{2n} \\ ... & ... & ... & ... \\ R_{n1} & R_{n2} & ... & R_{nn} \end{pmatrix} \tag{122}$$

$$[r_{ij}] = \begin{pmatrix} r_{11} & r_{12} & ... & r_{1n} \\ r_{21} & r_{22} & ... & r_{2n} \\ ... & ... & ... & ... \\ r_{n1} & r_{n2} & ... & r_{nn} \end{pmatrix} \tag{123}$$

are called the origin correlation matrix and the reduced correlation matrix respectively. Whenever we use the expression 'correlation matrix' without any further qualification we mean the reduced correlation matrix of (123). Similarly when we use the expression 'moment matrix' without further qualification, we mean the reduced moment matrix defined by (119). It is easily seen that correlation matrix (123) is obtained from moment matrix (119) by dividing the i-th line by $\sqrt{m_{ii}}$ and dividing the j-th column by $\sqrt{m_{jj}}$. This procedure we may refer to as the *normalization* of moment matrix (119).

In the following we shall as much as possible avoid the notion of partial correlation coefficients, because as we shall see these partial correlation coefficients are misleading in a great number of cases, and exactly in those cases which are of greatest importance in an analysis of economic data. Indeed we shall introduce a set of other coefficients which are based on an analogy with the *scatter coefficient* which we already have introduced in the case of two variables. Furthermore, we shall consider the general problem of determining *linear regressions* in several variables. The coefficients built on the analogy with the scatter coefficient in the case of two variables will prove to be valuable tools in determining those cases where the linear regressions in several variables have a significance.

In order to be able to handle the general problems of regression in n variables in a convenient way, it will be necessary to introduce the notion of *determinants*. Before we proceed to a discussion of the regression problems we shall give some of the elementary rules regarding determinants.

In the case of two variables we saw that we encountered rather frequently an expression of the form $m_{11}m_2 - m_{21}m_{12}$. This expression is a simple example of a determinant. It will be found convenient to write this expression in the following symbolic form:

$$\begin{vmatrix} m_{11} & m_{12} \\ m_{21} & m_{22} \end{vmatrix} = m_{11}m_{22} - m_{21}m_{12}. \tag{124}$$

When we write the expression considered in the form (124) we make immediately a connection with the *moment matrix* in the case of two variables. There is this difference, though, that the expression to the left in (124), that is to say, the *determinant* is a well defined *magnitude*. It is a *number* whose size can be given in the ordinary numerical way, while the moment matrix is a purely *symbolic* expression, which does not stand for a quantity, but only as the entity of all the numbers that occur as its element. Thus there is an essential difference between a matrix and a determinant. However to any matrix we may associate a determinant. In the two-dimensional case here considered we may start from the notion of a two-dimensional matrix and compute the magnitude which is defined by the computation rule in (124). This magnitude which is attached to the two-rowed matrix we shall call the *determinant value* of the matrix. What we have to do now is to generalize this notion to multi-rowed determinants.

In order to indicate that it is here a question of defining quite generally the notion of determinant without special reference to the case where the elements of the determinant are the moments m_{ij}, we shall denote the elements generally by a_{ij}. The magnitude of the determinant we shall denote D, so that a two-rowed determinant will be defined by the computation rule

$$D = \begin{vmatrix} a_{11} & a_{12} \\ a_{21} & a_{22} \end{vmatrix} = a_{11}a_{22} - a_{21}a_{12} \tag{125}$$

Rule (125) can be easily remembered when we imagine that we draw the two *diagonals* in the determinant to the left in (125). The value of the determinant is simply equal to the product of the quantities in the diagonal which goes from the upper left-hand corner to the lower right-hand corner minus the elements in the other diagonal. This rule we shall call the *crossing rule*.

In the case of a three-rowed determinant we have a similar crossing rule. We simply imagine that underneath the determinant we write as a forth and fifth row respectively the first and second row. Then we form the three down sloping diagonals $a_{11}a_{22}a_{33}$, $a_{21}a_{32}a_{13}$ and $a_{31}a_{12}a_{23}$, and the three up sloping diagonals $a_{31}a_{22}a_{13}$, $a_{11}a_{32}a_{23}$ and $a_{21}a_{12}a_{33}$. And then we take the sum of all three down sloping diagonals and from this we subtract the sum of the three up sloping diagonals. That is to say, a three-rowed determinant is defined by the computation rule

$$D = \begin{vmatrix} a_{11} & a_{12} & a_{13} \\ a_{21} & a_{22} & a_{23} \\ a_{31} & a_{32} & a_{33} \end{vmatrix} = \begin{matrix} a_{11}a_{22}a_{33} + a_{21}a_{32}a_{13} + a_{31}a_{12}a_{23} \\ -(a_{31}a_{22}a_{13} + a_{11}a_{32}a_{23} + a_{21}a_{12}a_{33}) \end{matrix} \tag{126}$$

For determinants of more than three rows there does not exist any such simple rule of computation as those which we have here developed for two-rowed and three-rowed determinants. For multi-dimensional determinants we shall use a definition which proceeds by recurrence. That is to say we define a four-rowed determinant by building on the definition of the three-rowed and we define a five-rowed determinant by building on the definition of the four-rowed, and so on. In order to exhibit how this recurrence definition works it will be necessary first to define what we understand by the *adjoint* of a two-rowed and a three-rowed matrix. We have already seen how we defined the adjoint of a two-rowed matrix. The adjoint of the two-rowed matrix (a_{ij}) is defined as the two-rowed matrix (a_{ij}^*), where the elements a_{ij}^* are determined by crossing out the line and column intersecting in the element a_{ij} of the original matrix and then *taking what is left*, introducing the sign $(-1)^{i+j}$. That is to say, we have

$$[a_{ij}^*] = \begin{pmatrix} a_{22} & -a_{21} \\ -a_{12} & a_{11} \end{pmatrix} \tag{127}$$

Similarly the adjoint (a_{ij}^*) of a three-row matrix (a_{ij}) is defined thus

$$[a_{ij}^*] = \begin{pmatrix} (a_{22}a_{33} - a_{32}a_{23}) & -(a_{21}a_{33} - a_{31}a_{23}) & (a_{21}a_{32} - a_{31}a_{22}) \\ -(a_{12}a_{33} - a_{32}a_{13}) & (a_{11}a_{33} - a_{31}a_{13}) & -(a_{11}a_{32} - a_{31}a_{12}) \\ (a_{12}a_{23} - a_{22}a_{13}) & -(a_{11}a_{23} - a_{21}a_{13}) & (a_{11}a_{22} - a_{21}a_{12}) \end{pmatrix} \tag{128}$$

That is to say, we have

$$a_{11}^* = +(a_{22}a_{33} - a_{32}a_{23}) \quad a_{31}^* = +(a_{12}a_{23} - a_{22}a_{13}) \quad a_{21}^* = -(a_{12}a_{33} - a_{32}a_{13})$$
$$a_{12}^* = -(a_{21}a_{33} - a_{31}a_{23}) \quad a_{32}^* = -(a_{11}a_{23} - a_{21}a_{13}) \quad a_{22}^* = +(a_{11}a_{33} - a_{31}a_{13})$$
$$a_{13}^* = +(a_{21}a_{32} - a_{31}a_{22}) \quad a_{33}^* = +(a_{11}a_{22} - a_{21}a_{12}) \quad a_{23}^* = -(a_{11}a_{32} - a_{31}a_{12})$$

$$\tag{129}$$

The notion of adjoint can be utilized to develop a very useful formula for the determinant value of a matrix. If we take the two-row determinant D defined by (125) we see that if we pick out the first *column* of this determinant and also the first column of the adjoint (127) and form the products of the corresponding elements in the original matrix and the adjoint matrix, the sum thus obtained will exactly be equal to the value of the determinant. We namely have

$$a_{11}a_{11}^* + a_{21}a_{21}^* = a_{11}a_{22} - a_{21}a_{12} = D \tag{130}$$

Furthermore we see that we obtain exactly the same result by picking out the *second* column of the original matrix and the second column of the adjoint. We namely have

$$a_{12}a_{12}^* + a_{22}a_{22}^* = -a_{12}a_{21} + a_{22}a_{11} = D \tag{131}$$

and we also see that we would get exactly the same result by picking out any of the rows, for instance, by picking out the first row in the original matrix and the first row in the adjoint, or by picking out the second row in the original matrix and the second row in the adjoint. The formulae thus obtained for the value of our two-row determinant we shall call the formulae for development according to columns or rows. For instance, in (130) we say that our determinant is *developed according to the first column*, in (131) we say that it is developed according to the second column, and so on.

Exactly similar formulae for the development according to rows or columns exist in the case of three-row determinants. The three-rowed determinant D defined by (126) may be developed according to its first row, thus

$$a_{11}a_{11}^* + a_{12}a_{12}^* + a_{13}a_{13}^* = a_{11}(a_{22}a_{33} - a_{32}a_{23}) - a_{12}(a_{21}a_{33} - a_{31}a_{23})$$
$$+ a_{13}(a_{21}a_{32} - a_{31}a_{22}) = D \qquad (132)$$

and it is easy to verify that we have a similar formula for the development according to the second row, according to the third row, according to the first column etc.

The formula for development according to rows or columns here indicated furnishes a means of defining higher rowed determinants by recurrence. Thus we may now disregard the original and *direct* definition of a three-rowed determinant given by (126) and define the value of a three-row determinant as the result we would get by developing it according to a row or according to a column.

This definition would be unique. And it would only involve that we had already beforehand defined the two-rowed determinant. Similarly, we may now proceed one step further and define the value of a four-rowed determinant as the result which we would get by developing it according to a row or a column. By actually carrying out the computations we would find that the result thus obtained is independent of which row or column we pick out. This definition of the magnitude of a four-rowed determinant involves only that we have already beforehand defined a three-rowed determinant. Similarly we might define a five-rowed determinant as the result obtained by developing it according to a row or column, and this definition would only involve the knowledge of what is meant by a four-rowed determinant. Thus we might continue and generally define a n-rowed determinant.[2]

If we pick out a certain number of rows from a matrix and the same number of columns and form the determinant of the elements occurring in the intersection points between the rows and columns thus selected, this determinant is called a *minor* of the matrix. If a matrix contains a q-row minor that is different from zero, while all higher rowed minors vanish, then the matrix is said to be of rank q. Minors which are such that their diagonal elements are also diagonal elements of the original matrix are called *principal* minors.

The notion of determinants and the notion of the adjoint of a matrix can be used to give a simple solution of a system of linear equations. First suppose that we have a system of homogenous linear equations, that is a system of the form

$$a_{11}x_1 + a_{12}x_2 + \ldots + a_{1n}x_n = 0$$

$$a_{21}x_1 + a_{22}x_2 + \ldots + a_{2n}x_n = 0 \qquad (133)$$

$$\ldots\ldots\ldots\ldots\ldots\ldots\ldots\ldots\ldots\ldots\ldots\ldots\ldots\ldots$$

$$a_{n1}x_1 + a_{n2}x_2 + \ldots + a_{nn}x_n = 0$$

where the coefficients a_{ij} are given constants, and the quantities $x_1, x_2, \ldots, x_n$ are the unknowns. One of the rules of elementary algebra is that such a system of linear equations has a solution when, and only when, the determinant of the coefficients, that is to say, the determinant

$$a = \begin{vmatrix} a_{11} & a_{12} & .. & a_{1n} \\ a_{21} & a_{22} & .. & a_{2n} \\ .. & .. & .. & .. \\ a_{n1} & a_{n2} & .. & a_{nn} \end{vmatrix} \qquad (134)$$

is equal to 0. Furthermore, if in the adjoint coefficient matrix

$$[a_{ij}^*] = \begin{pmatrix} a_{11}^* & a_{12}^* & .. & a_{1n}^* \\ a_{21}^* & a_{22}^* & .. & a_{2n}^* \\ .. & .. & .. & .. \\ a_{n1}^* & a_{n2}^* & .. & a_{nn}^* \end{pmatrix} \qquad (135)$$

there exists at least one row which does not consist exclusively of zeros, then the solution of system (133) is obtained by putting the quantities $x_1, x_2, \ldots, x_n$ proportional to the quantities in this row, that is to say, if the k-th row in the adjoint (135) is such that it does not consist exclusively of zeros, then the solution of system (133) is

$$x_1 = ca_{k1}^*, \quad x_2 = ca_{k2}^*, \ldots, x_n = ca_{kn}^* \qquad (136)$$

where c is an arbitrary factor of proportionality $\neq 0$. This shows that the quantities $x_1, x_2, \ldots, x_n$ are not determined uniquely by (133).

It is only the $(n-1)$ ratios between them that are determined by the system. This fact is also obvious from the very shape of system (133). We namely see that we may divide the whole system through by one of the unknowns and thus get a system where we only have $n-1$ unknowns, namely, the ratios of the original unknowns to one of them. If it so should happen that there did not exist any row in (135) which did not consist exclusively of zeros, that is to say, if every single element in (135) should be equal to 0, then (136) would not give the solution of system (133). In this case there still would exist a solution of (133), only the indeterminateness would now still be greater than the one which is exhibited in (136). The unknowns $x_1, x_2, \ldots, x_n$ would now depend not only on one arbitrary parameter c as in (136), but would depend on two or even more arbitrary parameters. Also, in this case it would be possible to indicate what the solution of system (133) is by building on the notion of determinants and adjoints. But the situation would be more complex. For instance, we would have to consider the adjoints of each one of the elements (a_{ij}^*) of (135). But we shall here not go any further into this most general case of a system of homogeneous linear equations.

Now let us consider an inhomogeneous system of linear equations, that is to say, a system of the form

$$a_{11}x_1 + a_{12}x_2 + \ldots + a_{1n}x_n = b_1$$
$$a_{21}x_1 + a_{22}x_2 + \ldots + a_{2n}x_n = b_2$$

$$\cdots\cdots\cdots\cdots\cdots\cdots\cdots\cdots\cdots\cdots\cdots\cdots$$

$$a_{n1}x_1 + a_{n2}x_2 + \ldots + a_{nn}x_n = b_n \tag{137}$$

where at least one of the coefficients $b_1, b_2, \ldots, b_n$ is $\neq 0$. One of the elementary rules of algebra is that this system has a solution ($x_1, x_2, \ldots, x_n$) when, and only when the determinant of the coefficients a_{ij}, that is to say, the determinant defined by (134) $\neq 0$. If this is the case, then the solution of the system is given by the following rule: in order to obtain x_1 replace the first column in the original coefficient determinant (134) by a column consisting of the elements ($b_1, b_2, \ldots, b_n$), and divide the result thus obtained by the coefficient determinant a defined by (134). Similarly, in order to obtain x_2 replace the second column in the original coefficient determinant (134) by a column consisting of the elements ($b_1, b_2, \ldots, b_n$) and divide the result thus obtained by the determinant a. Similarly, x_3 is obtained by replacing the third column in (134) by the column ($b_1, b_2, \ldots, b_n$), and so on.

In terms of the elements of the adjoint (135) this rule may be expressed thus: the magnitude of the unknown x_1 is obtained by multiplying the elements in the first column of the adjoint (135) by the corresponding elements ($b_1, b_2, \ldots, b_n$) and dividing the result by the determinant a defined by (134). That is to say, we have

$$x_1 = (b_1 a_{11}^* + b_2 a_{21}^* + \ldots + b_n a_{n1}^*)/a = \sum_j b_k a_{k1}^* / a \tag{138}$$

and similarly

$$x_2 = (b_1 a_{12}^* + b_2 a_{22}^* + \ldots + b_n a_{n2}^*)/a = \sum_k b_k a_{k2}^* / a \tag{139}$$

Quite generally we may write the solution of the system (137) in the form

$$x_j = \sum_k b_k a_{kj}^* / a \tag{140}$$

If we write $x_1', x_2', \ldots, x_n'$ instead of $b_1, b_2, \ldots, b_n$ in the right member of (137), this system will be looked upon as defining a *linear transformation* from the variables x to the variables x'. The transformation is called *non-singular* if the coefficient determinant a defined by (134) is $\neq 0$.

By the algebraic tools here developed it is now easy to solve the linear regression and correlation problems in n variables.

First we define the adjoint moment matrix

$$[m_{ij}^*] = \begin{pmatrix} m_{11}^* & m_{12}^* & .. & m_{1n}^* \\ m_{21}^* & m_{22}^* & .. & m_{2n}^* \\ .. & .. & .. & .. \\ m_{n1}^* & m_{n2}^* & .. & m_{nn}^* \end{pmatrix} \tag{141}$$

The elements of this matrix are defined by the rule expressed in formulae (127) and (129) and the corresponding rule for higher magnitudes of n. Similarly we define the adjoint correlation matrix

$$[r_{ij}^*] = \begin{pmatrix} r_{11}^* & r_{12}^* & .. & r_{1n}^* \\ r_{21}^* & r_{22}^* & .. & r_{2n}^* \\ .. & .. & .. & .. \\ r_{n1}^* & r_{n2}^* & .. & r_{nn}^* \end{pmatrix} \tag{142}$$

The elements of the adjoint matrix may be expressed by the elements of the adjoint moment matrix thus

$$r_{ij}^* = \frac{\sqrt{m_{ii}m_{jj}}}{m_{11}m_{22}...m_{nn}} m_{ij}^* \tag{143}$$

This is easily seen by actually working out the elements of the adjoint correlation matrix. By the same sort of reasoning as we applied in the case of the variables (see formula (57)), we see that the problem of the elementary regressions in the case of n variables may be formulated thus.

Consider the function:

$$G = \sum_t (a_0 + a_1 \cdot {}_t x_1 + a_2 \cdot {}_t x_2 + ... + a_n \cdot {}_t x_n)^2 \tag{144}$$

The i-th elementary regression, that is to say, the linear relation between the variables $x_1, x_2, ..., x_n$ which is obtained by minimizing the sum square in the direction of the x_1 axis is a relation of the form

$$a_0 + a_1 x_1 + a_2 x_2 + ... + a_n x_n = 0 \tag{145}$$

where the coefficients $a_0, a_1, ..., a_n$ are determined by minimizing function (144) under the assumption that a_i is *a constant not to be determined by the minimizing conditions*, and that the other coefficients $a_0, a_1, ..., a_n$ shall be determined by the minimizing conditions.

Let us denote the partial derivatives of function (144) with respect to the quantities $a_0, a_1, ..., a_n$, thus

$$G_j = \frac{dG}{da_j} = 2\sum_t (a_0 + a_{1\,t}x_1 + a_{2\,t}x_2 + ... + a_{n\,t}x_n) \cdot {}_tx_j \tag{146}$$

where by convention we put $x_0 = 1$. From (146) we see that the equation $G_0 = 0$ reduces to $a_0 = 0$. Therefore *all the elementary regressions pass through the mean.* Consequently the n elementary regressions may simply be written in the form (133). The i-th equation in system (133) represents the i-th elementary regression, that is to say, the regression obtained by minimizing the sum squares taken in the direction of the x_i axis.

Since all the elementary regressions pass through the mean, the problem of determining the coefficients of these regressions may be formulated by considering the function

$$G = \sum_t (a_1 \cdot {}_tx_1 + a_2 \cdot {}_tx_2 + ... + a_n \cdot {}_tx_n)^2 \tag{147}$$

whose partial derivatives are

$$G_j = \frac{dG}{da_j} = 2\sum_t (a_1 \cdot {}_tx_1 + a_2 \cdot {}_tx_2 + ... + a_n \cdot {}_tx_n) \cdot {}_tx_j \tag{148}$$

That is to say

$$G_j = 2(a_1 m_{1j} + a_2 m_{2j} + ... + a_n m_{nj}) \tag{149}$$

This shows that the coefficients $a_{i1}, a_{i2}, ..., a_{in}$ of the i-th elementary regression must satisfy the $(n-1)$ equations obtained from

$$a_{i1} m_{1j} + a_{i2} m_{2j} + ... + a_{in} m_{nj} = 0 \tag{150}$$

by putting $j = 1,2 ...$ (except i) $... n$. Since the coefficients a_{ii} are not to be determined by the minimizing conditions we may dispose of them in such a way as to obtain a simple and symmetric form of the solution. This is obtained by disposing of the coefficients a_{ii} in such a way that we get

$$a_{i1} m_{1i} + a_{i2} m_{2i} + ... + a_{in} m_{ni} = m \tag{151}$$

where m is the determinant value of moment matrix, that is to say

$$m = \begin{vmatrix} m_{11} & m_{12} & .. & m_{1n} \\ m_{21} & m_{22} & .. & m_{2n} \\ .. & .. & .. & .. \\ m_{n1} & m_{n2} & .. & m_{nn} \end{vmatrix} \tag{152}$$

If this is done we may look upon the set of coefficients $a_{i1}, a_{i2}, ..., a_{in}$ of the i-th elementary regression as being defined by the system of n equations

$$a_{i1}m_{1j} + a_{i2}m_{2j} + ... + a_{in}m_{nj} = me_{ij} \quad (j = 1, 2 ... n) \tag{153}$$

where the symbol e_{ij} is defined as equal to 0 when $i \neq j$, and equal to 1 when $i = j$. Now it is easy to see that the system of n equations which is obtained from (153) by putting $j = 1, 2 ... n$ is satisfied if we put

$$a_{ij} = m_{ij}^* \tag{154}$$

where m_{ij}^* are the elements of the adjoint correlation matrix. This shows that the i-th elementary regression L_i is simply the regression

$$m_{i1}^* x_1 + m_{i2}^* x_2 + ... + m_{in}^* x_n = 0$$

That is to say, the n coefficients of the i-th elementary regression are simply the n equations that are written in the i-th row in the adjoint correlation matrix.

We shall now see how the orthogonal mean regression is determined. Let a_0, $a_1, a_2..., a_n$ be the coefficients of the orthogonal mean regression. That is to say, we write the orthogonal mean regression in the form (145). By a generalization to n dimensions of formula (29) we see that the square of the distance from the point $(x_1, x_2, ..., x_n)$ in the scatter diagram to the plane of (145) is equal to

$$\frac{\left(a_0 + a_1 x_1 + a_2 x_2 + ... + a_n x_n\right)^2}{a_1^2 + ... + a_n^2} \tag{155}$$

The determination of the orthogonal mean regression is therefore equivalent with the problem of determining the coefficients a in such a way that the function obtained by extending the summation over t to expression (155) becomes as small as possible.

Taking the derivative with respect to a_0 of the sum square thus obtained we see immediately that we have $a_0 = 0$. Therefore we may reduce the problem to determining the coefficients $a_1, a_2, ..., a_n$ in the function

$$G = \frac{\sum \left(a_1 \cdot_t x_1 + a_2 \cdot_t x_2 + ... + a_n \cdot_t x_n\right)^2}{a_1^2 + ... + a_n^2} = \frac{\sum_{ij} a_i m_{ij} a_j}{\sum_i a_i^2} \tag{156}$$

in such a way that this function becomes as small as possible. The summation Σ_{ij} in (156) is defined by letting i run from 1 to n, and for each magnitude of i thus obtained letting j run from 1 to n. By forming in the usual way the derivatives of function (156) and equating each of the derivatives to 0, we see the coefficients $a_1, a_2, ..., a_n$ must be such as to satisfy the following system of n homogenous linear equations.

$$\sum_k (m_{ik} - Ge_{ik}) a_k = 0 \tag{157}$$
$$(i = 1, 2...n)$$

Now from what we have seen in our discussion of linear equations we know that system (157) has a solution (different from the trivial solution $a_1=0$, $a_2=0,\ldots$, $a_n=0$) when, and only when, the determinant of the coefficients is equal to 0. That is to say, we must have

$$\begin{vmatrix} m_{11} & G & m_{12} & .. & m_{1n} \\ m_{21} & m_{22} - G & .. & m_{2n} \\ .. & .. & .. & .. \\ m_{n1} & m_{n2} & .. & m_{nn} - G \end{vmatrix} = 0 \tag{158}$$

This is an algebraic equation of the n-th degree in G. It can be proved that the equation (158) has only real non-negative roots, and from the way in which we have deduced equation (158) we see that the smallest of the roots of this equation will be the magnitude which the function to be minimized, namely, (156) gets when the coefficients are given those magnitudes which will minimize the function. The procedure of solving the problem of the orthogonal mean regression will therefore be this: form equation (158) and determine the smallest of the roots of this equation. When this is done, form the system of homogeneous linear equations (157) and solve this system for the quantities $a_1, a_2, \ldots, a_n$. The coefficients a as thus determined are then the coefficients of the orthogonal mean regression. The latter part of the problem, namely, the problem of solving system (157) may be given in the following simple explicit solution: Let

$$s_{ij} = m_{ij} - Ge_{ij} \tag{159}$$

where G is the smallest root of (158).

The quantities s_{ij} being defined by (159) form the matrix (s_{ij}) whose elements are the quantities s_{ij}, and form the adjoint (s_{ij}^*) of the matrix (s_{ij}). Then any row in the adjoint (s_{ij}^*) may be taken as representing the regression coefficients $a_1, a_2, \ldots, a_n$. If G is determined as a solution of equation (158) it may be shown that it does not matter which one of rows of the adjoint (s_{ij}^*) is selected as representing the coefficients a, since all the rows of (s_{ij}^*) will be proportional. The only thing which we have to take account of is that if one of the rows of (s_{ij}^*) should consist exclusively of zeros (which may happen in some exception cases), then we must not choose this row but another of the rows (s_{ij}^*).

In practice where the quantities entering into system (157) are determined by a more or less inexact numerical computation the rows of (s_{ij}^*) will in general not be exactly proportional. Therefore it might make a slight difference which one of the rows we choose. It will consequently be desirable to have a rule by which we could, so to speak, average the results obtained by selecting the various rows. This may be done in the following way: determine the signs of the coefficients $a_1, a_2, \ldots, a_n$ by the signs of the elements in any of the rows of (s_{ij}^*). (If the numerical computations are not too inexact the signs in all the rows of (s_{ij}^*) will be compatible.) When the signs of the coefficient a are thus determined the magnitudes of these coefficients may be computed by the formula

$$a_i^2 = s_{ii}^* \qquad (160)$$

That is to say, the magnitude of the coefficient a_i (apart from its sign) is put equal to the square root of the i-th diagonal element in the adjoint of the matrix (s_{ij}) defined by (159). It may be proved that if G is exactly the solution of (158) this determination of the coefficients a_i will give exactly the same determination as the one obtained by putting the coefficients proportional to the quantities in a row in the adjoint (s_{ij}^*).

We now proceed to the *diagonal* mean regression. The determination of the orthogonal mean regression, as above explained, is a very laborious one. As a matter of fact, it is so laborious that in practice it will hardly ever be a question of applying it except for the particular case $n=2$ for which the explicit solution is given in formula (69). Furthermore, the orthogonal mean regression has the serious drawback that it is not invariant for a change in the units of measurement of the variables. The diagonal mean regression is a regression which is obtained by modifying the formula of the orthogonal mean regression in such a way that the regression obtained becomes simple enough to be actually handled and further such that it becomes independent of the units of measurement. The principle of this modification is very simple. If the quantity G entering into the determination of the orthogonal mean regression is inexactly computed we have seen that we will get different results accordingly as we select one or another of the rows of the matrix (s_{ij}^*). Furthermore, some of these determinations of the coefficients a may, so to speak, deviate to one side of the correct determination and others to the opposite side. It is just in order to compensate these opposite deviations that we computed the magnitude of the orthogonal mean regression coefficients by formula (160). Moreover, we see that the magnitude G which enters into the determination of the orthogonal mean regression *is a small quantity*. It represents the sum square of the perpendicular deviations from the regression plane in the case where this sum square is rendered as small as possible. In the case where we have a perfect linear relationship between our variables the quantity G here considered will be rigorously equal to 0. As a first approximation we might therefore say that is *actually is 0*. And then proceeding on this approximation, determine the regression coefficients by (160). The coefficients thus obtained are the diagonal mean regression coefficients. That is to say, the diagonal mean regression is a regression of the form

$$a_1 x_1 + a_2 x_2 + \ldots + a_n x_n = 0 \qquad (161)$$

where $x_1, x_2, \ldots, x_n$ designate the variables measured from the means and the coefficients $a_1, a_2, \ldots, a_n$ are determined by attributing to them the signs of any of the rows in the adjoint correlation matrix (m_{ij}^*) (assuming that the signs of these rows are compatible) and then putting the magnitudes of these coefficients equal to the square root of the diagonal elements in the adjoint correlation matrix. That is to say, by putting

$$a_i^2 = m_{ii}^*$$
(162)

In the case of three variables the explicit solution for the diagonal mean regression coefficients is

$$
\begin{aligned}
a_1^2 &= m_{22}m_{33} - m_{32}m_{23} \\
a_2^2 &= m_{11}m_{33} - m_{31}m_{13} \\
a_3^2 &= m_{11}m_{22} - m_{21}m_{12}
\end{aligned}
$$
(163)

where m_{ij} is the product moment of the variables x_i and x_j (taken about the means). In all those cases where the signs of the rows in the adjoint moment matrix are compatible, the diagonal mean regression furnishes a very good solution of the linear regression problem. It generally gives a very satisfactory fit and it is not very laborious to compute. Furthermore, it has the above-mentioned advantage that it is invariant for a change in the units of measurement.

In the case of n variables the fundamental moment formula takes on the form

$$
m = \begin{vmatrix}
m_{11} & m_{12} & .. & m_{1n} \\
m_{21} & m_{22} & .. & m_{2n} \\
.. & .. & .. & .. \\
m_{n1} & m_{n2} & .. & m_{nn}
\end{vmatrix}
= \frac{1}{n!} \sum_t \sum_u \cdots \sum_v
\begin{vmatrix}
_tx_1 & _tx_2 & .. & _tx_n \\
_ux_1 & _ux_2 & .. & _ux_n \\
.. & .. & .. & .. \\
_vx_1 & _vx_2 & .. & _vx_n
\end{vmatrix}^2
$$
(164)

The subscripts $t, u \ldots v$ in the right member of (164) run independent of each other through all the observation points. The fundamental moment formula shows that the moment determinant m, that is to say, the determinant value of the moment matrix, can never be a negative quantity, and furthermore, it is rigorously equal to 0 when the variables $x_1, x_2, \ldots, x_n$ are linearly dependent.

In this case the rows of the determinant in the right member of (164) will namely always be proportional and it is easy to see that any determinant where two rows are proportional must be equal to 0. If we 'normalize' the moment determinant, that is to say divide the i-th row by $\sqrt{m_{ii}}$ and divide the j-th column by $\sqrt{m_{jj}}$ we obtain the correlation determinant

$$
r = \begin{vmatrix}
r_{11} & r_{12} & .. & r_{1n} \\
r_{21} & r_{22} & .. & r_{2n} \\
.. & .. & .. & .. \\
r_{n1} & r_{n2} & .. & r_{nn}
\end{vmatrix}
$$
(165)

This correlation determinant we may take as an expression for how close the set of n variables $x_1, x_2, \ldots, x_n$ comes to being linearly dependent. The determinant r will namely always be lying between 0 and 1. It will be all the smaller the closer the set of variables comes to being linearly dependent, and it will be rigorously 0, when and only when the variables are rigorously linearly dependent. The square root of the determinant r we shall call the *collective scatter coefficient* and we denote it σ, that is to say, we put

$$s = +\sqrt{r} \tag{166}$$

It is easy to see that in the case $n=2$, the collective scatter coefficient as here defined reduces to the collective scatter coefficient which we have already defined above. And it may be proved that the collective scatter coefficient in n dimensions admits of a geometrical interpretation analogous to the geometric interpretation we gave of this coefficient in the case $n=2$.[3]

3.2 Types of clustering in scatter diagrams and the non-significance of partial correlation

I now proceed to a discussion of the extreme cases of linear dependency and perfect correlation between statistical variables. It is true that these extreme cases are not the ones which are most likely to occur in practical applications. Nevertheless a discussion of these extreme cases is essential for a rational interpretation of that is really involved in the notion of correlation in several variables, and particularly for the interpretation of partial and multiple correlation coefficients which are close to unity.

For the simple correlation coefficient the case is clear enough. The simple correlation coefficient between two variables is equal to unity when and only when one variable is proportional to the other (each variable being measured from its mean). Geometrically interpreted: the simple correlation coefficient is close to unity when and only when the swarm of observation points in the two-dimensional scatter diagram is clustering around a straight line through the origin. For partial and multiple correlation coefficients, however, the case is not quite so clear.

For more than two variables we have to distinguish between different *types of clustering*. For three variables, for instance, it might happen that the swarm of observation points in the three-dimensional scatter diagram is clustering around a plane through the origin, but is highly scattered within this plane.[4] The plane may be far from containing any of the axes. Or it may be a plane containing, say, the x_1 axis, that is, a plane perpendicular to the (x_2, x_3) plane. Again it might happen that the swarm of observation points is clustering not only around a plane but even around a straight line in this plane. For several variables the number of different cases is of course much greater. *And each one of these various cases has a very definite significance, which it is important to study.*

A rigorous analysis of these various cases is however usually neglected. And the practical application of the theory is often limited to the mechanical use of computation formulae under some simple assumptions, for instance the assumption that the partial correlation coefficient for the pair of variables (x_i, x_j) means the same thing as the simple correlation coefficient for (x_i, x_j) would have meant if the material has been, not what it actually is, but a material where all the other variables had been constants. (Which assumption is reasonably plausible only if the distribution of the variables is normal.)

The reason for not analysing the various types of clustering by the classical methods of correlation is easily understood. It will presently appear that the partial and multiple correlation coefficients and other classical correlation parameters become undefined in those cases of linear dependency which illustrate the various types of clustering. And in practical cases which approach these extreme cases, the classical correlation parameters lose their real significance.

The scatter coefficient and the coefficients of linear importance always preserve a sense. These notions will be employed here for discussion and classification of the various cases of linear dependency and the corresponding types of clustering.

In the first part of the discussion the rigorous algebraic point of view will be adopted. Subsequently the statistical integration of the algebraic criteria will be discussed. The methods to be used are rather simple. In fact, they are mostly based on the formula we have called the fundamental moment formula. This is another reason why a rigorous analysis of linear dependencies and the corresponding types of clustering should not be neglected in the study of correlation between statistical variables. From the discussion in this section it will immediately follow in which cases the definition of the classical correlation parameters preserves a sense.

Supposing the variables to be measured from their means, we lay down the following definitions.

The n-dimensional set of observational variables $x_1, x_2, \ldots, x_n$ is said to be linearly dependent, or to be a *collinear* set if there exists identically in t at least one linear relation of the form

$$a_1 \cdot {}_t x_1 + a_2 \cdot {}_t x_2 + \ldots + a_n \cdot {}_t x_n = 0 \tag{167}$$

where the coefficients $a_1, a_2, \ldots, a_n$ are independent of t and not equal to zero. If no such relation exists, the set is called linearly independent or *non-collinear.*

If there exists identically in t exactly p $(0 \leq p \leq n)$ distinct linear relations of the form (167), the set is said to be *p-fold collinear* or *p-fold flattened.* By p distinct linear relations of the form (1) is meant p linear relations, such that not one of them can be derived as a linear combination of the others, with constant coefficients.

From the theory of linear equations it follows that this definition of a p-fold collinear set is equivalent with the following: an n-dimensional set is p-fold collinear when and only when there exists at least $(n-p)$ dimensional sub-set $x_u, \ldots,$ x_v which is non-collinear and such that each of the remaining p variables identically in t, can be expressed as a linear combination of $x_u, \ldots, x_v$ with constant coefficients. Evidently, if the remaining p variables can be expressed a linear combination of $x_u, ..., x_v$ with constant coefficients, any of the n variables x_1, $x_2, ..., x_n$ can. A p-fold collinear n-dimensional set is therefore a set, which by a non-singular linear transformation can be transformed into a set where p of the variables are ineffective and $q = n - p$ of the variables are effective.

Geometrically interpreted a p-fold collinear n-dimensional set is a set for which the swarm of observation points in n-dimensional space are (rigorously) crowded in a certain $q = n - p$ dimensional plane through the origin (but not in a lower dimensional plane). This q-dimensional plane is called the *perfect regression plane* for the set, $q = n - p$ is called the *rank* of the *unfolding capacity* of the set, p is called the *flattening* of the set.

If $p = 0$, that is if the rank of the set is equal to its dimensionality, the observation points are scattered in n-dimensional space. There is no flattening, and the set is non-collinear.

If $p = 1$, that is if there exists exactly one linear relation of the form (167), the set is called *simply collinear*. In this case the flattening is 1, and the rank is exactly one less than the dimensionality of the set. There exists a perfect $(n-1)$ dimensional regression plane.

If $p > 1$, the set is called *multiply collinear* or *multiply flattened*. There now exists a perfect regression plane of lower dimensionality than $(n-1)$.

A simply collinear n-dimensional set $x_1, x_2, ..., x_n$ is called a *closed* set if all the n coefficients $a_1, a_2, ..., a_n$ in the linear relation which holds good for the set, are different from zero. This definition of a closed set is equivalent with the following: an n-dimensional set is closed if there exists at least one relation of the form (167) involving all the n variables (i.e. all the coefficients $a_1, a_2, ..., a_n \neq 0$) and no relation of the form (1) involving less than n variables. In fact, from this definition follows that the set must be simply collinear. For if there exist two (or more) distinct relations of the form (167) we can eliminate one variable and obtain a relation involving at most $(n-1)$ variables.

Geometrically interpreted a closed n-dimensional set $x_1, x_2, ..., x_n$ is a simply collinear set, the perfect $(n-1)$ dimensional regression plane of which *does not contain any of the axes* $x_1, x_2, ..., x_n$. In this case each one of the variables in the set can be expressed in terms of the others.[5]

I shall now consider necessary and sufficient criteria for the cases defined above. For shortness the moment matrix (m_{ij}) and the correlation matrix (r_{ij}) will be denoted (m) and (r) respectively.

I shall assume the set x to be an effective set, i.e. none of the variables is identically zero. In this case each minor contained in (m) is equal to or different from zero according as the corresponding minor of (r) is equal to or different from zero. In particular (m) and (r) have the same rank.

From the purely algebraic point of view one is only concerned with the cases where the set x has rigorously the property of being collinear, closed, etc. Criteria for these cases may be derived either from the properties of (m) or from the properties of (r). From the statistical point of view (which will be discussed subsequently) we have however to take account also of cases where the set x only 'comes near' to having the properties in question, the sense of 'coming near to' being defined by the values (close to zero or close to unity) of the determinant (r) and its minors. It is therefore preferable to state also the rigorous algebraic propositions in terms of the properties of (r). It should be noticed that in order to ascertain the rank of (r) it is sufficient to inspect its *principal* minors, for (r) is symmetric.

We have already seen that the set x is collinear when and only when $r-0$. A generalization of this is the following proposition: *the observational set x is of rank q (i.e. its flattening is $p=n-q$) when and only when the correlation matrix (r) is of rank q.* We shall not enter upon the proof of this proposition here.

In order to find a linearly independent q dimensional sub-set contained in the set x, we have to inspect the q rowed principal minors of (r). Any sub-set $x_u, \ldots, x_v$ such that the correlation determinant for this sub-set is different from zero, is a linearly independent set and can be used for expressing all the variables in the set x.

If the number n of variables is equal to number N of observations, the set is always collinear. More generally: if $N \leq n$, the rank of the set is at most equal to $N-1$, i.e. its flattening is at least equal to $n-N+1$. This simply follows from the fact that N points $_1x, \ldots, _Nx$, between which there exists the linear relation $\Sigma_t \, _tx = 0$ (or any homogeneous linear relation), must necessarily lie in an $N-1$ dimensional plane through the origin of x (and they might even lie in a lower dimensional plane).

This fact is also revealed by the rank of (r). All the N and higher rowed minors of (r) must namely now be zero.

From the preceding proposition we immediately infer the following: *a necessary and sufficient condition for a set x to be simply collinear is that $r=0$ and that at least one of the diagonal elements r_{ii}^* in the adjoint correlation matrix (r^*) is different from zero.*

If an n-dimensional set is collinear, it is always possible, at least in one way, to pick out a sub-set of $(n-1)$ variables in terms of which the one remaining variable can be expressed linearly. But it is by no means certain that *any* of the variables can thus be expressed in terms of the others. *The variable x_i in a simply collinear set can be expressed linearly in terms of the other variables when and only when $r_{ii}^* \neq 0$.* For x_i can evidently be expressed in terms of the other variables when and only when x_i occurs in the one existing relation which holds good for the simply collinear set, that is, when and only when the remaining $(n-1)$ variables do not by themselves form a collinear set, i.e. when and only when $r_{ii}^* \neq 0$.

From this we further conclude: *a necessary and sufficient condition for a set x to be a closed set is that $r=0$ and all the diagonal elements r_{ii}^* of the adjoint correlation matrix are different from zero.*

In a simply collinear set, a given row (column) of the adjoint moment matrix (m^*) will consist exclusively of zeros when and only when the diagonal element in the row (column) is equal to zero. For if (m^*) is of rank 1, we have $m_{ij}^{*2} = m_{ii}^* m_{jj}^*$ $(i, j = 1, 2, \ldots, n)$, where at least one of the $m_{ii}^* \neq 0$. The same rule holds good for the adjoint correlation matrix.

The last relation also shows that in a simply collinear set in a given element r_{ij}^* of (r^*) will vanish when and only when at least one of the two quantities r_{ii}^*

and r_{jj}^* vanishes. If either r_{ii}^* or r_{jj}^* (or both) vanishes, the partial correlation coefficient between x_i and x_j, namely

$$\bar{r}_{ij} = -\frac{r_{ij}^*}{\sqrt{r_{ii}^* r_{jj}^*}} \qquad (168)$$

will consequently be of the undefined 0/0 form. If r_{11}^* vanishes, the multiple correlation coefficient r_i will be of the form 0/0. Hence: *if all the partial (or all the multiple) correlation coefficients in a simply collinear set shall have a meaning, the set must be a closed set.* In a closed set all the $\bar{r}_{ii}$ and all the r_i have an absolute value equal to unity. The case of a closed set might therefore also be designated as the case of perfect correlation.

If the simply collinear set is not closed, all those partial correlation $\bar{r}_{ij}$ will be undefined which are situated in the matrix $(\bar{r})$ in a row (or a column) whose corresponding diagonal element in (r^*) is zero.

If the set is multiply collinear, the indeterminateness is ever greater. In this case (r^*) is of rank 0, and therefore each and all of the partial and multiple correlation coefficients of highest order undefined.

We now proceed to a statistical interpretation of the notion of types of clustering, and particularly to an interpretation of this notion in the procedure of fitting lines and planes to a given scatter diagram. The point of view which will be adopted is thus the regression point of view, although one or two occasional references will be made to the frequency aspect of the problem.

The procedure of determining an analytic relation between a certain number of statistical variables has a conceptual background somewhat like this. We have in our mind a certain pattern, according to which variations in statistical variables can be of three kinds. *Accidental* variations are variations due to the fact that a great number of variables have been overlooked, consciously or unconsciously, each of the variables being however of minor importance. *Disturbances* are variations due to the fact that one single, or a certain limited number of highly significant variables have been overlooked. *Systematic variations* are variations which show a certain regularity (in time or space), this regularity being taken as a criterion that no really relevant variables have been overlooked.

This classification does not pretend to be anything like satisfactory from a philosophical point of view. A critical reader will for instance find the troublesome problem of causality hidden in practically every line of the definitions. Furthermore the distinction between what shall be considered as accidental variations and disturbances is not sharp. To some extent the distinction depends on the complexity of the problem and on the relative perfection (or deficiency) of the empirical and rational tools of investigation which are at present at our disposal. Thus, in economics we are actually often forced to throw so much into the bag of accidental variations that this kind of variations comes very near to take on the character of disturbances. In such cases it would perhaps be more rational to introduce a hierarchic order of types of variations, each type corresponding to the overlooking of variables of a certain order of importance.

Nevertheless, I think that the rough three-fold distinction which has been made above will be sufficient for our purpose, so that it shall not be necessary to enter upon a lengthy philosophical discussion.

Then we proceed to the determination of an analytic relation between a certain number of statistical variables, we assume, implicitly or explicitly, that if the considered set of variables really forms a complete set of relevant variables, and if the accidental variations could be eliminated, so that only the systematic variations were left, then the variables would satisfy a certain functional relation (anyhow for some limited time or space considered). In fact, this assumption is really involved in the definition of systematic variations as distinguished from accidental variations and disturbances. The character of this functional relation is an important feature in any statistical problem, and in many problems it is the one important thing in which we are interested. A statistical fitting procedure, performed with a tentative analytic formula, is an attempt to get rid of the non-significant accidental variations and thus obtain some idea of the character of the functional relation which exists between the systematic variations.

As I see it, any statistical fitting procedure can be considered from this point of view. This interpretation seems rather natural. It is not, however, the only one which has been advanced. The set of n elementary regressions is sometimes considered as a unity, and as such contrasted with the unique regression obtained by some kind of mean regression method. It is contended that in principle only a regression of the latter type represents an approximation to the functional relation between the systematic variations and that the set of n elementary regressions represents an entirely different notion, namely the notion of stochastic relation, the stochastic relation being not a unique relation such as the functional relation, but a plurality of relations, namely as many relations as there are variables. It is claimed that this distinction is fundamental and characteristic for the distinction between the mechanical and the statistical conception of 'law'.

In my mind this interpretation is fallacious. The difference between the various conceivable regressions is a difference in assumption as to *how* the accidental element has actually manifested its presence in the material at hand, this difference in assumption entailing a difference in the technique by which the regression coefficients are determined. In the case of a mean regression the assumption and the technique is more symmetric in the variables than in the case of the elementary regressions. In a certain type of problem the technically best approximation to the functional relation between the variables will therefore be furnished by a mean regression, in another type of problem it will be furnished by one particular of the elementary regressions. It is only in the technical sense that a mean regression is 'mean'. Otherwise there is no difference between a mean regression and one particular of the elementary regressions. And it does not seem plausible to pick out in the infinity of possible techniques, that particular kind of technique which leads to the system of elementary regressions, and erect it into a principle, the conceptual importance of which should be comparable with the basic importance of the idea of functional relationship. There certainly does exist a difference between the conceptual schemes of a mechanical and a statistical law, but not in the sense that the first is something unique, the second something pluralistic. The difference, as I see it, is that the first is a law conceived so as to admit of no exceptions, the second a law which really admits of exceptions, just because the accidental variations are thought of as being superimposed on the systematic variations.

Another point which should be noticed in connection with the conception of regression and functional relation is that the partial and multiple correlation coefficients (and the generalizations of these parameters to curvilinear regression) are not primarily descriptive of the character of the systematic variations, but are essentially indicators of the presence of accidental variations and disturbances. In the exaggerated importance which in recent years has been attributed to computation of partial and multiple correlation coefficients, one has lost sight to some extent, it seems to me, of the fact that one of the essential things we are after is the character of the regression relation itself.

After these preliminary remarks we may turn to the notion of types of clustering. Let a statistical material covering N observations on n variables be given. And suppose we want to investigate the character of the systematic variations in the variables, by assuming as a tentative analytic formula the linear function.

In all practical cases the moment matrix, and hence the correlation matrix, will be non-singular. This in itself does not, however, tell us very much from statistical point of view. The essential question from the statistical point of view is if the deviation of r from zero is significant or not, that is if the deviation of r from zero is really descriptive of the systematic variations in the variables. Even if the systematic variations of the variables are such that they would give rigorously $r = 0$, *the slightest amount of accidental variation introduced would at once make r positive, not zero.* If r is considered from the sampling point of view, assuming the ideal universe in question to have r rigorously equal to zero, the mathematical expectation of an actually observed r would not be zero but some positive quantity. And the probability of an observed $r = 0$ would be virtually zero. An actually observed value of r has therefore to be viewed in the light of some criterion of the significance of its deviation from zero. And similarly for the other scatter parameters, that is, for the principal minors of r, respectively the square roots of r and its principal minors.

For a rigorous analysis it would be highly desirable to have an exact criterion for the significance of observed magnitude of the scatter parameters, in the form of formulae of the mathematical expectations and standard deviations of these quantities, or better still: in the form of complete theoretical distributions. At present I have no such formulae to offer. But nevertheless we have a rough criterion by which to judge the scatter parameters' closeness to zero, namely the fact that all these quantities are lying between 0 and 1 and are limited by the formulae and propositions of above. We are thus virtually in the same position with regard to judging the magnitude of the scatter parameters as we are with regard to judging the magnitude of those classical correlation parameters for which mathematical expectations, standard deviations or complete theoretical distributions are not available at present. This sort of criterion is certainly not ideal. But if it is used with care, I believe that it is far better than no criterion at all. And it is perhaps not vain to hope that it shall ultimately be possible to derive the necessary formulae for giving a more definite meaning to the scatter parameters' closeness to zero.

In view of the algebraic facts indicated above it is clear that the notions of simply collinear sets and closed sets must be important from the statistical point of view.

Suppose for instance that the scatter coefficient $s = \sqrt{r}$ for an n-dimensional set is found to be not significantly different from zero, indicating that the observation points in the n-dimensional scatter diagram come close to lying in a plane. This in itself is not sufficient to make it a plausible procedure to pick out one of the variables, say x_i, and compute the regression of x_i on the remaining $(n-1)$ variables. This procedure would have no meaning if $\sqrt{r_{ii}}$ is not significantly different from zero, while at least one other diagonal element in (r^*) is significantly different form zero. For in this case the $(n-1)$ dimensional plane around which the observation points are clustering is *not significantly different from a plane which contains the x_i axis*, the points being highly scattered within this plane. The regression which would have a meaning would therefore be a regression between (all or some of) the remaining $(n-1)$ variables, *not a regression involving x_i*. The variable x_i has nothing to do in the linear regression system. From the point of view of linear regression x_i is a superfluous variable drawn into observation. The n-dimensional set is not a closed set. If we would compute the regression of x_i on the other variables in this case, the whole system of regression coefficients of b_{ij} would be artificial. Computing the regression of x_i on the other variables would namely now mean forcing the quantity $\sqrt{r_{ii}^*}$ (whose deviation from zero is non-significant) into the coefficients b_{ij} as a denominator.

The question may arise: is not this exactly the kind of thing which would show up in the multiple and partial correlation coefficient? If the actual distribution of the observations is such that the variable x_i is a superfluous variable in the above sense, would not the partial correlations $\bar{r}_{ij}$ and the multiple correlation r_i necessarily have small numerical values? The answer is: they would not. On the contrary, the definition of the partial and multiple correlation coefficients is such that *when the remaining $(n-1)$ variables taken by themselves come close to forming a collinear set, the partial correlation $\bar{r}_{ij}$* between the superfluous variable x_i and any of the remaining variables, respectively the multiple correlation rx_i between x_i and the set of the other $(n-1)$ variables, may assume any value, in particular these parameters might come close to unity, *thus making it appear perfectly legitimate to compute the regression of x_i on the other variables.*

I shall take the case $n=3$ as an illustration. Let r_{12}, r_{13} and r_{23} be the simple correlation coefficients in the set (x_1, x_2, x_3). We put $r_{12}=ph$, $r_{13}=qh$, $r_{23}=\varepsilon\sqrt{1-h^2}$ ($h^2 \leq 1$), where ε is the sign of r_{23} and the square root is taken positive. Now consider p, q and h as arbitrary quantities. The consistency condition which characterizes the case where r_{12}, r_{13} and r_{23} are correlation coefficients for a set of real variables is

$$0 \leq R = h^2(1 - (p^2 - \varepsilon \cdot 2pq\sqrt{1-h^2} + q^2))$$

By studying the two conics in (p, q) coordinates

$$p^2 - \varepsilon \cdot 2pq\sqrt{1-h^2} + q^2 = 1$$
$$\varepsilon = \pm 1$$

which have the shape indicated in Figure 3.9, we see that the consistency condition is certainly satisfied for all values of $h^2 \leq 1$ if the point (p, q) is situated in the inner square of Figure 3.9, that is if

$$|p| + |q| \leq 1 \tag{168}$$

In terms of p, q and h we have (using Professor Yule's notation for the partial and multiple correlation coefficients)

$$r_{12.3} = \left(p - \varepsilon q\sqrt{1-h^2}\right) / \sqrt{1-q^2 h^2}$$
$$r_{13.2} = \left(q - \varepsilon p\sqrt{1-h^2}\right) / \sqrt{1-p^2 h^2}$$

$$R_{1(23)} = \sqrt{p^2 - \varepsilon \cdot 2pq\sqrt{1-h^2} + q^2}$$

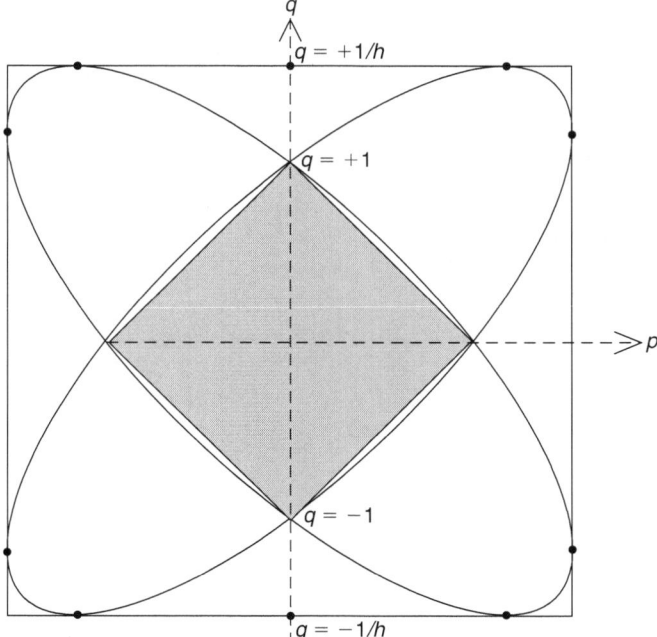

Figure 3.9 Partial and multiple correlation coefficients ($n=3$).

where all the square roots are taken positive. Further the standard error of estimates of x_1 as a linear function of x_2 and x_3 is

$$\sigma_{1.23} = \sigma_1 \sqrt{1 - R_{1(23)}^2}$$

where σ_1 is the simple standard deviation of x_1.

Therefore if p and q are chosen as two arbitrary number independent of h and satisfying (168), we have at the limit for $h \to 0$.

$$r_{12.3} = p - \varepsilon q$$
$$r_{13.2} = q - \varepsilon p$$

$$R_{1(23)} = |p - \varepsilon q|$$

Now, the limiting process $h \to 0$ means that we construct a case where the observation points in the three-dimensional scatter diagram (x_1, x_2, x_3) come close to lying in a plane containing the x_1-axis (i.e. a plane perpendicular to the x_2x_3 plane). But in this plane the observation points are far from clustering around a straight line. In other words, we construct a case where the set (x_1, x_2, x_3) comes as near as we want to being a simply collinear but not a closed set, namely a set where there exists a linear relation between x_2 and x_3 taken by themselves, but where there is no approach whatsoever to a linear relation between x_1 and the other variables. The case is one where x_1 is a superfluous variable drawn into observation.

Nevertheless we can specify the case by disposing of p and q in such a way that for a sufficiently small h, any of the partial correlation coefficients between the superfluous variable x_1 and one of the other variables, for instance the partial correlation coefficient $r_{12.3}$, comes as near as we please to any number between -1 and $+1$. Or the multiple correlation coefficient $R_{1(23)}$ can be brought as near as we please to any number between 0 and 1. For r_{23} positive we may for instance choose $p=-q=0.5$. At the limit for $h \to 0$ we get $r_{12.3}=+1$, $r_{13.2}=-1$, $R_{1(23)} = 1$ and $\sigma_{1.23}=0$. Choosing $p=q=0.5$ we get $r_{12.3}=r_{13.2}=0$, etc.

The case $p=q=0.5$ is particularly illustrative. All criteria seem to indicate that it would be perfectly legitimate to compute the regression of x_1 on the two other variables. We have maximum partial and multiple correlation and minimum standard error of estimate. And still such a regression would have no sense.

If we had computed the scatter coefficient s and the coefficients of linear importance

$$s = h\sqrt{1 - (p^2 - \varepsilon \cdot 2pq\sqrt{1-h^2} + q^2)}$$
$$\sqrt{r_{11}^*} = h$$
$$\sqrt{r_{22}^*} = \sqrt{1 - q^2 h^2}$$
$$\sqrt{r_{33}^*} = \sqrt{1 - p^2 h^2}$$

where all the square roots are taken positive, the real character of the relation between the variables would at once have been revealed, for we have at the limit for $h \to 0$.

$$s = \sqrt{r_{11}^*} = 0 \quad \text{and} \quad \sqrt{r_{22}^*} = \sqrt{r_{33}^*} = 1$$

$s = 0$ means that there exists at least one linear relation between the three variables $\sqrt{r_{22}^*} = 1$ (or $\sqrt{r_{33}^*} = 1$) means that there does not exist more than one such relation, and $\sqrt{r_{11}^*} = 1$ means that the one existing relation is a relation between x_2 and x_3.

It is easy to construct numerical analysis examples which illustrate this type of clustering. I constructed for instance three series x_1, x_2, x_3 where x_1 was a combination of words in English, each letter being attributed a value according to its place in the alphabet, x_2 consisted of digits picket at random in a logarithmic table, and x_3 was nearly a linear function of x_2. This case happened to give a high negative value for $r_{12.3}$ and high positive values for $r_{13.2}$ and $R_{1(23)}$. But the value of $\sqrt{r_{11}^*}$ (and therefore necessarily the value of s) turned out to be comparatively small, while $\sqrt{r_{22}^*}$ and $\sqrt{r_{33}^*}$ were significantly different from zero, indicating the presence of a linear relation between x_2 and x_3 and the lack of a linear relation involving x_1.

The conclusion is that before proceeding to the computation of the classical correlation parameters, it will be advisable to take a general survey of the type of clustering, using the scatter coefficient and the coefficients of linear importance, and if necessary the scatter coefficients for the lower dimensional sub-sets.

In particular it is essential to determine if the set (assumed approximately collinear) comes near to being a closed set, and if not to pick out those sub-sets which come near to being closed. It is only for the approximately closed sub-sets thus determined that the classical correlation parameters have a real significance. In particular it is only for a rigorously closed set the term perfect correlation has a meaning.

The following might serve as a general scheme for the analysis. First compute the simple correlation coefficients, i.e. the elements of the correlation matrix (r). If the scatter coefficient $s = +\sqrt{r}$ is close to unity, there is no use trying to express any of the variables linearly in terms of the others.

If s is reasonably close to zero, the diagonal elements r_{ii}^* in the adjoint matrix should be computed. If none of the quantities r_{ii}^* are normal, the set may be considered as a closed set and if desired the regression coefficients and other classical correlation parameters computed in the usual way.

If some of (but not all) the quantities $\sqrt{r_{ii}^*}$ are very small, the set may still be considered as a simply collinear but no longer as a closed set. Those variables x_a for which $\sqrt{r_{ii}^*}$ is very small might be left out and the rest of the variables treated as a closed set. If it is desired not to leave the variables x_a out completely, one might compute the regression in the usual way, however not compute the regression of any of the x_a on the other variables.

If all the quantities $\sqrt{r_{ii}}$ are very small, the set should be considered as multiply collinear. In this case there will exist at least two sub-sets which may be considered as closed sets and treated separately. These closed sub-sets are determined by an inspection of the (n-2) rowed and eventually the lower rowed principal minors of the correlation matrix (r). If there exists at least one q rowed principal minor of (r), the positive square root of which is not a very small quantity, while the positive square roots of all the higher rowed principal minors of (r) are very small, then the given n-dimensional set should be considered as $p-n-q$ fold collinear (p-fold flattened). There now exist exactly p closed sub-sets which may be treated separately. These p sub-sets are determined in the following way. Pick out the q-dimensional sub-set $x_u, \ldots, x_v$ which is such that the scatter coefficient for the sub-set is the greatest of all q-dimensional scatter coefficients. This q-dimensional sub-set might be called the *basis set*. The basis set is the q-dimensional sub-set which comes nearest to being an uncorrelated set. Now consider in turn the $p(q+1)$-dimensional sub-sets obtained by adding to the basis set one of the variables which are not in the basis set. Each of these p sub-sets comes close to being a simply collinear set and might be analysed as such. In particular the set might be reduced to a closed set by omitting all those variables x_a which are such that the square root of the corresponding element in the ($q+1$) rowed adjoint correlation matrix for the sub-set is a very small quantity. The variables which will eventually be omitted by this rule are necessarily variables occurring in the basis set. The one variable which is added to the basis set will never be omitted.

Notes

1 Yule, G.U. (1926) 'Why do we sometimes get nonsense-correlation between time series – a study in sampling and the nature of time series', *Journal of the Royal Statistical Society*, 89: 1–64.
2 The above formulae may be summarized by saying that the product sum of a row (or column) in the determinant and *the same* row (or column) in the adjoint, is equal to the value of the determinant. On the other hand it is easy to see that if we select a *different* row (or column) in the adjoint, the result is always zero.
3 The coefficient $\sqrt{r_{ii}}$ is called the coefficient of linear importance of the variables x_i in the set ($x_1, x_2, \ldots, x_n$). It is the absolute magnitude of the coefficient of the i-th variable in the diagonal mean regression when the variables are reduced to standard coordinates.
4 For the sake of brevity I use the expression 'within the plane' although not all the points (perhaps none of them) are rigorously lying in the plane. The meaning is that the points are highly scattered in directions parallel to the plane.
5 If the regression plane in a simply collinear set contains the x_i-axis, the coefficient of x_i in the perfect regression equation is equal to 0, that is the equation does not contain x_i, and it is consequently impossible to express x_i in terms of the other variables.
6 Editors' note: See pp. 000–000.
7 Editors' note: See pp. 000–000.

Index

Italic page numbers indicate boxes not included in the text page range. **Bold** page numbers indicate figures not included in the text page range.

An environmentally friendly book printed and bound in England by www.printondemand-worldwide.com

PEFC Certified

This product is
from sustainably
managed forests
and controlled
sources

www.pefc.org

This book is made entirely of sustainable materials; FSC paper for the cover and PEFC paper for the text pages.

#0354 - 030314 - C0 - 234/156/11 - PB